STATE
WATER
POLICIES

STATE WATER POLICIES

A Study of Six States

Jurgen Schmandt, Ernest T. Smerdon
and Judith Clarkson

PRAEGER

New York
Westport, Connecticut
London

Library of Congress Cataloging-in-Publication Data

Schmandt, Jurgen.
  State water policies.

  Includes index.
    1. Water-supply—Government policy—United States—
States—Case studies. 2. Water resources development—
Government policy—United States—States—Case studies.
I. Smerdon, Ernest T. II. Clarkson, Judith. III. Title.
HD 1694.A5S27   1988   333.91'00973   88-15257
ISBN 0-275-93132-3 (alk. paper)

Library of Congress Catalog Card Number: 88-15257
ISBN: 0-275-93132-3

First published in 1988

Praeger Publishers, One Madison Avenue, New York, NY 10010
A division of Greenwood Press, Inc.

Printed in the United States of America

The paper used in this book complies with the
Permanent Paper Standard issued by the National
Information Standards Organization (Z39.48-1984).

10 9 8 7 6 5 4 3 2 1

CONTENTS

TABLES AND FIGURES

PREFACE

The Lyndon B. Johnson (LBJ) School of Public Affairs at the University of Texas at Austin has established interdisciplinary research on policy problems as the core of its educational program. A major part of this program is the year-long Policy Research Project, during the course of which two faculty members from different disciplines direct the research of ten to 20 graduate students of diverse backgrounds on a policy issue of concern to a government agency. This "client orientation" brings the students face to face with administrators, legislators, and other officials active in the policy process and demonstrates that research in a policy environment demands special talents. It also illuminates the occasional difficulties of relating research findings to the world of political realities.

This book is the result of a policy research project conducted in 1986-87 under a grant from the National Science Foundation. It was designed to discover and examine the ways in which the states are using innovative approaches to solve problems in the field of water resource management and research, especially in light of decreased participation from the federal government over the past several years. Participants in the project conducted extensive interviews with local and state government officials, and derived additional information from agency reports and other publications.

With the federal government currently playing a less active role in water project funding and water research support, it is important that the states fill the void. State and local officials now generally accept the fact that the beneficiaries of water projects must pay for them through user fees, taxes, or by some other method. However, the issue of research in water resources and related environmental areas is another matter. Usually, state-supported research has focused on a single problem or a narrow set of problems, as opposed to long-range research.

In addition, as priorities shift from water resource development to management, the states are the more appropriate level of government to initiate and administer programs. Therefore, states must become effective supporting partners in water resource management and research.

The Policy Research Project participants examined water resource management programs and efforts to perform long-range research projects in six states. The field research was conducted by 12 graduate students. They began with a preliminary review of approximately 13 states. Six that had strong, new, water resource management-research programs were selected. Students collected materials from various sources and later traveled to the states to conduct interviews with administrators and staff within the programs. The final stage involved integrating the information obtained from publications and interviews, and analyzing the data.

A conference with support from the National Science Foundation, discussing the many important issues described in this report, will be held in November 1988. Officials who provided information for this report will be invited to attend or present papers regarding their state's programs. This effort will be a part of a conference sponsored by the Center for Growth Studies, Houston Area Research Center, as a component of a multiyear study of the changing policy roles of state governments.

We would like to thank the many people involved in the compilation of this study: the students, who spent many hours researching the information and interviewing state officials; Marilyn Hunt, who coordinated much of the data collection and compilation; and Susan Roush, who spent numerous hours typing the many revisions to the manuscript. We are also grateful to those state officials who so generously gave of their time as interviewees, and in particular, Bruce Baker, James Hearney, William Johnston, William Lord, David Moreau, and Rex Woods, for reviewing appropriate chapters. We hope that no factual errors have been included in the text. However, the authors accept full responsibility for accuracy.

Finally, it should be noted that the views or findings of this study are not necessarily endorsed by the National Science Foundation, which provided financial assistance, the LBJ School of Public Affairs, nor The University of Texas at Austin.

ACRONYMS

GENERAL
    EPA   Environmental Protection Agency
    gpd   Gallons per day
    maf   Million acre-feet
    mgd   Million gallons per day
    NSF   National Science Foundation
    USGS   U.S. Geological Survey

ARIZONA
    AMA   Active Management Area
    CAP   Central Arizona Project
    DWR   Department of Water Resources
    FICO   Farmers Investment Company
    GMA   Groundwater Management Act
    SAWARA   Southern Arizona Water Resources Association
    WRRC   Water Resources Research Center

CALIFORNIA
    AHI   Aquatic Habitat Institute
    CPS   California Policy Seminar
    CVP   Central Valley Project
    DWR   Department of Water Resources
    SWP   State Water Project
    SWRCB   State Water Resources Control Board
    WWD   Westlands Water District

FLORIDA
    DER   Department of Environmental Regulation
    DNR   Department of Natural Resources

WMD	Water Management District

NORTH CAROLINA
COG	Council of Governments
DEM	Division of Environmental Management
DNRCD	Department of Natural Resources and Community Development
NCSU	North Carolina State University
UNC	University of North Carolina
WRRI	Water Resource Research Institute

TEXAS
LCRA	Lower Colorado River Authority
TDWR	Texas Department of Water Resources
TSPE	Texas Society of Professional Engineers
TWC	Texas Water Commission
TWDB	Texas Water Development Board
TWRI	Texas Water Resources Institute

WISCONSIN
DNR	Department of Natural Resources
TDP	Transferable Discharge Permit
UW	University of Wisconsin
WGNHS	Wisconsin Geological and Natural History Survey
WRC	Water Resources Center

STATE
WATER
POLICIES

WATER POLICY: THE EVOLUTION OF FEDERAL AND STATE ROLES

INTRODUCTION

The development and management of water resources have followed a complex path over the course of the last century. While the development of the nation's water resources has had important regional impacts (more than a third of federal funds have been spent in the West and another third in the South),[1] the nation as a whole has been affected by the massive effort: "Water resource development and management in the United States has created 12,000 miles of waterways, irrigated 30 million acres of land (and drained an even larger area), provided water supplies for countless cities and industries, directed tons of concrete and earth at thousands of streams which, from time to time, overflow their banks and harnessed more than 30 million kilowatts of electric power capacity."[2]

An analysis of these events is interesting in and of itself, but also serves to illustrate the changing roles of various levels of government. Local governments have long been instrumental in planning and advocating water projects. State governments developed and implemented water law. In addition, the federal government financed, in the interests of economic development and public welfare, many major projects that were beyond the means of local governments or the private sector. This rationale has been particularly applicable for larger water development projects, which may encompass several river basins in more than one state. In addition, a great deal of the expertise required for such ambitious projects was often more readily available at the federal level.

Several factors have contributed to a change in attitude toward federally funded water development projects. Increasingly, during the 1960s and 1970s, various groups questioned the economic efficiency of expensive new water projects. In addition, prompted by the limits to growth debate and the 1973 energy crisis, an increasingly large sector of the public became aware of the alarmingly high rates of degradation and depletion of many critical natural resources. Concern about the environment also caused the public to take new interest in water issues.

With limitations in water supply threatening to impede the long-term economic growth of some areas of the country and with the feasibility and cost-effectiveness of additional water supply projects decreasing, there is now an urgent need to develop new policies that incorporate better management of existing water supplies. As part of the search for new policies, a shift in responsibilities is under way. This study to determine what new policies are being developed and how institutions are adapting to these changes. The discussion focuses on three issues. First, to what extent better management of existing water supplies has replaced the promotion of additional water supply projects as the prevailing public policy. Second, if we are going to develop public policies based on better management of available resources, from where will the initiative and funding come. Third, who will provide the additional support for the research and related studies needed to make future technical and policy advances possible.

This study follows these three themes by documenting how state governments--and organizations within states, such as water districts, river authorities, and regional water compacts--are increasingly called upon to resolve water policy issues. Whereas the federal government was a major player when water development projects were the preferred approach to water management, now that the emphasis has changed from development to better management of existing resources, its role is declining, and state governments are assuming a more active role. We ask what policy initiatives the states have taken and whether they are providing the necessary support for the research needed to develop new policies and techniques.

TRADITIONAL FEDERAL AND STATE ROLES

Beginning in the last century, the federal government assumed responsibility for a variety of projects designed to promote growth and economic development. In 1824, following a decision by the Supreme Court vesting the Congress with power over navigation within all of the states, an appropriation was made to remove some minor obstructions to navigation from the Ohio and Mississippi Rivers. Over the years, the Corps of Engineers has become responsible for projects that include development of the Great Lakes, dredging of port facilities, and the maintenance of the Gulf Intracoastal Waterway. Currently, the United States has 25,000 miles of commercially navigable waterways, including 9,000 miles in the Mississippi River Basin.[3]

With the passage of the 1902 Reclamation Act, the Congress assumed responsibility for water resources development, flood control, and economic development. Fifteen years later, it acted to control flooding on the Mississippi River and in 1936 authorized a national flood control program. The Tennessee Valley Authority (TVA) began the development of the entire Tennessee River Basin in order to control devastating floods and stimulate economic growth in the South. Whereas the Corps of Engineers assumed primary responsibility for flood control and land drainage in the eastern United States, the Bureau of Reclamation was principally concerned with irrigation projects in the 17 western states. Under the 1902 Reclamation Act, these western reclamation projects were to be funded from the proceeds of public land sales; costs would be repaid within ten years with no interest charge. In 1926 the repayment period was extended to 40 years, and in 1939 legislative changes allowed for contracts to be written to reflect the productivity of different classes of land within the project area. As interest rates rose and hydroelectric revenues were applied to costs associated with irrigation, the value of subsidies to farmers increased, in some cases approaching 90 percent.[4] In California's Central Valley Project, only 5 percent of the total $931 million spent on the project's irrigations facilities over the last 40 years has been repaid to date.[5]

Federal subsidies for water development projects extended long after their initial goals had been realized. Two primary reasons have been cited for this:

1. A great variety of constituencies, including the federal agencies themselves, benefited from these projects. In geographical terms, "there was something for everyone," and support in Congress for a project in one member's district could be traded for support for one in another, or for votes on an entirely different issue. This became the basis for "pork barrel" politics.

2. The method of appropriating money for financing the projects invited drawn out project development. In trying to appear restrained in its budget requests, Congress would authorize projects and provide a modest level of funding for the first year. When funding levels exceeded acceptable goals, the solution was often to reduce the budget by spreading the financing period over a longer time period. For instance, the 1971 request included $821 million for the Corps of Engineers' projects, of which only $16 million represented appropriations for new projects. One million dollars of this was recommended for the start of the Tennessee-Tombigbee Waterway, estimated to involve a total cost of $320 million.[6]

Federal spending for construction, operation, and maintenance of water resource projects peaked in 1966, averaging $4.2 to $6.1 billion (in 1984 dollars) for the 1960s, and declining to $3.4 billion in 1984. The Congressional Budget Office concluded that this decline was a result of both budgetary pressures and an inability of the Congress and the executive branch to agree on the appropriate role of the federal government in making investments in water resources.[7] Since 1977, spending at the state level has increased to partially compensate for this, but with many water projects already built, there has been a steady increase in operating expenditures.

Two major themes characterize changes in water policy since 1970. The withdrawal of the federal government, which has also occurred in other public policy areas, has been paralleled by a shift from a predominantly development-driven approach to one of better management of existing supplies. It is hard to say whether there is any direct relationship between these two trends. The federal government has, in the interests of public welfare, assumed responsibility for many major projects, often citing economies of scale as a justification for expenditure of public funds. On the other hand, in most cases, states are responsible for the allocation of water rights. In western states, where constraints on water availability are getting serious, states have devised their own specific methods, based on appropriative rights, for administering water rights. Federal lands and federal projects involving water must respect existing appropriative rights and, more recently, have been required by the Supreme Court to abide by state laws and regulations pertaining to the operation of water development projects.[8]

The Legal Basis for Federal and State Roles

Understanding these developments and the resulting shifts in the roles of federal and state governments is essential for comprehending today's water policies. A closer look at the historical record will help to place in context the new state initiatives discussed in subsequent chapters.[9] Primarily a state responsibility, the main issue in water law has been the right to water. The right to surface water has been addressed as part of property law. Two opposing approaches have developed over time and continue to influence policy today. The eastern United States followed the riparian rights approach originally developed in England. Under this concept, lakes and streams are considered as private waters, and the owner of the bordering land has the right to make "reasonable use" of them. While the owner can modify both quantity and quality of water use, those modifications must be within bounds of reason and in keeping with the purpose for which the land was dedicated. In recent times, some states have further restricted riparian water rights; the use must not interfere with other uses and adequate flow must be maintained. In times of water shortages, some users may have higher priorities than others. To implement these policies, states require permits for withdrawal so that the quality of the water can be protected and waste can be guarded against. Updating the definitions of beneficial use and establishing priorities among them is a key task for current state water policies.

The western United States, by contrast, followed the doctrine of "first in time, first in right." To appropriate water, the user need only demonstrate availability of water in the source of supply, show an intent to put the water to beneficial use, and give priority to more senior permit holders during times of shortage. The doctrine of "prior appropriation" goes back to times when mining and agriculture were dominant economic activities, which could only be performed if access to large amounts of water were guaranteed. Rights to the water are lost if the individual does not use it. This obviously deters conservation. The practice of conferring water rights, which have the characteristics of property rights, today remains a formidable obstacle to setting social and economic priorities for water use.

Ground water rights tend to be less individualistic, because nobody can own an aquifer, which may underlie the property of many owners. The common law of unlimited withdrawal was first restricted by rules of reasonable use, which give equal rights to all overlying landowners. A variant to this approach is used in parts of California and Arizona. Under the correlative right rules, water is allocated in proportion to the extent of ownership of the overlying land. The most widely used system in the West today goes beyond these limitations by appropriating specific water rights to users and establishing priorities among them.[10] Again, implementation of this policy depends on the issuance of permits by state agencies. Texas is the most notable case where no statewide method of restricting ground water usage exists; it retains the common-law approach of unlimited withdrawal.

Major controversies over water rights continue to be fought at the state level, in some cases resulting in interstate conflicts that have to be resolved by the courts. However, this does not mean that the states provided strong leadership and were prepared to resolve controversial allocative decisions that extend beyond the mandate of the responsible state agency.[11] To the contrary, until recently most states avoided taking action by following a three-pronged strategy: supporting federal water projects that were sought by their constituents; leaving hard decisions to the courts; and, for those issues that could not be resolved by the courts,[12] encouraging opposing interest groups to find solutions among themselves. Particularly in states confronting water shortages, policymaking by comfortable neglect will not do in the future, and hard choices will have to be made.[13]

Federal water law is more restricted in scope. It deals with the powers, projects, programs, and properties of the federal government.[14] In many respects, state law is the basis for federal water rights. For example, section 8 of the Reclamation Act of 1902 requires the federal government to proceed in conformity with the laws of the state "relating to the control, appropriation, use, or distribution of water." Accordingly, the Bureau of Reclamation and the Forest Service have had to obtain water rights from state water law officials.

Yet there have been many cases where the federal government has claimed reserved water rights. As early as 1899, the Supreme Court held that states cannot deny water rights to the United States that are needed for the beneficial use of government property. In 1908, the Supreme Court ruled in *Winters* v. *United States* that the federal government can reserve water rights on Indian reservations. Reserved rights, in contrast to appropriated rights under state laws, become effective from the date land was set aside, not from the date water was first diverted. This interpretation was first advanced by the federal government in 1955 and was first used in

1963 to claim reserved water rights on other federal lands, such as national parks and forests. The states, along with the timber and mining industries, as well as property owners, feared the loss of first-user priorities and vigorously fought expansion of the reserved rights doctrine. The Supreme Court again supported federal claims. In *Arizona* v. *California* (1963) the court held that state law did not apply to federal reclamation projects.[15] In 1978, however, the Court was more respectful of states' rights and restricted federal reserved rights to specific needs that were essential to the planned use of the land. This interpretation is part of the decision in *United States* v. *New Mexico*, which rejected federal efforts to expand the reserved water rights of national forests to protect instream water for fish and wildlife. Such an expansion of the reserved rights doctrine, according to the Court, infringed upon the historic role of states in water allocation.[16]

In summary, it would appear that the federal government has had a very restricted role in the overall management of water resources. The courts have repeatedly affirmed that its right to water is comparable to those of any other water user. Allocation of water to federal projects may be governed by the same state laws as those that apply to other water users. Thus, the federal government has not been in a position to provide leadership in developing a more just or beneficial system for the allocation of water. In fact, some see the history of shared federal and state responsibilities in water management as antagonistic.[17] As a result, the development of innovative schemes for allocating increasingly scarce water resources will have to begin at the state level. In searching for solutions, states have two main approaches from which they can select. They can regulate water allocations to the most beneficial uses, or they can allow the market to achieve this goal.[18] Arizona's approach, discussed in a later chapter, follows the first approach. Other states, among them California and Florida, find it difficult to develop the policy consensus needed for redistribution and are experimenting with market-based allocation schemes.

THE IMPACT OF FEDERAL ACTIONS
Evaluating the Federal Policy

The methods used to evaluate and justify federally financed water projects have evolved over the last 50 years. The Flood Control Act of 1936[19] specified that the benefits of federal projects should exceed costs. The act specifies that "the federal government should be prepared to undertake such investments...if the benefits to whomsoever they may accrue exceed the costs." During the 1950s, the Interagency Committee on Water Resources developed guidelines requiring uniform data for the purpose of evaluating projects. An influential handbook of practices for the economic analysis of river basin projects was published. On October 6, 1961, the president requested the secretaries of Interior, Agriculture, the Army, and Health, Education, and Welfare to review existing standards and recommend improvements. Their report was published as Senate Document

97 and replaced the 1958 handbook. In 1973, this document was superceded by the "Principles and Standards for Planning Water and Related Land Resources," developed by the Water Resources Council as a result of the Water Resources Planning Act of 1965.[20] The standards delineated in this document were intended to provide for uniformity and consistency in comparing and judging the beneficial and adverse effects of alternative plans.

Between 1979 and 1981, the Water Resources Council published sections of "Principles, Standards and Procedures for Planning Water and Related Land Resources." Methods were developed to quantify national and regional economic development benefits of water projects, as well as to evaluate environmental quality benefits and other social effects. These standards were never fully incorporated into federal water planning procedures and in 1983 were replaced by nonbinding "Principles and Guidelines" that emphasized economic benefits.[21]

These events attest to the fact that concern was developing pertaining to evaluation of proposed projects. Increasingly, there was a realization that the benefits of some projects were not as great as had been claimed during the planning stages, and that they did not justify the expenditure of public funds. In 1970, the Brookings Institution concluded that the rate of return required of federal water projects was very low by almost any reasonable standard and that the definition of benefit associated with many projects was very questionable. Compared with a 10-15 percent return on most private industrial investments, the return on the majority of Corps projects was closer to 5 percent. Some Bureau of Reclamation projects actually lost money.[22]

In many cases, the real rate of return in terms of overall national productivity was actually much less than the numbers suggest. For instance, in the case of some irrigation projects, the farm output on the newly irrigated lands was in effect matched by a reduction in output in other parts of the country. At that time, the Department of Agriculture was spending about $4.5 billion to restrict the production of agricultural output. In the case of flood control projects, investment in the floodplain was often accelerated, and in some cases it was reported that flood damage increased after the completion of projects.[23]

The National Water Commission was established in 1968 to make an overall assessment of water issues. The commission's purpose was to review present and anticipated national water resource problems, consider the economic and social consequences of water resource development, and advise on specific water resource matters. Working with the Water Resources Council, the commission produced its final report in 1973.[24] It concluded that water development projects are no longer the primary factor that drives economic growth in a given area. With more industrialization, other factors, including the performance of the national economy, increasingly influence regional economic growth. The commission believed that increased emphasis must be placed on the management of existing water developments as a means of improving regional growth potential, rather than relying on new projects. Otherwise, water development will be ineffective for regional growth purposes and may simply result in the redistribution of economic activities.[25]

The report provides a comprehensive evaluation of the institutions involved in water development and how they interact to affect the planning process. Numerous recommendations were made, including greater involvement of the lower levels of government that are nearest the problem. The issue of cost-sharing policies is pertinent to the present discussion. The commission noted inconsistencies among types of projects and granting agencies in the cost-sharing arrangements. In the past, this has sometimes led to the construction of more costly projects, such as reservoirs rather than levees, because this option is less costly for the local community. While not disapproving of cost-sharing arrangements, the commission recommended new policies consistent with six specific goals. Direct beneficiaries of water projects should be obligated to repay all project costs allocated to services for which they benefit. Subsidies are only justified if they serve some compelling social purpose. The recommendations are based on the principle that: "appropriate cost-sharing policies should provide incentives for the selection of efficient projects that will lead to progress toward water resources policies that are in harmony with other national programs and policies."[26]

Controlling Federal Outlays

The 1970s: A Period of Transition
The debate about cost sharing and how much the federal government should subsidize water development projects continued throughout the 1970s and the first half of the 1980s. Many groups, including those in the emerging environmental movement, contended that, as long as the federal government footed the bill, wasteful water development projects would continue to be built, while economic efficiency dictated better management of existing supplies.

By 1978, no administration had successfully consolidated cost-sharing policies for federal water projects. President Carter proposed the development of a national water policy. Conservation and nonstructural methods, such as better management, were now a national priority. He intended beneficiaries to pay a larger part of project costs; structural methods for flood control would be subject to the same 20 percent state share that applied to nonstructural measures. The president regarded his proposals for greater state sharing of costs as a way of increasing their roles and responsibilities in water policies, as well as a deterrent to undesirable projects. He proposed a large expansion of federal funds for state water planning and technical assistance. The states viewed this as federal intrusion, and the National Governors' Association developed its own policy paper.[27]

In assigning states the primary authority and responsibility for water management, the governors' position did not conflict with that of the president. However, to some extent, the issue had already become an area of confrontation. Soon after coming to office, the president announced a "hit list" of 32 water projects that would not be funded.[28] Following negative reaction in Congress, he then ordered a review of federal water projects for which appropriations were under consideration. He announced his opposition to 18 of them and requested major changes in five.[29] This added to the perception that the states were being asked to increase their share of the costs without commensurate gains in policy and program development.

By the time he left office, President Carter appeared to have achieved very little. States were not providing front-end money, and the independent review of projects by the Water Resources Council was doomed because the Council was slated for abolition in the Reagan budget.[30] However, this period does seem to have marked a turning point in the general attitude toward federal financing of water projects. It was not until 1986 that the controversy over cost sharing was resolved and new legislation enacted. The end result has been that no new projects were authorized between 1976 and 1986.

Water Quality Management

Closely associated with the issues of water quantity and how available water supplies should be allocated is the issue of water quality. By 1970, it was realized that many of the nation's rivers were becoming unfit for wildlife and recreational uses. In addition, agricultural, municipal, and industrial pollution had adverse consequences for downstream users, who were being forced to spend increasing amounts to restore adequate water quality. The Federal Water Pollution Control Act[31] authorized the Environmental Protection Agency (EPA) to set minimum water quality standards for each river segment according to a classification system. This 1972 legislation authorized $18 billion for the first three years of construction grants for waste water facilities and increased the federal share of costs from 50 to 75 percent. These grants grew to an annual outlay of about $6 billion in 1977, falling to $2.6 billion in 1984 (the federal share reduced to 55 percent).[32]

The Reagan Administration

The Reagan administration has had a much more limited agenda in terms of water resources. Its primary goal has been to reduce spending on domestic programs. With the momentum for increased cost-sharing building, the administration had the opportunity to reduce spending on water development projects. However, its position has been influenced by its close association with western farmers. In 1983, Assistant Secretary of Defense for Civil Works (responsible for the Army Corps of Engineers) William Gianelli proposed, with the approval of the Office of Management and Budget, new cost-sharing arrangements for federal water projects. He recommended that states, cities, and other users pay all of the costs of municipal and power use costs and at least 35 percent of flood control and irrigation use costs. Later, in testimony before Congress, he appeared less firm about ensuring nonfederal financing prior to the start of the project. Also, despite approval of the policy by the Cabinet Council on Natural Resources, Interior Secretary James Watt later wrote a letter to the chairman of the Environment and Public Works Subcommittee on Water Resources, insisting that "cost-sharing arrangements will be established on a case-by-case basis."[33]

Congress has also predictably been divided on the issues. Representatives from eastern states, where older water supply systems are often in a state of disrepair, are reluctant to continue supporting subsidies for western irrigation projects. However, two bills (HR 3678 and S 1739), introduced in 1984, contained limited cost-sharing provisions. Anticipating a presidential veto, the House Democratic leaders abandoned the attempt to get water development projects approved in 1984. In trying to develop broad support, by providing "something for everyone"--$800 million annually of low-interest loans to repair aging water supply systems and increased spending for environmental protection--the house bill authorized $18 billion in new water projects, with little increase in cost sharing.[34]

The Omnibus Water Resources Development Act (HR 6), which finally became law in November 1986, authorized the Corps to undertake 260 new projects at a cost of $16.3 billion. Of this, $4.3 billion will be funded from nonfederal sources, covering 100 percent of hydroelectric project costs and municipal and industrial supplies, 35 percent of agricultural water supply costs, and 50 percent of recreational water costs.[35]

Compared with the stance on development projects, the administration has been more firm in its desire to cut the sewage-treatment-plant construction program. The EPA estimated that a further $90 to $106 billion was required to complete the program started in 1973; the administration requested $23 billion.[36] In reauthorizing the Clean Water Act, Congress approved, in November 1986, $18 billion for construction of sewage treatment plants and $2 billion for pollution control programs. The president pocket vetoed the bill, claiming excessive cost. In January 1987, he again vetoed the same bill (HR 1), following almost unanimous passage in both houses. The veto was overridden.[37]

Emerging Issues and Policy Implications

Despite many problems, there has been a general improvement in surface water quality. The situation for ground water is different. It is becoming abundantly evident that degradation of ground water is a major problem, especially in specific localities. With limitations in surface water supplies being noted in the 1970s, people increasingly turned to ground water as a source. It provides 40 percent of all water used for irrigation and 80 percent of all water used in rural areas. However, such usage may have peaked as overdrafting has resulted in the decline of water tables and increased pumping costs in some areas. In other instances, salt water intrusion, particularly in coastal areas, has resulted in a deterioration in water quality. For areas that rely heavily on ground water, pollution of any kind, natural or man-made, is a serious problem, because it is likely that once an aquifer is contaminated, it will be costly and sometimes impossible to restore the water to acceptable quality. Salt contamination is also a problem in arid areas, particularly in the Southwest, that rely heavily on surface water for irrigation. In the Colorado River basin in the Southwest, two factors combine to aggravate the problem. Enormous amounts of water are removed from the river, both by evaporation from reservoirs and for irrigation purposes. In addition, the return flow contains salt leached from croplands, and this adds to the already significant level of natural salts. The results are often costly. For example, in order to meet its treaty obligations with Mexico, the United States has constructed a $234.1 million desalting plant in Yuma, Arizona.[38] Annual operating expenses are expected to be high.

Nunn and Ingram[39] claim that most of our problems arise from market imperfections and unwise government policies, including narrow-purpose programs, long-established subsidies, and inappropriate legal constraints. Changes in policy will necessarily create bitter conflicts as agricultural interests are pitted against municipal needs. Current water-use patterns in many ways reflect the fact that, at the federal level, different agencies have been established to represent each of these different interests. For instance, the U.S. Bureau of Reclamation built storage dams and other water supply projects in an attempt to develop the West and provide each farmer with the opportunity to work up to 160 acres. Later, the 160-acre-farm size limit was abandoned. Currently, less than 3 percent of the farms encompass 31 percent of the land served by these projects.[40] With a reduction in the role of the federal government, the states now have the opportunity to develop more comprehensive solutions that best fit their individual needs and establish the basis for economic growth.

STATE-FEDERAL RELATIONS

This realignment of state and federal responsibilities also appears to be the case in other public policy issues. For instance, a recent study on science and technology policy demonstrated considerable activity at the state level in order to promote economic development.[41] These authors claim that the states are not usurping a new role, but resuming one evident prior to the depression and the Second World War, periods that required more centralized decision making. Despite the claims of the Reagan administration, the trend toward decentralization has been in effect for some time. In the early 1970s, the Nixon administration initiated many cost-sharing programs with state and local governments. In addition, the new environmental awareness, which fostered legislation such as the Clean

Water Act,[42] has increasingly resulted in the requirement that states initiate programs in order to meet federal standards. Thus, in exchange for more individualized programs, the states are having to assume more of the financial burden. This does not necessarily result in the expenditure of large amounts of public funds. New initiatives in science and technology policy show state governments working in close cooperation with universities and the private sector, acting as a catalyst rather than directly administering their own programs.[43]

The withdrawal of the federal government from many of the issues associated with water resources could provide an opportunity for the states to develop individualized programs and coordinated management plans. Each state has a unique set of climatic, environmental, and economic factors that color its attitude toward water management. In some cases, the issue has been forced upon the states as the allocation of limited water supplies emerges as a political issue. Other states are more farsighted and are implementing plans for the optimum use of this resource.

Implications for Water Policy

In 1980, the U.S. Water Resources Council published a report entitled *State of the States: Water Resources Planning and Management*. It attempted to assess the ability of the states to assume responsibility for water resources planning and management. It concluded that only two states, Florida and Delaware, had fully comprehensive approaches with planning and management functions consolidated in one agency. The other states had a variety of programs, often dispersed among different units of government. Only 12 to 15 states were developing formal state water plans.[44]

However, progress at the state level was being made. Between 1960 and 1980, the number of state and local water resources employees increased from about 70,000 to about 115,000, while the number of federal employees remained constant. State and local expenditures for all water resources purposes increased from $89 per capita ($16 billion) in 1960 to $111 per capita ($25 billion) in 1980 (in 1980 dollars). In addition, the capability to finance water resource development at the state and local level had also progressed. For 1980-2, the 50 states combined had issued almost $8 billion in water resources general obligation and revenue bonds.[45]

What does this mean in terms of specific programs in individual states? Only one thing can be said for sure: each state has its own unique set of environmental parameters and economic forces. Each state has developed its own response to managing its water resources. The most significant factor that determines much of the response is climate. Although different states have developed different mechanisms, based on their individual historical and cultural roots, the most striking differences derive from issues of abundance. Annual rainfall in the United States ranges from less than 5 inches in the deserts of the Southwest to 50 inches or more in southeastern states and more than 100 inches in the coastal Pacific Northwest. In general, the East is humid and the West is arid. Another factor that compounds the problem is the variations in population distribution. Initially spurred by federally subsidized water development projects, some of the fastest growing states are those with the driest climates. As a result, in the driest western states, per capita consumption is 1,200 gallons per day (when all uses are considered), compared with 120 gallons per day in the East.[46] In the lower Colorado River basin of the Southwest, consumption already exceeds renewable supply. Often the deficit is made up from ground water and severe overdrafting is apparent in many areas. With consumption continuing to increase, some states are being forced to address the issue of allocating priorities among uses.

It is apparent that differences in climate and population density will have a major impact on water availability and use patterns. At the time when water policies at the federal level were driven by the desire to develop western states, the emphasis was on providing dependable water supplies for irrigated agriculture. Many of these states have favorable climates, which more recently has led to a population boom. With the realization that water supplies are limited in these dry western regions, the traditional agricultural interests are often in direct competition with municipal and industrial users for dependable supplies. As a result, in these states, the current focus has shifted from water development to better management of existing supplies. With the federal government withdrawing from water resource management, the question is how effective are the states in taking the initiative and addressing this issue.

NOTES

1. U.S., Congress, Joint Economic Committee, Subcommittee on Economic Goals and Intergovernment Policy, *Hard Choices: A Report on the Increasing Gap between America's Needs and Our Ability to Pay for Them* (Washington, D.C.: Government Printing Office, 1984).

2. Charles J. Cicchetti et al., "Benefits or Costs? An Assessment of the Water Resources Council's Proposed Principles and Standards," in *Benefit-Cost and Policy Analysis 1972*, eds. William A. Niskanen et al., (Chicago: Aldine, 1973), p. 431 (hereafter cited as "Benefits or Costs?").

3. National Water Commission, *Water Policies for the Future; Final Report to the President and to the Congress of the United States* (Washington, D.C.: Government Printing Office, 1973), pp. 111-114 (hereafter cited as *Water Policies*).

4. Terry Anderson, *Water Crisis: Ending the Policy Drought*, (Baltimore, Md.: The Johns Hopkins University Press, 1983), pp. 45-52 (hereafter cited as *Water Crisis*).

5. Mohamed T. El-Ashry and Diana C. Gibbons, *Troubled Waters: New Policies for Managing Water in the American West* (Washington, D.C.: World Resources Institute, 1986), p. 13.

6. Charles Schultze, with Edward Hamilton and Allen Schick, *Setting National Priorities: The 1971 Budget,* (Washington, D.C.: The Brookings Institute, 1970), p. 167 (hereafter cited as *Setting National Priorities*).

7. U.S., Congress, Congressional Budget Office, *The Federal Budget for Public Works Infrastructure* (Washington, D.C.: U.S. Government Printing Office, July 1985), p. 68 (hereafter cited as *The Federal Budget*).

8. California v. U.S., 438 U.S. 645 (1978).

9. The following discussion is based on Warren Wiessman, Jr. and Claire Welty, *Water Management: Technology and Institutions* (New York: Harper and Row, 1985). See in particular, chapter 3, "Water Policy and Institutions."

10. Anderson, *Water Crisis,* p. 97.

11. One notable example is the variety of methods and the extent to which different states have accommodated instream (wildlife) needs within the appropriations doctrine.

12. Helen Ingram, Nancy Laney, and John R. McCain, "Water Scarcity and the Politics of Plenty in the Four Corners States," *Western Political Quarterly* 32 (1979): 298-306 (hereafter cited as "Water Scarcity").

13. The strategy of legislative avoidance has been documented in a study by Robert Salisbury and John Heinz (cited in Ingram, Laney, and McCain, "Water Scarcity").

14. Frank J. Trelease, "Uneasy Federalism--State Water Laws and National Water Uses," *Washington Law Review* 55 (1980): 751-775.

15. Milton H. Jamail, John R. McCain, and Scott J. Ullery, *Federal-State Water Use Relations in the American West* (Tucson, Ariz.: University of Arizona, Office of Arid Land Studies, 1978).

16. Ingram, Laney, and McCain, "Water Scarcity."

17. Margaret S. Hrezo and William E. Hrezo, "From Antagonistic to Cooperative Federalism in Water Resources Development," *American Journal of Economics and Sociology* 44 (1985): 199-214.

18. "Water in America," *The Economist* (October 4, 1986): 37.

19. 33 U.S.C. 701a.

20. For a critique of the document see Charles J. Cicchetti et al., "Benefits or Costs?," p. 432.

21. U.S., Congress, Congressional Budget Office, *Efficient Investments in Water Resources: Issues and Options* (Washington, D.C.: U.S. Government Printing Office, August 1983), p. 18 (hereafter cited as *Efficient Investments*).

22. Schultze, *Setting National Priorities,* p. 163.

23. Schultze, *Setting National Priorities,* p. 165.

24. National Water Commission, *Water Policies.*

25. National Water Commission, *Water Policies,* p. 58.

26. National Water Commission, *Water Policies,* pp. 485-499.

27. Leonard Wilson, *State Water Policy Issues* (Lexington, Ky.: The Council of State Governments, 1978), pp. 4-12 (hereafter cited as *State Water Policy*).

28. Dean Schooler and Helen Ingram, "Water Resource Managment," *Policy Studies Review* 1, no. 2 (1981-82), pp. 243-254.

29. Wilson, *State Water Policy,* p. 23. President Carter subsequently signed an appropriations bill that included nine projects he opposed.

30. Schooler and Ingram, "Water Resource Managment."

31. 33 U.S.C., sections 1251-1376.

32. Congressional Budget Office, *The Federal Budget,* p. 56.

33. Lawrence Mosher, "Water Torture," *National Journal* (July 23, 1983), p. 1559 (hereafter cited as "Water Torture").

34. Timothy Clark, "Dry Spell Continues for Water Projects as Financing Agreement Eludes Congress," *National Journal* (November 3, 1984), pp. 2079-2082.

35. Sierra Club, "President Signs Mammoth Water Resources Bill," *National News Report* 18 (December 17, 1985), p. 4.

36. Lawrence Mosher, "Localities Begin to Challenge Government's Water Policy 'Vacuum'," *National Journal* (January 28, 1984), pp. 164-168.

37. Sierra Club, "Clean Water Bill Back on President's Desk," *National News Report* 19 (January 23, 1987), p. 1.

38. "Water-Short Colorado May Be Dammed if it Builds, Dammed if it Doesn't," *National Journal* (July 17, 1982), p. 1259.

39. Christopher Nunn and Helen Ingram, *America's Water: Current Trends and Emerging Issues* (Washington, D.C.: The Conservation Foundation, 1984), p. 34 (hereafter cited as *America's Water:*).

40. U.S., Department of Interior (cited in Nunn and Ingram, *America's Water,* p. 50).

41. Jurgen Schmandt and Robert Wilson, "State Science and Technology Policies: an Assessment," *Economic Development Quarterly* 2, no. 2 (1988), pp. 124-137 (hereafter cited as "State Science").

42. 33 U.S.C., sections 1251-1376.

43. Schmandt and Wilson, "State Science."

44. The Council of State Governments, *Water Resource Management, New Responsibilities for State Governments,* prepared for the 1980 Annual Meeting of the Interstate Conference on Water Problems, Cincinnati, Ohio, September 21-25, 1980.

45. Congressional Budget Office, *Efficient Investments,* p. 25.

46. Congressional Budget Office, *Efficient Investments,* p. 13.

STATE RESPONSES: AN OVERVIEW

BACKGROUND AND STUDY DESIGN

This section analyzes the factors that have resulted in a change in attitude toward water in the states that we have chosen to study. These themes are developed more fully in the chapters that follow. Here we attempt to identify unifying concepts. However, it is difficult to make general statements about the development of water policies at the state level. Some states have a long history of concern for their natural resources and have addressed water quantity and quality issues as they have arisen. Other states have taken a more laissez faire approach, leaving the courts to settle disputes or waiting for the federal government to force them to take action. Now that the debate about water issues in much of the country is focused on allocative decisions and limitations in water supply that could have an impact upon regional economic growth, this attitude is changing. As discussed in Chapter 1, the federal government is not about to finance additional water development projects, especially if the main objective is regional economic development. Thus, it is incumbent upon the states to take the initiative. If they perceive water resource management to be an integral part of their economic development, they will have to assume a policymaking rather than an administrative role.

Recently, this change has been exemplified by the recommendations of the National Groundwater Policy Forum. Chaired by Governor Bruce Babbitt, it explored the issue of federal versus state activity as the most appropriate means of protecting ground water. Following a series of nationwide public hearings, it published its final report in 1986. The main recommendation was that states bear the primary responsibility for ground water management, with local governments bearing a major responsibility for program implementation. The role of the federal government should be restricted to ensuring consistency and equity among states and providing technical support and oversight.[1]

In general, states are resisting further federal regulation of their resources. The trend in recent years has been for the federal government to enact legislation and the states to implement it. With decreasing amounts of federal financial support to accompany such programs, the states would prefer to initiate their own programs. One of the goals of the current study was to determine to what extent selected states had responded to problems in water resource management in a timely manner. Do states generally wait for federal regulation or some form of crisis to precipitate action?

Once action has been initiated, a great variety of responses are possible. These range from a comprehensive plan of action to a more piecemeal approach to the problem. The response will be fashioned by both institutional and technical considerations. In both cases, this will largely depend on whether the state has a history of addressing water management issues. If it does, it is likely that the institutions will already be in place, and in some cases, technical information, based on previous research activities, will be available. If the state does not have well-developed institutions, either new ones must be formed or the solutions are likely to be incremental.

This project was designed to ascertain the nature of state initiatives in making new water policy and addressing technical problems related to water management. We focused on the importance of institutional factors, the development of financing mechanisms, and the role of research in formulating new policies. In choosing the six states to be studied, the following were some important questions considered:

1. Does the state have a long-term water policy as evidenced, for example, in a comprehensive water plan?
2. Has the state developed new approaches for water management, and are such programs supported by innovative funding mechanisms?
3. Has the state developed a ground water policy?
4. Does the state provide the funds necessary for the support of water research and a mechanism for the integration of new findings into the development of policies?

Several states presented interesting cases and met the criteria delineated above. However, the size of the project staff and the travel budget made it necessary to restrict the size of the study. As a result, we selected six states, representing a variety of different approaches to addressing water resource issues: Arizona, California, Florida, North Carolina, Texas, and Wisconsin. Our choice was influenced by a desire to cover different geographical regions, as well as historical differences in addressing social and environmental concerns. Our study illustrates the importance of these factors; while some states developed water resource management plans as a matter of course, others waited for a critical situation to arise. We have focused on the most significant water policy issue in each state. In the case of the western states--Arizona, California, and Texas--the issue of better management of existing supplies was of primary concern, as opposed to a continuation of the policies mainly focused on additional water development projects. In Florida, North Carolina, and Wisconsin, water quality concerns are paramount. In each state chapter, we have included a case study that illustrates the development of programs at the state level to address pressing public policy problems that are not being solved by the federal government.

WATER PROBLEMS CONFRONTING THE STATES
Major Policy Concerns

Three of the states studied--Arizona, California, and Texas--are facing allocative decisions resulting from inadequate supplies in a significant part of their state. A summary of consumptive use patterns is shown in Table 2.1. These three states are some of the fastest growing states in the nation. Between 1960 and 1980, the population of Arizona doubled, and in Texas and California it increased by 50 percent (Table 2.2). Those high rates of growth, which are expected to continue, put a considerable strain on the states' resources. In some areas, it has become apparent that availability of

TABLE 2.1 Consumptive Use Patterns

State	Total consumption (mgd)					Per capita (gpd)		% of renewable supply
	Public supply	Rural use	Irriga-tion	Indus-trial	Total	all uses	excluding irrigation	
Arizona	340	32	4,000	170	4,542	1670	199	>100
California	1700	130	23,000	330	25,160	1062	91	34
Florida	330	100	1,500	550	2,480	255	101	<5
North Carolina	110	170	130	350	760	129	107	<10
Texas	640	400	8,000	1900	10,940	781	210	<25 (east) >60 (west)
Wisconsin	57	82	77	91	307	65	49	<5

Source: U.S., Department of the Interior, Geological Survey, *National Water Survey 1983--Hydrologic Events and Issues*, Water Supply Paper 2250 (Washington, D.C.: Government Printing Office, 1984), p. 27; Wayne B. Solley, Edith B. Chase, and William Mann IV, *Estimated Use of Water in the U.S. in 1980*, Geological Survey Circular 1001 (Reston, Va.: U.S. Geological Survey, 1983).

TABLE 2.2   Population by State, 1940-1980 (millions)

State	1940	1950	1960	1970	1980
Arizona	0.50	0.75	1.30	1.78	2.72
California	6.91	10.59	15.72	19.97	23.67
Florida	1.90	2.77	4.95	6.79	9.75
North Carolina	3.57	4.06	4.56	5.08	5.88
Texas	6.41	7.71	9.58	11.20	14.23
Wisconsin	3.14	3.43	3.95	4.42	4.71

Source: U.S., Department of Commerce, Bureau of the Census, *1980 Census of Population, Characteristics of the Population, U.S. Summary-- Number of Inhabitants,* vol. 1, ch. A, table 8.

water may be the factor that ultimately limits the rate of economic development.   In fact, out-of-state eastern investors have cited water management problems as a reason for showing some reluctance to invest in Arizona.[2]

Despite the fact that, in general, agricultural uses of water are no longer rapidly increasing in Arizona, the demands of fast growing municipal and industrial uses are creating conflicts between different user groups. As in all western states, allocation of surface water has traditionally been determined by the prior appropriation doctrine, with little control over ground water use. Thus, in the past there have been few restrictions placed on water use; in general, a permit for surface water has been issued subject only to the need to protect supplies to more senior permit holders. The legal basis for allocating water under this scheme served Arizona well when agriculture and mining formed the basis for economic development. However, as municipal and industrial demands increase, it is often argued that greater economic benefit from existing water supplies could be gained by other allocative methods, including those that rely on market factors. Such a decision has already been forced upon Arizona. When data for irrigated acreage are analyzed (Table 2.3), little increase (5 percent) is evident in Arizona between 1959 and 1978, whereas greater increases were shown in California (18 percent) and Texas (29 percent). Irrigation in Texas has exhibited remarkable growth since 1940 as a result of ground water development on the High Plains, but recently shows a leveling trend.

Although Arizona has the severest deficit in water supply (Table 2.1), similar use patterns exist in certain parts of California and Texas, where the driest areas have long relied on irrigated agriculture as the basis for their economy. The large geographical diversity that exists in both of these states, with annual rainfall varying considerably from one part to another, compounds the problems associated with reaching a political consensus on water policy. In the past, southern California has relied heavily on the transfer of water from more northern areas in the state. However, recent attempts to extend the State Water Project, by building the Peripheral Canal, were rejected by the voters. This appears to indicate a change in attitude toward water development projects. Similarly, voters in Texas marked the end of an era when, in 1981, they rejected a financing plan that could have led to importation of water from other states.

TABLE 2.3 Irrigated Acreage, 1940-1978 (millions of acres)

State	1940	1950	1959	1969	1978
Arizona	0.65	0.95	1.05	1.07	1.10
California	4.20	6.50	7.40	7.30	8.70
Texas	0.90	3.00	5.50	6.80	7.10
All other states	12.40	15.50	19.30	23.90	33.00

Source: U.S., Department of Commerce, Bureau of the Census, *1978 Census of Agriculture*, vol. 4, Irrigation (AC78-IR) (Washington, D.C.: Government Printing Office, 1982), table 1, pp. 146-147.

The three remaining states in our study--Florida, North Carolina, and Wisconsin--face different priorities in the area of water resource management. With annual rainfall in excess of 50 inches, they do not have general water supply problems, even though North Carolina and Wisconsin have experienced considerable growth since 1940 and Florida's 1980 population is five times that of its 1940 population (Table 2.2). These three states have been preoccupied with water quality problems. Both North Carolina and Wisconsin have fostered the growth of industries that have traditionally discharged by-products into natural water courses. In Florida, the largest source of water pollution is agriculture. Agricultural development in south Florida was facilitated by federally sponsored land-drainage projects. Newly reclaimed lands are some of the most fertile in the country, and intensive agriculture, involving the use of fertilizers and pesticides, has contributed to ground water contamination. In addition to agriculture, the economic prosperity of the state is dependent upon its recreational resources, which have encouraged the growth of tourism and the relocation of retirees. This diversity has resulted in conflicts between different groups. The very flood control and reclamation projects that brought the initial development now threaten the ecological balance that is necessary to maintain a high quality of life and the wildlife that attracts tourists.

Specific Policy Issues

The 1970s saw a change in attitude toward the environment and the management of natural resources. Realizing that many of these resources, including water, were available in finite quantities, management, both in terms of quantity and quality, became an important public policy issue. However, sometimes the political will to implement change was lacking, and it took some kind of an incentive or crisis to bring about a change in attitude toward water resources. Although water is often the basis for economic growth, it has no direct market value, and ground water, for instance, has traditionally been subject to the right of capture.

Increasing population pressures, together with the withdrawal of federal funds for new projects, have affected the ability of states to develop new water supplies. The three western states that were chosen each have had to face the fact that their ability to continue developing new supplies is severely limited. Different factors have been instrumental in fostering a change in attitude, and the resulting policies are also very diverse. Arizona, one of the driest states in the nation, has, to a large extent, been dependent upon federally funded water development projects for irrigated agriculture. However, following authorization of the Central Arizona Project (CAP) in 1968, the federal government proceeded to impose certain conditions upon the state. Irrigators that accepted CAP water were required to reduce their ground water usage accordingly, in order to alleviate the problem of severe overdrafting of ground water. Using the leverage of federal dollars, the U.S. Department of the Interior insisted that Arizona enact meaningful ground water management legislation as the price for the continued construction of the CAP.[3]

A change in water management policies in California also reflects a change from a predominantly development-oriented approach to one of wiser management of existing supplies. However, in this case, most of the impetus for change has come from within the state. California has always been an active participant in the development of its water resources. In fact, in the 1930s it was responsible for planning the Central Valley Project as the initial stage of the State Water Plan. Revenue bonds were approved by the voters, but could not be sold because of the depression. Financing was then arranged through the Federal Reclamation Act. Later, the state built the State Water Project. While there continues to be pressure to develop the state's water resources further, financial constraints, together with the increasing reluctance of residents in the northern part of the state to allow further transfers of "their" water to the south, have forced a greater emphasis on conservation and reuse of water. The California drought of 1976-77 provided the necessary impetus for legislation to facilitate conservation, including the formation of the Office of Water Conservation within the Department of Water Resources.

Although geographically Texas resembles California in some ways, with the driest areas dependent upon irrigated agriculture, these areas do not have the population base necessary to give them the political clout required for water development projects to replace depleted ground water supplies. Considerable effort in the 1960s and 1970s was directed at developing plans for the importation of water from other states. However, three attempts to obtain voter approval for financing were all unsuccessful. The state still lacks a political consensus on how to address water management issues. In 1981, the lieutenant governor took a leadership position in the formulation of more realistic water policy goals that are in tune with a greater emphasis on water management. It took two legislative sessions to enact a package of legislation (the Texas Water Plan), which was overwhelmingly approved by the voters in 1985. With its primary emphasis on financing local water projects, the legislation did stipulate that conservation provisions be included in projects involving state financial assistance.[4]

Not all states have needed external factors or impending crises for them to act. In Wisconsin, for instance, there has been an historic commitment to progressive, activist government and a commitment to conservation. As a result, state officials have readily addressed water quality problems and are often ahead of the federal government on these issues. Consensus committee procedures characterize the Wisconsin legislature, and this method enabled environmentalists and solid waste disposers to resolve their differences outside the floor of the legislature. The resulting 1983 Groundwater Act provides for the monitoring of threatened aquifers, the replacement of contaminated water supplies, the cleanup of ground water hazards, and compensation to victims of well contamination.[5]

Increased attention to water quality issues has been forced upon many states. In 1951, North Carolina passed significant water quality legislation that enabled the state to begin building the water institutions necessary for effective water resource management. Although the standards set in the Federal Water Pollution Control Act of 1972 were more stringent than those set by the state, North Carolina had taken an important step forward by developing water quality standards and classifying streams according to the "best use" of each segment. In Florida, phosphate-mining activities and agricultural runoff are significant causes of ground water pollution, and storm water is a major source of surface water contamination. Beginning in the early 1970s, Florida started to address these problems by developing a comprehensive plan that considered water resources within the context of land development planning. The unprecedented growth of the early 1970s made Florida the fastest growing state in the nation. Increasing public awareness of the potentially devastating effects of uncontrolled growth, together with a severe water shortage in south Florida in 1971, provided the impetus for legislative reform of the state's land-use regulatory system. In addition, it was realized that the federal reclamation projects had resulted in the destruction of many critical wildlife habitats, which are important to its flourishing tourist industry.

APPROACHES TO WATER MANAGEMENT

It is evident from an analysis of the factors that prompted state action on water resource management that attitudes toward this issue vary enormously. This is also reflected in the type of response elicited. Some states have attempted to take a more comprehensive approach, while others have enacted legislation to address specific issues. However, despite attempts by some states to enact comprehensive water management plans, this has not always led to the most effective and far-reaching policies. In fact, attempts to enact and later implement such plans may have the opposite effect, as opposition groups either impose compromises upon those plans prior to enactment or subject their provisions to judicial review during implementation. Pelham claims that enactment of comprehensive programs may produce less effective controls than ad hoc approaches, as implementation is often more difficult than enactment.[6] A review of such plans in the selected states serves to illustrate the point.

In 1972, Florida enacted the first of a series of legislative actions aimed at comprehensive land-use planning, including water resource management. The Florida Environmental Land and Water Management Act of 1972 authorized the Administration Commission (consisting of the governor and six elected state officers) to designate areas of critical state concern. Following such designation of the Florida Keys, the Florida Supreme Court held that the legislature could not delegate legislative power to regulate land use to an administrative agency.[7] Throughout the 1970s and early 1980s, Florida grappled with the problems of state comprehensive planning. Legislation enacted in the early 1970s was criticized on the grounds that it depended upon procedural review rather than a policy base. By 1985, the State Comprehensive Plan, incorporating the State Water Use Plan, was adopted.[8] The plan has been criticized because it does not contain a clear statement of legislative policy and the lack of a funding mechanism.[9] However, the State Water Use Plan does provide for the restoration of 62,000 acres of degraded lakes, 220,000 acres of degraded wetlands, and 98 miles of degraded rivers by the year 2005.[10]

Similar problems have confronted other states. Arizona has the most comprehensive legislation for the management of ground water. Prompted by *Farmers Investment Co.* v. *Bettwy*,[11] the Groundwater Management Commission was formed in 1977, and eventually the 1980 Groundwater Management Act was passed.[12] Designed to achieve safe yield in ground water usage by the year 2025, it restricts development in areas that do not have an ensured long-term supply and limits agricultural uses of water. Despite some specific provisions, such as a prohibition on new agricultural projects, the act has been criticized because there are no specific mechanisms for ensuring that the goal of safe yield by 2025 will be attained.

In Texas, similar problems have arisen. Despite the adoption of the Texas Water Plan by the state agencies and the passage of some significant water legislation in 1985, attempts at comprehensive planning have often resulted in procedural rather than substantive provisions.[13] Voters, who approved a bond package to finance water development projects in 1985, accepted the weak provisions to control water use; passage of more stringent controls was not a politically viable option. The end result of such a vague mandate is that the legislature passes its responsibility for policymaking to the state agencies and, in some cases, ultimately to the courts.

In California, the Department of Water Resources is responsible for the California Water Plan, first prepared in 1957 and most recently updated in 1983. It attempts to inventory water supplies, predict future demand, and prescribe water management plans.[14] The lack of a comprehensive water-use plan is probably a result of the state's geographical diversity. The state has succeeded in enacting legislation to encourage water conservation and increase the transferability of water rights, but schemes to increase the water supply to southern California are constantly under attack by northern voters. The Office of Water Conservation, created within the Department of Water Resources as a result of the 1976-77 drought, coordinates public education programs aimed at reducing both municipal and agricultural demand.

Other states have also developed specific programs to facilitate better management of water resources. In Wisconsin and North Carolina, water quality issues have been paramount. Both states have developed innovative programs to address specific problems in this area. High levels of pollution in the Fox and Wisconsin Rivers led to the development of a system of wasteload allocation based on the assimilative capacity of the rivers in order to improve water quality, without placing an undue burden upon the industries responsible. In North Carolina, the significance of their Pollution Prevention Pays Program has been recognized by the EPA and is being used as a model for the rest of the country.

Where comprehensive legislation has been enacted, the importance of institutional factors has been recognized. In particular, new institutions may be created specifically to facilitate the integration of different levels of government. The basis for the integrated approach to water management in Florida was the establishment of five water management districts, each with taxing authority, under the Department of Environmental Regulation. Similarly, in Arizona, four active management areas were established under the Department of Water Resources. In both of these states, additional funding mechanisms were devised to support the new programs. A real estate tax implemented in Florida to finance land acquisition as part of the Save Our Rivers and Save Our Everglades Programs, together with bonding capacity, is expected to raise almost $1 billion in the next 20 to 25 years.[15] In Arizona, the Groundwater Management Act provides for a ground water withdrawal fee intended to cover the cost of the administration of the program, as well as engineering feasibility and site design studies.

Other states have developed innovative funding mechanisms to support specific programs. The Texas Water Development Board receives revenues from the Agricultural Soil and Water Conservation Trust Fund, established in the state treasury and funded with $10 million.[16] In Wisconsin, the entire 1983 Groundwater Act is financed by user fees levied against solid waste disposers and totaling $1.5 million per year.[17] In an effort to increase public awareness of the importance of water conservation, the Texas Society of Professional Engineers initiated an education program for schoolchildren. They elicited financial support from the private sector to match a Texas Water Development Board grant, and the current Phase II Program is funded at $249,500.[18]

THE ROLE OF WATER RESEARCH

Research support in many fields has, to a large extent, traditionally been the responsibility of the federal government. Many of the issues that need to be addressed in the area of water management are in the public sector and of general interest, extending beyond state boundaries. As a result, states have been reluctant to fund this and most other types of water research. Although the states have a desire to participate in such efforts, in the past they have relied on federal leadership to provide the necessary funds.

In 1964, the U.S. Office of Water Resources Research was authorized by the Water Resources Research Act.[19] The goal of the program is to develop new technology and more efficient methods for resolving local, state, and nationwide water resource problems. Formerly an independent research office within the Department of the Interior, it has undergone several administrative reorganizations and is currently part of the U.S. Geological Survey (USGS). The office does not maintain its own research facilities, but provides a small noncompetitive annual grant to support one state university water-resources research institute in each state. In 1986 each institute received an annual allotment of $119,000.[20] Each state is required to provide matching funds in the form of faculty salaries and over-head expenses. A small competitive grant program, which requires a progressively rigorous nonfederal matching of funds (now $1.5 nonfederal to $1 federal and scheduled to go to 2 to 1), has been administered by USGS since 1985. This program, originally part of the Office of Water Resources Research, was transferred in 1982 to the Bureau of Reclamation, and subsequently to USGS. In recent years, its funding has been subject to reduction, due to pressure from the Office of Management and Budget to eliminate the program. However, congressional support resulted in the reconstitution of the program, and its annual budget has increased from $2.5 million in 1985 to $4.4 million in 1987.[21] Other water resources research projects funded by USGS are administered regionally and include matching state and local grant funds. Since 1980, increases in the annual budget for these projects have not kept up with the rate of inflation.[22]

Several federal agencies, including EPA, U.S. Department of Agriculture, U.S. Department of Defense, and the National Science Foundation, have funds for water research, both in the form of competitive grants and as intramural programs. As a result, it is very difficult to obtain accurate estimates of funding trends. Despite the fact that there does not appear (so far) to have been a reduction in the level of federal support for this type of research (Table 2.4), the perception at the state level is that the federal government is not providing the support that is needed. This has probably resulted from an increased awareness of the need for water research and the development of many new programs within state institutions, thereby increasing the competition for existing funds. In Wisconsin, total annual federal grant funds averaged $618,028 for the years 1975-80, whereas the comparable figure for 1981-85 is $181,210.[23]

Some states, such as California, appropriate money specifically for research of water issues. Traditionally a well-funded institute, the California Water Resources Center receives most of its $1.2 million annual budget from the state.[24] In Arizona, the Water Resources Research Center is funded through the state university. In 1984 its annual budget doubled to $500,000.[25] State support for the Water Resources Center in Wisconsin is limited and reflects the reluctance of the legislature to fund research as opposed to monitoring activities. However, a large interdisciplinary program exists in the Institute of Environmental Studies at the University of Wisconsin. In Texas, state support for research is available through dedicated funds administered by the Texas Water Development Board. Since 1981, $8.1 million has been used to finance water-related planning studies and research projects.[26]

TABLE 2.4 Annual Federal Appropriations for Water Research ($ millions)

	1965	1968	1971	1974	1977	1980	1983
Actual amount	70	125	162	174	240	350	460
Adjusted to 1965 value	70	105	115	104	120	125	160

Source: B. B. Berger and D. Ullman, "Some Practical Considerations for Assessing Federal Water Resources Research Support" (paper delivered at National Conference on Water Resources Research, Chevy Chase, Md., February 1985).

Other innovative sources of funds are being developed in a variety of states. The North Carolina Water Resources Research Institute has been able to increase its funding through a cooperative arrangement with local governments. The North Carolina Urban Water Consortium is a group of six cities committed to research and technology transfer that will result in higher quality and more cost-effective water supplies for urban residents. Prompted by water quality problems and overdrafting of the Cretaceous Aquifer, each participating city contributes $10,000 annually to the research effort of the consortium.[27] Cities also contribute additional funds to support research projects that benefit them directly. In Wisconsin, industry and private foundations are becoming important sources of funds. Since 1979, the Water Resources Center has received a series of grants from Wisconsin Power and Light Co., and in 1986, it obtained a significant grant from the National Nonpoint Source Pollution Institute, a nationwide organization funded by private industry.[28] In California, the San Francisco Bay Aquatic Habitat Institute was created to provide a coordinated, permanent, long-term monitoring program in order to complement ongoing studies about currents, chemistry, and biology of the bay-delta system. It is a nonprofit corporation funded by industrial and municipal dischargers of waste water pollutants, as well as federal and local governments.[29]

The limited commitment of state funds to research, in most cases, reflects the limited role that research plays in the formulation of state water policy. Formulation of the Arizona Groundwater Management Act depended entirely on reaching a political consensus, not on scientific considerations. The increase in funding for research in Arizona has been directed toward a series of water issue papers designed to alert legislators and other members of the water community to policy problems. An attempt has been made to broaden the previously technical orientation of the Water Resources Research Center so that it could better represent interdisciplinary research. A related example comes from the Tucson Active Management Area, where the Southern Arizona Water Resources Association, sponsor of a basinwide management study, has successfully integrated policymakers into the planning process.

Through grants and other means of support to local governments and university departments, the Water Resources Research Institute in North Carolina has participated in research related to water resources policy, planning, and management. This has helped to shift the emphasis from water development research to water management research. A similar change in emphasis is occurring in California. Here research activities include studies on water conservation policies, water pricing policies, the development of improved planning criteria, potential institutional conflicts associated with specific development and management alternatives, and an analysis of changing attitudes toward water rights. In Texas, the shift in focus at the Water Resources Institute at Texas A&M University has been from predominantly agricultural to water quality issues, and the water research program at The University of Texas at Austin is directed more to water quality and improved water management.

GENERAL OBSERVATIONS

1. In most states, the primary emphasis in water policy has changed from one of development to one of better management of existing supplies. This is particularly evident in western states, where allocative problems already exist. It is also evident that where the issue is being addressed, the initiative is arising at the state level. Even in cases where federally funded projects, such as cases in California and Florida, have had adverse side effects, the state is taking the initiative in seeking solutions.

2. Several progressive states are developing comprehensive water-use plans, which allocate priorities between water uses and foster long-term economic goals. There is also a growing awareness of the relationship between water quantity and water quality issues. Unlike the federal government, state governments often have a single water resources department, which is conducive to the formulation of more comprehensive

water resource policies that integrate environmental and economic considerations.

3. The development of comprehensive water plans is often associated with institutional changes. Regional water management districts, which are responsible for the implementation of new policies, are an integral part of such plans in Florida and Arizona.

4. The reduction in the role of the federal government in water policy, particularly in providing funding, has been phased in over the last 15 years. In the 1970s, despite a reduction in funds for water development projects, a considerable amount of money was allocated for sewage and water treatment facilities. Now that treatment facilities are widespread, the federal government has reduced its financial commitment, retaining primarily its regulatory role.

5. Although water resource management is a pressing environmental issue, the federal government does not appear to be willing to reverse the trend and provide additional funds. In contrast to its former active participation in water development projects, the federal government is leaving it up to the states to develop their own plans and provide most of the necessary financial support.

6. The general reduction in federal funds for domestic programs is creating financial problems for many states. In some cases, new funding mechanisms are being created as an integral part of new programs. Environmental programs are no exception. Florida, Wisconsin, and Arizona have successfully implemented new fees to cover the cost of their water resource management programs. Other states, such as Texas, California, and Wisconsin, have enlisted the help of private industry.

7. With federal dollars for water research not keeping up with increasing demand, the states are having to decide whether they are willing to support such programs. A state's commitment to water research seems to reflect its level of commitment to research and education in general. California has always provided a high level of support for research, including water research. In Wisconsin, a well-funded university provides an environment conducive to research, which is funded by a variety of sources, including private industry.

8. Although the states are searching for ways to improve water management and fund essential research, there is much that remains to be done. As the Wisconsin case illustrates, it appears that local sources may only be willing to fund water research directed at specific problems and applications. Thus, if the federal government does not fund basic research in water resources, some needed advances, such as improving water quality and detoxifying hazardous pollutants, may go unattended.

9. Our survey of the water policies of six diverse states indicates that states have responded to water issues in their own peculiar manner. Despite similar problems, for instance in western states, there is no uniformity in response. Whereas California has been developing a state water plan for more than 50 years, Texas has been much slower in addressing water issues that are critical for its economic development. It is also evident that, in

those states that are addressing water policy issues, there is an effort to use a more comprehensive approach. Based on such a small survey, it is impossible to determine how extensive such policies are. However, we have determined that states are capable of dealing with water resource management issues, often using quite innovative approaches.

NOTES

1. The National Groundwater Policy Forum, *Groundwater: Saving the Unseen Resource, Proposed Conclusions and Recommendations* (Washington, D.C.: The Conservation Foundation, November 1985).

2. Interview with Dr. William Lord, director, Water Resources Research Center, Arizona, January 12, 1987.

3. Arizona Water Commission, *Inventory of Resources and Uses; Phase I: Arizona State Water Plan* (Phoenix: Arizona Water Commission, 1975), p. 47.

4. Tex. Water Code Ann. Section 17.125 (Vernon 1985).

5. Harvey E. Wirth, *Wisconsin's Groundwater Law and Regulation, A History: 1948-1985* (Document presented to the Water Resources Center, University of Wisconsin-Madison, 1986), p. 127 (hereafter cited as *Wisconsin's Groundwater Law*).

6. Thomas G. Pelham, *State Land-Use Planning and Regulation* (Lexington, Mass.: D. C. Heath and Co., 1979), p. 6 (hereafter cited as *State Land-Use Planning*).

7. Pelham, *State Land-Use Planning*, pp. 123-125.

8. Robert C. Apgar, "Florida's State Land Development Plan," *Florida Environmental and Urban Issues* XIII, no. 3 (April 1986), p. 4.

9. Northwest Florida Water Management District (NFWMD), *Tenth Annual Conference on Water Management in Florida, Abstracts*, Public Information Bulletin 86-1 (Havana, Fla.: NFWMD, October 1986), pp. 12-13.

10. Victoria Tschinkel and Gilbert Berguist, "The State Water Use Plan: Where Do We Go From Here?," *Florida Environmental and Urban Issues* XIII, no. 3 (April 1986), pp. 5-9.

11. Farmers Investment Co. v. Bettwy, 113 Ariz. 520, 558 P. 2d 14 (1976).

12. ARS 45-401 *et seq.*

13. Tex. Water Code Ann. Section 17.147 (Vernon 1985).

14. Department of Water Resources (DWR), *The California Water Plan: Projected Uses and Available Water Supply to 2010*, Bulletin 160-83 (Sacramento, Calif.: DWR, December 1983), pp. 15-16.

15. NFWMD, *Tenth Annual Conference on Water Management in Florida*, p. 4.

16. Texas Water Development Board (TWDB), *Statement to Water District and River Authority Study Committee* (Austin, Tex.: TWDB, September 19, 1986), pp. 5-6.

17. Wirth, *Wisconsin's Groundwater Law*, p. 127.

18. Interview with E. D. Dorchester, P.E., division engineering manager, Texas Electric Service Company, former chairman, Texas Society for Professional Engineers, Water Education Council, May 18, 1987.

19. Public law 88.379.

20. R. Steifel, "Water Resources Research in the FY 1987 Budget," *AAAS Report XI: Research and Development, FY 1987* (Washington, D.C.: American Association for the Advancement of Science, 1987).

21. Interview with Frank Coley, USGS, March 31, 1987.

22. Interview with Bill Boney, district chief, Water Resources Division, USGS, March 31, 1987.

23. Documents for site visit team, Water Resources Center, University of Wisconsin, Madison, Wisconsin, March 1986.

24. Interview with Rex Woods, assistant director, Water Resources Center, University of California, Davis, January, 1987.

25. Interview with William Lord, January 12, 1987.

26. Texas Water Development Board (TWDB), *Proposals Funded by the Research and Planning Fund* (Austin, Tex.: TWDB, March 1987), p. 10.

27. Interview with David Moreau, director, Water Resources Research Institute, Raleigh, North Carolina, January 12, 1987.

28. Documents for site visit team, Water Resources Center, University of Wisconsin, Madison, Wisconsin, March 1986.

29. The San Francisco Bay Aquatic Habitat Institute, "Bylaws" (March 12, 1986).

ARIZONA

BACKGROUND
Historical Factors

Salt River Project

Arizona experienced its first substantial population increase with accelerated westward migration following the Civil War. Farmers from the East brought with them the knowledge, skills, and desire to establish a new agricultural base in the West. By 1869, an irrigation system had been developed in the Salt River Valley, and agricultural development flourished until severe floods, followed by droughts between 1890 and 1900, reinforced the need for flood control and water storage facilities on the Salt and Verde Rivers.[1]

In 1902 the U.S. Congress passed the Federal Reclamation Act in response to the need for water development throughout the West. In order to take advantage of the benefits that could be derived from this act, the Salt River Valley Water Users' Association was established in 1903.[2] A year later, after the association agreed with the Department of the Interior to take over the administrative and operational functions upon completion of the water project, the construction of Roosevelt Dam was authorized.

A number of other dams followed, creating what is known today as the Salt River Project, the first multipurpose reclamation project in the United States. Besides Roosevelt Dam, the components of the project are: Mormon Flat Dam, completed in 1926; Horse Mesa Dam, completed in 1927; and Stewart Mountain Dam, completed in 1930.[3] The Salt River Project also included two dams on the Verde River: Bartlett Dam, completed in 1939; and Horseshoe Dam, completed in 1945.

The Colorado River Compact

Although western water policy was "driven" at the federal level, in the sense that the federal government provided the necessary resources to build water projects, the federal government ostensibly did not get involved in the policy implications of a particular project. Nonetheless, the Bureau of Reclamation played a major role in water development in the West and took the lead in the reclamation effort on public lands. The burden was on the states to take the initiative, by proposing a project and then securing federal funding for its construction. Similarly, it was up to the states to agree among themselves as to the apportionment of interstate waters impounded by federally sponsored water projects. If the states failed to come to an agreement, then the courts would settle the dispute by decree. The Salt River Project illustrates this approach. The bottom line, however, was that, while the federal government was instrumental in providing the means for water development, it did not get involved (except where federal lands and Indian reservations were concerned) in determining the ends to which the newly developed water should be put.

Accordingly, while a number of states, including Arizona, sought to enlist federal aid to develop the Colorado River, this aid was conditional upon the states reaching an agreement on how to apportion the water among themselves. In 1922 the seven Colorado River Basin states (Arizona, California, New Mexico, Nevada, Utah, Wyoming, and Colorado) signed a compact for the apportionment of the water supply of the river and its tributaries. The compact divided the Colorado River Basin into two subbasins, Upper and Lower, and apportioned to both basins 7.5 million acre-feet (maf) of water annually.[4] The Lower Basin, however, was given the right to increase its beneficial consumptive use by one maf annually.

Boulder Canyon Project Act

The Boulder Canyon Project Act of 1928 authorized the construction of Hoover Dam and Power Plant and the All-American Canal. In addition, it provided for apportionment of water among the Lower Basin states, and authorized the Secretary of the Interior to execute contracts for Boulder Canyon Project water, subject to the terms of the Colorado River Compact.[5]

The provisions of the act stipulated that it would take effect upon the fulfillment of either of two conditions: (1) that all seven states ratify the Colorado River Compact, or (2) that six of the states, including California, ratify the compact, and that California agree to limit its consumptive use of water.[6] The first condition was not met until 1944, because Arizona was not satisfied with the terms of the compact. The second condition, however, was fulfilled, making the act effective as of June 25, 1929.

The Boulder Canyon Project Act, which created Hoover Dam and Lake Mead, also authorized the States of Arizona, California, and Nevada to enter into an agreement apportioning the 7.5 maf of water allocated to the Lower Basin under the compact. The three states, however, were unwilling to accept this formula for apportionment, and in 1952 Arizona filed suit in the U.S. Supreme Court against California.[7]

In 1963 the Court concluded that the Congress, by enactment of the Boulder Canyon Project Act, had provided its own method of allocating waters among the Lower Basin states and this method applied to the first 7.5 maf of mainstream water. However, the Court essentially agreed with Arizona, allowing that inflows from the tributaries of the Colorado should not be included in the water to be divided, but should remain for the exclusive use of each state. The court decree apportioned the first 7.5 maf per year of Colorado mainstream water available to the three Lower Basin states as follows: Arizona, 2.8 maf per year; California, 4.4 maf per year; and Nevada, 0.3 maf per year. Any excess above 7.5 maf was apportioned 50 percent to California and 50 percent to Arizona.[8]

Critical Issues

Beginning in the 1950s, Arizona experienced tremendous growth in agriculture, particularly in cotton farming. As a result, there was a corresponding increase in water demand, and agricultural interests became a powerful political force in Arizona. Although cotton farming declined after cotton prices dropped, a great deal of the land brought into production for cotton farming remains in other types of agricultural production.

Concurrent with the increase in agriculture, Arizona grew more populous and more urban. As urban demand for water increased, it competed directly with agricultural needs in the Salt River Valley. The competition was more indirect in other areas. These demographic changes gave Arizona water politics two separate dimensions. First, there was a need to increase total available water resources to provide for the increased demand from both the agricultural and urban sectors. Second, there was a conflict concerning allocation of the existing available water supply between urban-industrial and agricultural users.[9] Presently, agriculture accounts for 89 percent of annual consumptive use. Cities represent only 7 percent of consumptive use, and the remaining 4 percent is used for mining, power generation, and for fish and wildlife (see Table 3.1).

Although Arizona's water policy has focused almost exclusively on the development of surface water supplies, it is ground water that has permitted Arizona to reach its present level of development. Unlike surface water, ground water is essentially "free" water that is easily developed by any private landowner. On an annual basis, Arizona uses much more ground water than surface water to meet its agricultural, domestic, and industrial needs. Each year, however, the state consumes far more ground water than nature replenishes. Historically, most of the ground water pumped has been for agricultural purposes. Annual volumes of pumped ground water increased from 200,000 acre-feet in 1920 to nearly 1.5 maf in 1940. As of 1977, 5 maf were being pumped annually, representing several times the natural replenishment rate. The depletion of ground water approaches 100 times the rate of renewable supply in some of the smaller hydrologic basins. Ground water is being depleted in the Tucson area at over three times the natural recharge rate; in the Phoenix area at 11 times the replenishment rate; and in the agricultural areas of Pinal County at 12 times that rate.[10]

TABLE 3.1 Estimated Water Use in Arizona, 1965-80

	1965	1970	1975	1980
Population (millions)	1.58	1.78	2.25	2.72
Consumption by Use (offstream)				
Total (mgd)	3,081	4,824	5,876	4,542
Public supply	110	160	200	340
Rural use	19	44	66	32
Irrigation	2,900	4,500	5,400	4,000
Industrial	52	120	120	170
Per capita (gpd)				
all uses	1,950	2,710	2,612	1,670
excl. irrigation	115	182	222	199
Withdrawals by source				
Total (mgd)	6,300	6,800	7,800	7,900
Ground water	4,200	4,200	4,800	4,200
Surface water	2,100	2,600	3,000	3,700

Source: U.S. Geological Survey, _Estimated Use of Water in the United States, 1965; Estimated Use of Water in the United States, 1970; Estimated Use of Water in the United States, 1975; Estimated Use of Water in the United States, 1980_, Geological Survey Circulars 556, 676, 765, and 1001 (Reston, Va.: U.S. Department of the Interior, 1968, 1972, 1977, and 1983).

The Central Arizona Project
In order to address its rapidly increasing demand for water, Arizona looked to the largess of the federal government to sponsor yet another major water project. The Central Arizona Project (CAP), authorized by the Colorado River Basin Act of 1968, is intended to provide the conveyance and storage facilities necessary to import a major portion (1.2 maf per year) of Arizona's remaining share of Colorado River water into the south central part of the state.

Early Legislative History. Arizona's fight for the authorization of the CAP lasted over 20 years, with the final version shaped by many political compromises. Much of the initial delay resulted from an inability of the states served by the Colorado River to agree on the apportionment of its waters. However, following ratification of the Colorado River Compact in 1944, Arizona and the Bureau of Reclamation agreed on the joint financing of feasibility studies for the utilization of Arizona's share of Colorado River water.[11] The results of the study were released in the 1947 Central Arizona Project Report. The report stated that additional water was needed in central Arizona to: (1) permit reduction of pumping and thus limit withdrawals from the ground water basin to its safe annual yield; (2) permit delivery of a supplementary supply to lands now inadequately irrigated; (3) permit delivery of an adequate supply to developed lands now idle for lack of water; (4) permit delivery of an adequate municipal supply to the City of Tucson; and (5) permit carrying of excess salts out of the basin.[12]

Hearings on bills authorizing the CAP were held during the Eighty-first and -second Congress. Twice Arizona Senators Carl Hayden and Ernest MacFarland succeeded in getting a bill passed in the Senate. However, opposition within the House Interior Committee defeated all efforts in the House. California representatives led the opposition, claiming that Arizona lacked title to the water to be used for the project.[13] Other critics "disputed the economics of the project, portraying it as a gigantic raid on the public treasury on behalf of agriculturalists who had overextended themselves and now wanted the taxpayers to come to their rescue."[14] The opposition won the first legislative bout. In 1951 the House Interior Committee passed a resolution postponing consideration of the CAP until the water rights issue was settled. Meanwhile, the interests actively backing the CAP had not passively awaited a decision by the Court. Almost as soon as it became apparent that Congress would not authorize the CAP, the state began to look at prospects of constructing the project without federal aid. The Central Arizona Project Association had provided considerable research assistance when the state legislature authorized the Arizona Interstate Stream Commission to pursue these investigations in association with the Arizona Power Authority. Subsequent economic studies by the state and the CAP Association "demonstrated the impossibility of the state financing a project that would require a considerable subsidy from power revenues for the water-delivery features of the project."[15]

This realization, coupled with the encouraging Draft Report by the special master, provided the impetus for Arizona to request a reappraisal of the project by the Bureau of Reclamation. In the resultant 1962 Appraisal Report, the bureau focused on the expanding urban and industrial demand in addition to the continuing agricultural needs.[16] When both direct and indirect benefits were included in the analysis, the benefit-cost ratio, on the basis of a 50-year pay-out period, was increased from 1.63:1.0 to 2.54:1.0. The rapid population increase and continuing ground water overdraft were cited as principal factors behind the new, improved ratio.[17] The 1962 plan contained only minimum changes from the original version.

Authorization. With the favorable appraisal study and the Supreme Court decision in 1963, two battles had been won for the CAP. However, victory could not be complete without winning the legislative battle, which had been postponed since 1952. The active supporters of the Colorado River Basin Bill were the two groups that would benefit most from the CAP: representatives of Arizona's water interests and the Bureau of Reclamation. Within Arizona the entity responsible for obtaining passage of the CAP bill was the Arizona Interstate Stream Commission. Created in 1948, the commission was composed of seven members appointed by the governor, with the approval of the Senate, for six-year terms.[18]

Beyond the perceived need for additional water, the general feeling was that it was Arizona's "turn" to have a project authorized to allow the development of its entitlement to Colorado River water. Arizona had successfully fought California's water development projects in the 1930s, had lost its authorization attempt of the 1940s, and then had spent 12 years in court. In the meantime, water development projects for other states, such as the Colorado River Basin Storage Project, had been authorized.

The five-man congressional delegation from Arizona shared the feeling that the CAP's time had finally arrived. They realized, however, that the project was strictly an Arizona issue. The passage of a bill containing the CAP would depend upon their ability to use influence, cash in past favors, and "to exploit the self-interest of others with influence in the legislative process by linking in one way or another their plans and desires to the success of the CAP."[19]

Despite the opposition of several significant political entities, the Colorado River Basin Project Act was signed into law on September 30, 1968. It established the CAP as a typical Bureau of Reclamation "multiple-purpose" project: "For the purposes of furnishing irrigation water and municipal water to the water-deficient areas of Arizona and western New Mexico through direct diversion or exchange of water, control of floods, conservation, and development of fish and wildlife resources, enhancement of recreation opportunities, and for other purposes...."[20]

Provisions of the Act. In response to the authorization of the CAP, the Central Arizona Water Conservation District, consisting of Maricopa, Pima, and Pinal Counties, was formed as the local entity responsible for the repayment of CAP costs. In December of 1972, the district and the Secretary of the Interior entered into a master repayment contract. The contract contains, at the insistence of the federal government, restrictions that must be incorporated into contracts with the ultimate users of CAP water.[21] First, CAP water is prohibited from being used to irrigate lands not having a recent history of irrigation (i.e., between September 30, 1958 and September 30, 1968). Second, contracts for CAP water must contain provisions to control expansion of ground water use for irrigation in the contract service area. Furthermore, pumpage of ground water from within a contractor's service area for any use outside that service area is prohibited, except where it is determined that surplus ground water exists or that drainage is required.

The two most significant provisions of the contract, however, in effect redirected Arizona water policy. First, the contract grants municipal and industrial users of CAP water a 100 percent priority over all agricultural uses in the event of shortages.[22] Additionally, the contract requires that irrigators accepting CAP water must reduce their ground water pumpage by the amount of project water that they receive.[23]

It is these provisions that finally provided the necessary "hammer" that forced Arizona to address its ground water overdraft problem. Using the leverage of federal dollars, the Department of the Interior insisted that the Arizona legislature enact meaningful ground water management legislation as the price for continued construction of the CAP.[24]

Ground Water Management

Efforts to control the overdrafting of ground water began in the 1930s, when the first of many study commissions was established and charged with submitting reform legislation. It was not until the 1940s, however, that anything of consequence occurred. At that time, the Department of the Interior insisted, as it would for the next 40 years, that the price of their support for the CAP was a commitment from the State of Arizona to restrict the increasing overdraft of its ground water. This pressure, and the strong insistence of Governor Sidney Osborn, led the state legislature to enact the 1948 Groundwater Code, which placed limits on new pumping in certain areas of the state that were designated as "critical areas." Even then, however, the 1949 act was criticized as inadequate to control and curtail ground water uses.

In 1953, the Supreme Court of Arizona confirmed in *Bristor* v. *Cheatham*[25] that the doctrine of reasonable use prevailed, meaning ground water could be pumped and put to beneficial use, subject only to a standard of reasonableness. The only actual limit to "reasonable use" established by the Arizona courts is that ground water may not be transported off the land from which it was pumped if pumping for use elsewhere would damage other property owners by adversely affecting the common supply. This rule of law was reaffirmed in subsequent court decisions, and ultimately led to the controversial decision in *Farmers Investment Co. (FICO)* v. *Bettwy* in 1976.[26]

In the FICO case, the court enjoined the transportation of ground water by a mining company from its wells located within a critical ground water area to its mill. This decision had profound implications for municipalities, as well as the mining industry, as it meant that they could not transport water pumped from outlying municipally owned lands into the cities for municipal water supplies. The FICO decision, coupled with the continued federal interest in linking completion of the CAP and final CAP allocations with ground water reform, renewed interest in a comprehensive reexamination of Arizona's archaic ground water laws, and ultimately led to the 1980 Groundwater Management Act.

STATE INITIATIVES IN WATER
RESOURCE MANAGEMENT
Policy Development

Groundwater Management Act of 1980
Study Commission. Although effective ground water management had been a prerequisite for the CAP since the beginning of the project, the Interior Department had not pressed the point. It was not until 1977 that the Interior Department resurrected its demand for ground water law reform and set a deadline for ground water management legislation.

The preparatory work that led to the 1980 Act was undertaken by the Groundwater Management Study Commission, established by the legislature in 1977. The commission proposed the year 2020 as a target date for the elimination of ground water overdraft, and recommended the purchase and retirement of farms as the method to achieve this goal. While agriculture favored this approach, the cities and mines found it totally unacceptable. The cities and mines thought that ground water should be considered a public resource governed by the same rules as surface water and believed that farmers did not have a property right that could be sold. The farmers, on the other hand, maintained that their right to use ground water was a property right that they could convey and that could not be taken by the government without just compensation.[27]

Negotiations among the different factions on the central issue of how to eliminate ground water overdrafting, as well as on a number of other issues, progressed over three years with frequent volatile sessions. Nevertheless, the work was kept on track amid renewed threats by the Interior Department to withhold CAP water allocations. Ultimately, following closed-door sessions, the factions reached a compromise, whereby an ambitious program of conservation was established, instead of relying principally on the retirement of farms. Under the conservation program, mines are required to use the latest available conservation method, consistent with a reasonable economic return; cities are subject to per capita water allotments set by the Water Resources Department; and agriculture's water use is limited by a "water duty," also established by the department.[28]

Furthermore, to partially satisfy agriculture's demand that farmers be compensated for the "confiscation" of their alleged property rights, starting in 2006, the department has the authority to purchase and retire "grandfathered" water rights, in order to achieve management goals.

Governor Babbitt's Role. Given the renewed federal pressure for ground water reform and the inability of the study commission to arrive at a consensus, the representatives of the three major interest groups--the cities, mines, and agriculture--began private negotiations in 1979. Within a few months, however, these negotiations broke down. At this point Governor Babbitt, at the request of the negotiators, agreed to mediate negotiations among the parties in a final attempt to reach a compromise. The governor presided over the group's meetings for the next six months, until a compromise bill was formulated. It was agreed that the bill proposed by the group would not be amended by the legislature.

All three interests agree that, without Babbitt's intervention, the 1980 law would not have been enacted. Because the rump group was not an officially established advisory committee or subcommittee of the Arizona Groundwater Management Study Commission, it was not subject to the open meetings laws. The press was aware that secret negotiations were taking place, but was never permitted to attend. For the most part, reporters realized that secrecy was necessary and did not object.

Babbitt's view of his role in the negotiations was that he was merely facilitating a compromise and not imposing his own views of ground water management on the group.[29] The governor reasoned that, because each group was ably represented, any bill that emerged from the rump group would be a reasonable compromise. Babbitt was able to bring these three differing interests together for a number of reasons. First, being the governor, the power of the office provided a certain amount of coercion. In addition, he understood the complex issues and was willing to involve himself in the details. Perhaps, most important was his negotiating style, which sought to achieve a consensus after a lengthy discussion of each issue. If a consensus was not reached, he decided the matter in favor of one group or the other. He chose the topics for discussion in such a way that all factions had some victories during the course of a negotiating session. Finally, he saved the most difficult issues for last, when the momentum to reach agreement was strongest. All those in the rump group realized the importance of the CAP for the state, and none of the groups wanted to be responsible for sabotaging it.[30]

In March 1980, the rump group reached an agreement on the basic framework of the act in a document called "Concepts for Agreement." The agreement called for strong state management and a program of conservation. Most importantly, the agreement met the two essential requirements of a workable ground water code in Arizona: "it satisfied most of the requirements of the three dominant political and economic forces in Arizona water politics, and, at the same time, established a mechanism for curbing ground water consumption."[31]

The full commission approved the agreement and translated its provisions into a bill. After this draft was completed a few months later, the rump group reviewed the proposed bill in detail. Although there were a few last-moment dramatics, when the interest groups could not agree on a few remaining unsettled issues, the governor simply announced that the negotiations had ended and that the bill would not be scrapped because of disagreement over a relatively minor issue.[32]

The commission approved the bill on June 6, 1980. On June 11, in a one-day session, the act was passed by both the House and Senate by wide margins. Although some legislators sought to amend the bill, it passed without any changes. Legislative leaders were able to obtain the cooperation of most legislators by stressing the urgency of the matter, the delicate nature of the compromise reached, and by promising some legislators that amendments would be considered in the next session.[33]

The next day, the bill was signed by Governor Babbitt. Because it had passed by an 80 percent majority, it became law immediately.

Groundwater Management Code. The code establishes the goal of eliminating ground water overdraft by 2025. It created the Department of Water Resources (DWR), which is responsible for all state-level surface and ground water management functions, except for water quality. At the local level, the code created active management areas (AMAs), in which mandatory conservation, enforced by civil and criminal sanctions, is required. The legislation creates four initial AMAs, which include most of Pima, Pinal, and Maricopa Counties, and the Prescott area in Yavapai County. These areas were determined by the commission as those areas of the state most in need of immediate comprehensive ground water management. Subsequent AMAs may be designated by the director of the DWR, based upon specified criteria, or by the election of local residents. The AMA boundaries generally must correspond to ground water basin boundaries.[34] Safe yield goals are set for all but the Pinal AMA.

Each agricultural user in an AMA will receive a "water duty," limiting its pumping to the minimum amount of water necessary for crops historically grown in the area. The law, in addition to providing grandfathered rights, provides for permits for new uses, although no new irrigated agriculture is permitted in AMAs. The code also requires that, whenever possible, new users must retire agricultural land by purchasing grandfathered water rights, rather than sinking new wells. Mines and other industries will be required to use the best conservation technology available. New development in areas where the developer cannot show an ensured 100-year water supply, from whatever source, is effectively prohibited. The director will have the power to limit per capita consumption in urban areas.

Environmental Quality Act of 1986
The 1980 Groundwater Management Act focused on the issue of ensuring future supplies of ground water through conservation of existing ground water resources. It was realized that, in addition to securing an adequate water supply, however, the quality of the available water is equally important. After passing the 1980 act, Arizona started to work on legislation to protect ground water quality, ultimately enacting the Arizona Environmental Quality Act of 1986.

History of the Act. Although Arizona had long been concerned about the availability of a dependable water supply, it had never seriously addressed water quality issues. While the state legislature passed acts to implement federal clean water policy, this legislation applied mainly to surface water quality. In 1977, however, the state attorney general issued an opinion in which the state Water Quality Control Council was required to promulgate water quality standards for ground water as well as for surface water and required the legislature to clarify existing law.35

In the early 1980s, however, the legislature was stalemated on environmental quality issues, as the two opposing interest groups cancelled each other out. On one hand, the mining and agriculture industries blocked strong environmental protection measures. On the other hand, the environmental lobby stopped weak legislation that purported to protect water quality.

Ground water quality resurfaced on the legislative agenda when, in 1984, the City of Tucson, which gets all of its water supply from ground water, found trichloroethylene contamination in city water supply wells. Although proposed ground water quality legislation filed in the 1984 legislative session failed, it was the turning point, eventually leading to successful legislation. Again, in 1985, proposed legislation clarifying the Arizona Department of Health Services' authority to implement a ground water quality permit program failed to pass.36

These two successive legislative failures led to the movement for a statewide referendum on the problem of ground water quality. In 1985, the Arizona Clean Water Advocates, a coalition that included the City of Tucson, the Sierra Club, Common Cause, and the Audubon Society, filed an initiative petition for comprehensive ground water quality protection.37 Although the initiative was scheduled for the November 1986 ballot, the advocates of the initiative made it clear that the initiative's real objective was to force the legislature to act on the ground water quality issue in the 1986 session. The strategy behind the initiative was a not-too-subtle "carrot and stick" approach to legislative action. Industrial and other interests opposed to strong ground water quality legislation were given one more opportunity to have their views incorporated into ground water legislation. If, however, a compromise could not be reached, the initiative proposed a "draconian" regulatory scheme that was much more comprehensive than had previously been proposed. Given the fact that there appeared to be strong public support for the initiative and that Governor Babbitt had endorsed it, this proved to be a sufficient incentive to bring all of the major interests to the negotiating table.

The Negotiating Process. The Groundwater Quality Act was created through a two-track negotiating process. The preliminary negotiations, initiated by Representative Hawke and Senator Lunn, set the stage and defined who the interested parties would be. The informal group consisted of various environmental and industry representatives. The group's approach sought to minimize the potential for conflict by first tackling and resolving the simple issues before dealing with the more difficult ones. Representative Hawke avoided formal notes and positions, but pointed out to the group when agreements had been reached on general concepts and language. Hawke, however, did not characterize the group's work as a consensus-building process, but rather as a process of drafting a document that expressed a "sense of the group." Ultimately, these negotiations led to the "Hawke draft," which provided the foundation for the broader negotiations of the Ad Hoc Water Quality Committee appointed by Governor Babbitt.[38]

When the Ad Hoc Water Quality Committee began its work, Governor Babbitt's intent had been for the committee to meet in the open in order to build public confidence in the draft legislation. As the committee got under way, however, open meetings resulted in posturing before the media, and the process bogged down. Babbitt therefore returned to the private negotiating process, which he had successfully used in negotiating the 1980 act. Once again, Governor Babbitt took on the role of mediator in attempting to reach an accommodation between the various interest groups. Key issues addressed and resolved by the committee included pesticide regulation, aquifer classification (how much ground water will be regulated), point of compliance (at what point is a violation of aquifer quality standards to be measured), and liability for pollution (who is responsible for cleanup costs and for how much).[39]

After three months of intensive negotiations, the governor's ad hoc committee reached agreement on legislation for ground water protection. Again, the legislative leadership warned that no substantive changes to the act would be allowed during its passage, and the respective interest group representatives that negotiated the act fully supported its passage and implementation.[40]

Provisions of the Act. The Environmental Quality Act of 1986 establishes regulatory authority to minimize pollution of aquifers and eliminate it where possible. Enforcement of the act is spread among six existing and new agencies, with a first-year appropriation totaling more than $4 million. The act created 150 new positions and the Department of Environmental Quality, giving it the authority to protect water and air quality. It also insulated the appropriation and new positions from a 1986 across-the-board cut in the size of state government.

Pesticide regulation is a key feature of the act, which directs the Commission on Agriculture and Horticulture to regulate the use of pesticides through a licensing and permitting system. Pesticide management areas are designated, and the use of certain pesticides is prohibited in areas around schools, day-care centers, health-care institutions, and residential neighborhoods.[41]

The act requires ground water quality standards promulgated by the agency to be based on economic, social, and environmental costs and benefits. It requires all aquifers to be inventoried and classified by June 30, 1987. A comprehensive aquifer-monitoring program is established to develop a statewide data base. Aquifer protection permits are required for all activities that have been found to pollute ground water.[42]

Implementation

The primary agency responsible for implementation of the Groundwater Management Act (GMA) is the DWR, whose director is appointed by the governor. The director of the DWR is responsible for developing management plans for each AMA (Phoenix, Tucson, Prescott, and Pinal) with the goal of reaching safe yield (defined as the long-term balance between ground water withdrawals and the annual amount of natural and artificial recharge) by the year 2025, except for the Pinal AMA, which is predominantly agricultural and has modified goals.[43] The DWR was also given authority to purchase and retire water rights in order to reach conservation goals.

Since its creation in 1981, the DWR has been oriented toward the administrative tasks of putting the new grandfathered water rights system into place. The GMA created three new types of water rights:

1. Irrigation Grandfathered Rights. These are rights to irrigate with ground water specific acres of land in AMAs that have been irrigated in the five years prior to the formation of the AMA. This right can be conveyed to others for farming purposes.

2. Type I Irrigation Grandfathered Rights. This is the right to use three acre-feet per year of ground water (or less if amount used on the land was less) by virtue of purchasing and retiring agricultural lands.

3. Type II Irrigation Grandfathered Rights. This right is based on nonirrigation withdrawals of ground water taking place as of June 12, 1980, but not associated with the retirement of irrigated land.[44]

The task of sifting through the applications for grandfathered rights has fallen on the active management areas. The preoccupation with this administrative task has made DWR and AMA activity more rudimentary than innovative during this first management period. As one AMA official put it, the idea during the first period has been to get people used to the idea of the GMA.[45]

Another administrative function performed by DWR pursuant to the GMA is the creation of per capita water usage standards for jurisdictions within the AMAs. Again, the responsibility of setting these standards falls on each AMA. Because each AMA has different patterns of water use, the nature of this responsibility varies across AMAs. In Tucson, for example, setting standards is relatively easy, resulting from a well-developed conservation ethic, present since 1976 (to be discussed more fully in a case study). Per capita water usage had already fallen to about the levels stipulated in the first Tucson management plan by the time the plan went into effect.

The situation in Phoenix is very different. With varying population density among the communities within the Phoenix AMA, meeting a single per capita standard is difficult. To cite just one example, each resident of the City of El Mirage uses 118 gallons of water per day, while residents served by the Paradise Valley Water Co. use 884 gallons per day.[46] This disparity can be attributed to such factors as the presence or absence of golf courses and the amount of green space in the community. The problem facing the Phoenix AMA is developing some standard other than per capita use that will both enforce conservation and reflect the lifestyles and patterns of usage throughout the AMA. The AMA is working on such a standard for the second management plan.[47]

Though these administrative tasks remain the primary concern of the DWR, the real test of DWR's enforcement powers will come in mid-1987, the first effective date of the GMA. At that time, major pumpers will be subject to cease and desist orders and fines of up to $10,000 for violating the limits set by their grandfathered rights. With the threat of stiff civil penalties, the DWR may test the respect and good will it has built up within the state in its first years of existence. The DWR has considerable statutory power, however, and the strict provisions and structure of the GMA enjoy broad support within the Arizona legislature.[48]

The implementation mechanisms of the Groundwater Management Act of 1980 show how water scarcity has brought about two fundamental changes in Arizona's political climate. The very structure of the act attests to the shift toward urban and away from agricultural interests. By building the act around the four AMAs, which contain 80 percent of the state's population and 69 percent of the state's overdraft, management of water is, for the first time, placed in state hands for the benefit of cities.[49] The act formally recognized the end of agriculture as the driving economic force. Second, by placing priority on urban over agricultural interests, the act recognizes a new role for water as an economic development tool in the state. In order to allow for greater urbanization and attract high-technology industries, the state had to allay the fears of eastern investors, who pointed to Arizona's water management problems as justification for curtailing investment in the state.[50] As a result, in order to ensure continued economic growth in the state, local control over water had to be sacrificed.

Financing

The financing mechanisms authorized by the GMA focus primarily on fee-levying authority given to DWR. The DWR will be able to control ground water withdrawals to some degree through pricing leverage, based on the "irrigation water duty" levied on holders of irrigation grandfathered rights.[51] However, the fees aren't large enough to control withdrawals alone. Their function is largely revenue producing. The irrigation water duty is essentially a pump tax, which has, or will have, three components: (1) a $.50 to $1.00 per acre-foot fee to finance administration of the act; (2) a charge not to exceed $2.00 per acre-foot to finance ground water augmentation schemes such as recharge; and (3) a fee, not to exceed $2.00

per acre-foot and not to be levied before 2006 for purchase and retirement of farmland.[52] With authority to levy fines of up to $10,000, the AMAs will have considerable leverage against violators. As of January 1987, no fines have been levied.[53]

Closer inspection of the act reveals several inconsistencies, which policymakers will need to address in the future. First, although agriculture uses 80 percent of the state's water and bears most of the burden to conserve, it is the group given the least incentive to conserve. While the type II water right allows the sale of water apart from the sale of land, the other rights allow the sale of water only in association with the sale of land. Thus, the farmer has no incentive to conserve beyond minimum legal requirements. The DWR has countered that, because ground water levels are declining and there are more rights than water, allowing the sale of water would result in more rights than water. With many rights chasing scarce water, one would expect the price of water to be bid upward and a more economically efficient allocation of water to come about.[54]

Another disturbing aspect of the GMA is its tendency to put off the day of reckoning until 2025, when the safe yield goal must be met. Present estimates place conservation from the first management plan at a 6 percent reduction in ground water withdrawals. With CAP water expected to eliminate 60 percent of the state's ground water overdraft, it is clear that much remains to be done to reach the goal of safe yield. Although it would be politically unrealistic to impose greater conservation measures in the first management plan, the history of inertia in water policy issues justifies concern about meeting goals set 40 years down the line. This fact underscores the need for Arizona to plan now, through research and other innovative programs, to meet these goals. Though the track record of the research community, thus far, has not been very good in terms of its ability to affect policy formation, efforts are being made to make research more responsive to the needs of policymakers.

THE ROLE OF WATER RESEARCH

Research has had very little impact on water policy formulation in the State of Arizona. This becomes evident through an examination of the method by which major water legislation gets passed in Arizona. The 1980 Groundwater Management Act was created by putting municipal, mining, and agricultural interests behind closed doors and forcing them, at Governor Babbitt and the federal government's insistence, to work out a compromise. There were no research findings used to support one management option over another. Indeed, there was an incentive *not* to rely on research findings, since they might give one side reason to be uncompromising.

The passage of the 1986 Groundwater Quality Act was accomplished in a similar way. Governor Babbitt recognized a need to pass legislation on water quality, but was unsuccessful in three legislative sessions. When environmentalists threatened to have a strict water quality referendum placed on the November 1986 ballot, Babbitt threw his support behind the initiative in hopes of forcing the legislature to act. Though legislators were anxious to avoid the referendum, they were unable to agree upon a bill. Again, Babbitt went behind closed doors to lead the negotiations that eventually produced a bill. As one might expect, the closed sessions were not for the purpose of reviewing research findings; political compromises were made. Arizona officials see the closed-door process as a price worth paying for what they see as substantive water legislation. As a consequence, little attention is paid to long-term policy goals.

Institutional Arrangements

Because availability of water has been the determinative factor shaping Arizona's development, there has been considerable effort devoted to research in water resources. For example, significant water-related research programs exist within the College of Agriculture, the College of Engineering and Mines, and the College of Arts and Sciences of the University of Arizona. In general, this research has not focused on water policy issues, as there has been little attempt to incorporate such findings into the policymaking process. Here we will discuss the extent to which policy research has been undertaken by three separate entities in Arizona: the Water Resources Research Center (WRRC) at the University of Arizona; private consultants for specific projects; and the DWR in the course of developing management plans. Research in Arizona generally is not used to shape policy. Rather, it provides policymakers with alternative approaches for meeting preestablished policy goals.

Water Resources Research Center
Since the state has taken a more active approach to water policy, the WRRC in recent years has tried to direct itself more to policy problems, as opposed to just hydrological concerns. However, according to Dr. William Lord, director of the WRRC, "the influence of academics generally, and this University in particular, upon state policymaking in the water area has been amazingly slight, given the kind of resources here."[55]

Since 1984, funding at the WRRC has increased from $250,000 annually to $500,000, although no money is appropriated for specific research projects. Most of the recent increase in funds is being directed toward a series of water issue papers and a new Water Information Program, a project to develop a computer data base on water information. The issue papers are designed to alert legislators and other members of the water community to policy problems. For example, the first paper was on the issue of stream adjudication of Indian water rights, and a forthcoming paper is on the feasibility of CAP water recharge. While the issue paper series is an attempt to broaden the technical orientation of the WRRC, it is recognized that it does not represent the kind of policy-related, interdisciplinary research in which universities should be engaged.[56] Although the center's long-term goal is to have an impact on policy formulation, that seems to be of secondary importance at this point. Given the recent increase in funding, which has been devoted to issue papers and the computer data base, the center may have to wait a few more years for the needed additional funds for policy research.[57]

Private Consultants

Research projects contracted by the state or localities to consultants are usually specific in nature with a technical bias. Occasionally they deal with institutional issues, which is an important component of policy research. One such study, funded by a 1986 legislative act, examines the economic and hydrologic impacts of water transfers in the Phoenix and Tucson areas. Existing state policies are not congenial to academic involvement early in the decision process, where it could be most useful. Instead, calls for assistance come at the data collection stage, when the problem has already been defined, or misdefined. The Tucson AMA now has several university researchers involved in such a data-collecting exercise.[58]

Department of Water Resources

The third and final area of research in Arizona to be discussed is the planning process undertaken by the DWR. If management plans are to be taken seriously, it is important that the DWR participate in policy formulation and respond to local concerns. In Tucson, for example, officials of the local AMA sit on the board of the Southern Arizona Water Resources Association (SAWARA), a nonprofit interest group active in water issues. The Tucson AMA also cultivates a close relationship with the Tucson Water Department, the AMA's largest water user. Thus, the planning process (and here the distinction between planning and research is not clear) is reciprocal and political. Though it lacks the clarity, for example, of the WRRC's efforts at coordinating all water resources research in the AMA, such a system more closely reflects the realities and challenges of long-term water policy research.

An example of a research effort undertaken by the DWR demonstrates the benefits of having a state agency involved in research, while also showing its limitations. In 1986, the DWR conducted a study entitled *Augmentation Options to Active Management Areas* as a means to survey the most promising augmentation options for the second management plan, which is scheduled to go into effect in 1990. The report identified ten augmentation options in three broad categories. The categories and specific options were:

I. Treatment of Nonpotable Water to Meet Specific Uses
   a. Desalination (Sea Water and In-State)
   b. Effluent Use or Recharge
II. Increase or Maximize Use of Runoff
   a. Weather Modification (In-State and Out-of-State)
   b. Watershed Management (In-State and Out-of-State)

     c.   Water Harvesting
     d.   Storm Runoff Capture
  III. Water Redistribution
     a.   Iceberg Harvesting
     b.   Importation of Water from Out of State
     c.   Maximize Utilization of CAP Water
     d.   In-State Water Transfers[59]

After discussing the details of each option, the report identified the top six as first priority for a feasibility study. The report rated the following options as most promising: in-state weather modification, in-state water transfers, in-state watershed management, effluent use and recharge, storm runoff and capture, and surplus CAP water.[60] Additional study was recommended to identify the breadth of knowledge about each alternative, the amount of additional water possible from each alternative, and the institutional constraints associated with the implementation of each.

This type of research can certainly be characterized as policy research, because it arrays the various options available to policymakers to meet a policy goal. In addition, by conducting these studies at the DWR level, the information is more effectively disseminated to the AMAs. However, the augmentation report also reveals some of the limitations, including limited staff resources, of research by the DWR. As valuable as this report is for laying out options for augmentation, some additional mechanism is needed to fill in the details in the report so that some of its recommendations can have an impact.

Two characteristics of the role of research in Arizona water policy should be emphasized. The first is that research has long been excluded from the policymaking process in Arizona. The second is that present research efforts in Arizona are limited to specific projects, which are designed to meet policy goals already established. Our case study on the Tucson AMA seeks to illustrate how the Tucson community is attempting to bring research into the policy process.

CASE STUDY: WATER POLICY DEVELOPMENT
IN THE TUCSON ACTIVE MANAGEMENT AREA

This case study will look at two examples of the role of research in the Tucson community. We will first examine Tucson's Artificial Recharge Demonstration Project, a joint effort of the city, state, and county. The recharge project represents an example of research being applied to a specific policy goal. The second part of the study will focus primarily on SAWARA, the sponsor of a basinwide management study. Although the basinwide study is not an AMA activity, it is the best example of policy research going on in the Tucson AMA. Both the recharge project and the SAWARA study are examples of studies taking place within an already determined policy environment. The main difference between the two is that the recharge project is technical in nature, while the SAWARA study is more policy oriented.

The prominent role of SAWARA is a common thread running throughout water policy in Tucson. The SAWARA is a nonprofit organization, established in November 1982, to ensure that the CAP would be completed to Tucson. Because this goal had such wide support in the community, SAWARA was able to attract a broad membership, which today includes prominent business leaders, environmentalists, university people, Tucson Water officials, and Tucson AMA officials. Since its establishment, SAWARA's areas of interest have extended well beyond the completion of CAP, as the remainder of the study shows. Perhaps the most important thing to note about SAWARA is that its broad base of membership gives it a great deal of credibility within the community and at the state level.[61]

Tucson Demonstration Recharge Project

The Arizona DWR, through the Tucson AMA and the Tucson Water Department, has begun implementing an artificial recharge demonstration project as a means of augmenting the city's water supply. The project plans to return treated effluent, excess CAP water, and storm water runoff to the aquifer for storage.[62] Using artificial recharge effectively is vital to water management in Tucson for two reasons. Effluent, whose supply is constant throughout the year, is used primarily in the summer months to water golf courses and parks.[63] In addition, it will ensure effective use of CAP water when it arrives in Tucson in 1991. Presently, there is limited demand for CAP water, and Tucson will not be using all of its 263,000 acre-feet per year allocation until several years after its arrival.[64] Artificial recharge will enable that water to be stored, thereby augmenting future supplies while maintaining the goal of safe yield.

It is worth noting that the recharge project does not represent original research, but is instead an application of existing research to a new policy situation. The feasibility of recharge was originally studied by the University of Arizona's WRRC in the 1960s, and in 1978 the Army Corps of Engineers began looking at recharge options in Tucson as part of the Tucson Urban Study.[65] However, it was not until legislation was passed authorizing a fee to finance such a project, that the state took an active role in recharge. Further action by the state in 1986, most notably HB 2209, has facilitated the development of recharge projects, by clarifying health and some (but not all) ownership issues surrounding recharge.

Enabling Legislation
The Tucson Demonstration Recharge Project was made possible by the 1984 legislation that authorized the Tucson AMA to begin such augmentation schemes during the first management plan. The GMA had authorized such initiatives for the second plan, but this subsequent leg-

islation was passed at the urging of Tucson AMA officials and the SAWARA, who felt that Tucson needed to be working on augmentation options sooner than 1990. The legislature's response was a bill permitting the Tucson AMA to levy an augmentation fee of $.50 per acre-foot of ground water withdrawal for the first three years of the project and up to $2.00 per acre-foot thereafter. The revenues, expected to be about $200,000 per year initially, will be used to finance engineering feasibility and site design studies, as well as construction, operation, and monitoring systems. The Tucson AMA is expected to sign intergovernmental agreements with Tucson Water and the Pima County Flood Control Authority; these entities will lend their expertise and financial assistance to the project.

The Artificial Groundwater Recharge and Underground Storage Projects Act of 1986 (HB 2209) set up a permitting process, administered by the DWR, to ensure that applicants have the financial ability to complete the project and that projects are hydrologically feasible. The bill also requires applicants to receive a water quality permit from the Department of Health Services. The water quality dimension of recharge is important because of the high quality of ground water already in the Tucson area. There seems to be little to fear from returning treated effluent to the ground; such effluent has been used for several years on golf courses and playgrounds in the city and has gained acceptance from the public. City and state officials are being cautious, however; the first health incident with effluent will set reuse plans back many years, and officials hope to avoid such an eventuality.[66]

Enactment of HB 2209 also established that a recharger is entitled to withdraw the same amount of water injected into the aquifer, less 10 percent, which remains in the ground to contribute to the safe yield goal. Although it did not clarify ownership rights to effluent (i.e., it is unclear whether recharged effluent is surface water, ground water, or whether a new class of water should be created), the bill did improve the prospects for recharge, by ensuring that those who do recharge will be able to withdraw what they have put in.

The Role of SAWARA

Of final interest to the recharge issue is the role SAWARA has played in generating public support. The SAWARA's newsletter, *WaterWords*, devoted an entire issue to explaining recharge to SAWARA members and the public in the summer of 1986. Because the SAWARA's members include businessmen and environmentalists, as well as faculty and AMA and Tucson Water personnel, it speaks with authority to those interested in water issues in Tucson. With its expertise and clout, the SAWARA can go to the political community and say, "this is what we need to do now."[67] The SAWARA has played an active and partisan role in public education and lobbying on water issues, something the AMA has been unable to do because of limited staff.

The Prospects for Basinwide Management in Tucson

The use of artificial recharge and other augmentation schemes, although an important part of efficient use of Tucson's water resources, will be beneficial only insofar as it takes place within a solid basinwide management structure. The idea of basinwide management dates back at least as far as 1976 and is presently under active consideration as a result of a 1986 study titled *Basin-Wide Management Alternatives for the Tucson Active Management Area*. While the concern here will be to evaluate the proposals recently put forth by the SAWARA, the City Council's water rate increase of 1976 left such an imprint on water politics in Tucson that those events warrant review.

The Tucson Water Rate Increase of 1976

In 1976, the Tucson Water Department expressed "its intent to effectively manage the water resources of the Tucson and Avra Valley Basins."[68] There were two reasons for such an effort. First, there was a very real crisis regarding the Tucson Water Department's ability to adequately serve Tucson's growing population. Indeed, the population in Tucson was 301,000 in 1976 and was expected to grow to 384,000 by 1986. The Tucson Water Department forecast serious capital improvement problems by 1981 and recommended rate increases, averaging 42 percent, to meet those needs.[69] Second, a group of environmentally oriented "New Democrats" had taken control of the City Council in 1976; to them water conservation represented a basic moral requisite.[70] Since high rates presumably would encourage conservation, the Tucson Water Department's recommendations had sympathetic ears at the council.

However, implementation of these rate increases had unfortunate consequences for the political careers of the New Democrats, who were recalled by the voters in January 1977. The recall of the New Democrats was not solely due to the fact that they raised water rates. They were "viewed as high-handed, arrogant, and disinterested in public participation."[71] Furthermore, low priority was given to the problem of political acceptability by the council's New Democrats.[72] The lesson to be drawn from this experience is not that attempts at basinwide management or other bold policy initiatives are unrealistic, but rather that the process one follows while attempting such ambitious initiatives is important.

The irony of the New Democrats' defeat is that their policies were not reversed, as their opponents had promised. The high rates remained in place and, more importantly, the new council embarked on a "beat the peak" campaign. Designed as a capital conservation tool (i.e., reduce peak demand for water so as to avoid the need for expensive system expansion), the campaign later became a water conservation tool. The overall result was a successful demand management policy--per capita pumpage fell from 189.4 gallons per day in 1976-77 to 147.5 gpd in 1978-79.[73] It also represented a retreat from the ambitious move toward basinwide management in favor of a more cautious, noncoercive approach.

Noncoercion and attention to political feasibility characterize the efforts at basinwide management being undertaken by SAWARA today.

SAWARA's Study of Basinwide Management for Tucson

The study of basinwide management began at the instigation of SAWARA in December 1983. Its objective was "to determine the effectiveness and equity of existing and alternative institutional mechanisms in balancing water supply and demand, while accommodating future demand and ensuring adequate water quality protection."[74] The SAWARA contracted with a consulting firm to perform the study.

On the face of it, it may seem strange that a private nonprofit organization has taken the lead on such an important issue. However, only the Tucson AMA and SAWARA have basinwide management as a primary concern,[75] and the Tucson AMA does not have the staff resources to conduct such a broad study.[76] In addition, the SAWARA's broad base of membership makes it an ideal forum from which to launch such a study. Its broadly based members had to arrive at a consensus before releasing the report, thus avoiding the risk of inciting a controversy that would render the study irrelevant.

Consciously or not, the SAWARA avoided the mistakes of the New Democrats in 1976. They paid attention to political feasibility by including the relevant actors (city, AMA, and university officials) in the study process. A committee of 36 SAWARA members, cutting across all facets of their membership, was the foundation for the study. Although it is too early to evaluate the study's impact, the fact that an AMA official sees the study as "a complementary part of our work" and agrees that "down the road we have to come to a unified regional management system" suggests that the report will be significant.[77] Careful attention to process, something neglected by Tucson Water officials in the 1970s, may pay off for the SAWARA in the 1980s.

The report itself recognizes that, although there is no present water crisis in the Tucson area, the current management system is not adequate to address the problems Tucson must confront in the future. Of great concern to the SAWARA is the lack of a basinwide funding mechanism that can raise sufficient capital to plan, build, and implement projects.[78] As a result, there is no consensus as to who should provide funds for large projects with basinwide benefits. One example is the recharge of ground water with excess CAP water. Though Tucson Water is going ahead with plans to conduct its own recharge program, the report notes an inequity in having one agency pay for a project that is likely to benefit everyone in the basin.

Despite the fact that the creation of a centralized management entity would be the most efficient option for the basin, the report notes that such an option would be contrary to six years of state action, designed to make the AMA a strong management entity. It would also undercut a value held very dear to localities in Arizona: some control over their destiny regarding water use. Consequently, for what amounted to political reasons, the SAWARA rejected this option, maintaining that the present system is designed to provide "maximum flexibility under a State framework of . . . management requirements."[79] The report, instead, recommends the enhancement of the existing management entities over the creation of a single new body or several limited management entities. Enhancement, according to the SAWARA, means improving efficiency, by "expanding the authorities of existing management entities and improving interrelationships among management entities."

While the enhancement recommendation has the political advantage of not destroying existing institutions, it nonetheless seems too general to have much impact. After receiving and approving the consultant's report, the SAWARA established several new committees to study those issues that seemed of most immediate concern to the Tucson area. The two issues chosen for study were: (1) water transfer, exchanges, and marketing; and (2) supply issues related to recharge, storage, and use of excess water.[80] Such issues as cost (e.g., financing recharge projects on a basinwide basis) will be considered by these committees.

As cautious as the SAWARA's recommendation may seem, it is important to realize that the approach is appropriate in light of traditional water policy in Tucson and Arizona. That tradition has been one of state policy action (e.g. the passage of the Groundwater Management Act) coming only after some external impetus (such as the threatened cutoff of CAP funds). The problem with this tradition, as we have seen, is that it has excluded research from the policymaking process. The SAWARA's attempt to bring policymakers into the research process, as illustrated in this example, may enhance the role of research in water policy formation.

CONCLUSIONS

1. One of the driest states in the nation, Arizona's early development was greatly facilitated by federal water supply projects. Together with readily available ground water, these projects fostered the growth of irrigated agriculture.

2. With increasing economic development and depletion of ground water supplies, Arizona looked to the federal government to build the CAP. A controversial project from its inception, its completion was conditioned upon the state addressing its ground water problems.

3. Under the leadership of Governor Babbitt, the 1980 Groundwater Act was formulated through a consensus process that involved all of the user groups. Its main feature is the goal of attaining safe yield in ground water usage by the year 2025, primarily by reducing agricultural usage of water.

4. Implementation of the act depended upon the formation of regional AMAs with the authority to develop policies to assist in the attainment of this goal. A pump tax was devised as a means of financing administration of the program and encouraging conservation.

5. In the past, research has not played a significant role in the development of water policy in Arizona and has not received much state funding. The formulation of the Groundwater Management Act depended mainly upon political, not scientific or engineering, considerations. However, the current director of the WRRC is encouraging the desirable greater emphasis on water policy research. In addition, local initiatives, such as the artificial recharge project, are under way. This research does not, in general, represent highly original efforts, but rather seeks to address issues within the existing policy framework.

6. In general, Arizona historically has taken a reactive stance in addressing water issues. Even in its attempts to formulate a ground water policy, it has stopped short of delineating a plan, and has merely stated a goal for the future. Water research continues to play a minor role in helping to address these issues, so far having only an incremental impact on water policy.

This chapter was written by John Horrigan and Alexander Schmandt.

NOTES

1. Arizona Water Commission, *Inventory of Resources and Uses; Phase I: Arizona State Water Plan* (Phoenix: Arizona Water Commission, 1975), p. 47 (hereafter cited as *Inventory*).
2. Arizona Water Commission, *Inventory*, p. 29
3. Arizona Water Commission, *Inventory*, p. 29.
4. Dean Mann, *The Politics of Water in Arizona* (Tucson: The University of Arizona Press, 1963), p. 68 (hereafter cited as *Politics of Water*).
5. Arizona Water Commission, *Inventory*, p. 70.
6. Arizona Water Commission, *Inventory*, p. 70.
7. Arizona v. California, 373 U.S. 546 (1963).
8. Arizona Water Commission, *Inventory*, p. 72.
9. Wesley Steiner, "Public Water Policy in Arizona," *State Government* 55, no. 4 (1982), p. 133 (hereafter cited as "Public Water Policy").
10. Steiner, "Public Water Policy," p. 133.
11. Richard Bergman and Kip Viscusi, *Damming the West*, Ralph Nader's Study Group Report on the Bureau of Reclamation (Washington, D.C.: Center for the Study of Responsive Law, 1972), p. 108.
12. Bureau of Reclamation, *Report on Central Arizona Project*, Department of the Interior, Project Planning Report No. 3-8b.4-2 (December 1947), pp. 153-154.
13. John Upton Terrell, *War for the Colorado River, Vol. I: The California Arizona Controversy* (Glendale, Ca.: Arthur H. Clark Co., 1965).
14. Mann, *Politics of Water*, p. 140
15. Mann, *Politics of Water*, pp. 130-131.
16. Mann, *Politics of Water*, pp. 130-131.

17. Bureau of Reclamation, *Central Arizona Project: Final Environmental Statement* (Washington, D.C.: Department of the Interior, 1972).

18. Mann, *Politics of Water*, p. 128.

19. Helen Ingram, *Patterns of Politics in Water Resource Development: A Case Study of New Mexico's Role in the Colorado River Basin Bill* (Albuquerque: The University of New Mexico, 1969), p. 21.

20. *Colorado River Basin Project Act of 1968*, 82 United States Statutes-at-Large 865.

21. James Egbert, "Arizona Water Resource Management Problems Created by the Central Arizona Project," *Arizona Law Review* 25 (1983), p. 223.

22. 40 U.S.C., section 1524(b)(3).

23. 43 U.S.C., section 1524(c).

24. Philip Higdon and Terence Thompson, "The 1980 Arizona Groundwater Management Code," *Arizona State Law Journal* (1980), p. 621.

25. Bristor v. Cheatham, 75 Ariz. 227, 255 P.2d 173 (1953).

26. Farmers Investment Co. v. Bettwy, 113 Ariz. 520, 558 P. 2d 14 (1976).

27. Desmond Connal, "A History of the Arizona Groundwater Management Act," *Arizona State Law Journal* (1982), p. 325 (hereafter cited as "History of Arizona").

28. Ariz. Rev. Stat Ann., sections 45-564 (A)(1) and (2).

29. Connal, "History of Arizona," p. 331.

30. Connal, "History of Arizona," pp. 331-332.

31. Connal, "History of Arizona," p. 333.

32. Connal, "History of Arizona," p. 325.

33. Connal, "History of Arizona," p. 325.

34. Arizona Groundwater Management Study Commission, *Final Report* (Phoenix, Ariz.: Department of Water Resources, June 1980), p. II-2.

35. Gordon Meeks, *Arizona Groundwater: Negotiating an Environmental Quality Act* (Denver, Colo.: National Conference of State Legislatures, January 1987), p. 15 (hereafter cited as *Arizona Groundwater*).

36. Meeks, *Arizona Groundwater*, pp. 16-17.

37. Meeks, *Arizona Groundwater*, p. 18.

38. Meeks, *Arizona Groundwater*, pp. 19-21.

39. Meeks, *Arizona Groundwater*, pp. 23-25.

40. Meeks, *Arizona Groundwater*, pp. 23-25.

41. Meeks, *Arizona Groundwater*, p. 11.

42. Meeks, *Arizona Groundwater*, p. 12.

43. Department of Water Resources (DWR) *Arizona Department of Water Resources Transition Report* (Phoenix: DWR, 1986), p. 14.

44. Zachery Smith, *Interest Group Interaction and Groundwater Policy Formation in the Southwest* (New York: University Press of America, 1985), pp. 152-153 (hereafter cited as *Interest Group Interaction*).

45. Interview with Steve Olsen, deputy director, Tucson AMA, January 13, 1987.

46. Department of Water Resources (DWR), *Management Plan: First Management Period: 1980-90, Phoenix Active Management Area* (Phoenix, Ariz.: DWR, December 1984), p. 68.

47. Interview with Frank Barrios, director, Phoenix AMA, January 14, 1987.

48. Interview with Senator John Hays, January 15, 1987.

49. Smith, *Interest Group Interaction*, p. 152.

50. *Arizona Department of Water Resources Transition Report*, p. 29.

51. Smith, *Interest Group Interaction*, p. 154.

52. Rodney T. Smith, *Troubled Waters: Financing Water in the West* (Washington, D.C.: The Council of State Planning Agencies, 1984), p. 112.

53. Interview with Steve Olsen, deputy director, Tucson AMA, January 13, 1987.

54. Michael McNulty and Gary Woodward, "Arizona Water Issues: Contrasting Legal and Economic Issues," *Arizona Review* (Tucson, Ariz.: University of Arizona, Division of Economic and Business Research, College of Business Administration, fall 1986), p. 6.

55. Interview with Dr. William Lord, director, Water Resources Research Center, Arizona, January 12, 1987.

56. Interview with William Lord, January 12, 1987.

57. Interview with William Lord, January 12, 1987.

58. Interview with William Lord, January 12, 1987.

59. Craig O'Hare, "Augmentation Options to Active Management Areas" (October 1986) (hereafter cited as "Augmentation Options").

60. O'Hare, "Augmentation Options," pp. 22-23.

61. Interview with Mary Beth Carlisle, executive director, SAWARA, January 12, 1987.

62. Department of Water Resources (DWR), *Management Plan: First Management Period: 1980-90, Tucson Active Management Area,* Special Supplement: Chapter IX Augmentation Program (Phoenix, Ariz.: DWR, October 1985), p. 4 (hereafter cited as *Management Plan*).

63. DWR, *Management Plan*, p. 7.

64. Interview with William Lord, January 12, 1987.

65. DWR, *Management Plan,* p. 4.

66. Interview with Kirke Guild, Tucson Water Department, January 13, 1987.

67. Interview with Kirke Guild, January 13, 1987.

68. William E. Martin et al., *Saving Water in a Desert City* (Washington D.C.: Resources for the Future, 1984), p. 15 (hereafter cited as *Saving Water*).

69. City of Tucson Budget, Fiscal Year 1986-87, p. B-1.

70. Martin et al., *Saving Water,* pp. 13-14.

71. Martin et al., *Saving Water,* p. 75.

72. Martin et al., *Saving Water,* p. 17.

73. Martin et al., *Saving Water,* p. 25.

74. *Basin-Wide Management Alternatives for the Tucson Active Management Area*, developed by Southern Arizona Water Resources Association (August 1986); report prepared by Rich and Associates, p. ii (hereafter cited as *Basin-Wide Management Alternatives*).

75. *Basin-Wide Management Alternatives*, p. 7.

76. Interview with Steve Olsen, January 12, 1987.

77. Interview with Steve Olsen, January 12, 1987.

78. *Basin-Wide Management Alternatives*, p. 35.

79. *Basin-Wide Management Alternatives*, p. 51.

80. *Basin-Wide Management Alternatives*, p. 61.

CALIFORNIA

BACKGROUND
Historical Factors

Water has been a controversial issue in California since the area was settled in the 1800s. California is the most populous state in the country, and the needs of the population, as well as the diverse needs of industry and agriculture, have put a tremendous strain on the water supply. The focus of the problem has been, and will continue to be, the conflict arising from development of areas with the least water. Whereas most of the precipitation occurs in the northern part of the state, water consumption is greatest in the highly populous south and the Central Valley, which depends on irrigated agriculture.

The rapid increase in population growth and water consumption during the last two decades is shown in Table 4.1. This trend is expected to continue with recent projections for the state indicating a population of 34.4 million by 2010--close to a 45 percent increase over 1980 levels. The southern coastal region, between and including Los Angeles and San Diego, is projected to account for half of that growth.[1] In contrast, nearly 70 percent of the state's precipitation falls in the northern third of the state. Southern California and the Central Valley receive only 5-20 inches of rainfall annually, with desert areas receiving near zero levels of precipitation.[2] Thus, the majority of the state's population resides in areas with the least amount of water, necessitating an extensive system of dams, reservoirs, pipelines, and aqueducts to service these areas.

TABLE 4.1 Estimated Water Use in California, 1965-80

	1965	1970	1975	1980
Population (millions)	18.4	20.0	21.1	23.7
Consumption by use (offstream)				
Total (mgd)	16,514	21,710	22,840	25,160
Public supply	1,300	1,400	1,500	1,700
Rural use	94	120	130	130
Irrigation	15,000	20,000	21,000	23,000
Industrial	120	190	210	330
Per capita (gpd)				
All uses	898	1,086	1,082	1,062
excl. irrigation	82	86	87	91
Withdrawals by source				
Total (mgd)	31,000	38,000	40,000	44,000
Ground water	14,000	18,000	19,000	21,000
Surface water	17,000	20,000	21,000	23,000

Source: U.S. Geological Survey, *Estimated Use of Water in the United States, 1965; Estimated Use of Water in the United States, 1970; Estimated Use of Water in the United States, 1975; Estimated Use of Water in the United States, 1980*, Geological Survey Circulars 556, 676, 765, and 1001 (Reston, Va.: U.S. Department of the Interior, 1968, 1972, 1977, and 1983).

Numerous mountain ranges and dense forests have often made the task of building distribution systems very difficult and costly. Most of the water development occurring in the nineteenth and early twentieth centuries was financed by the private sector. Individual cities and regions constructed canals and aqueducts for their own use. Even today, many privately financed irrigation agencies still supply water, without state or federal government financing, to the same lands that they have served for over 100 years. Of the approximately 40 maf annual usage, nearly 30 maf is delivered by the more than 2,500 local or private water agencies, via surface diversion and storage projects or ground water pumping.[3] The development of these private initiatives set a precedent for the development of the present, major comprehensive conveyance systems of the state: the state-operated State Water Project (SWP) and the federally operated Central Valley Project (CVP).

State Water Planning

All California water supply projects have been controversial to some degree. The 340-mile Los Angeles Aqueduct, completed in 1913, aroused the wrath of local farmers, and the construction of the Hetch Hetchy reservoir on the Tuolumne River as a water supply for San Francisco angered conservationists. In 1919, under the sponsorship of the California State Irrigation Association, a plan was developed to divert water from the Sacramento River for the purpose of irrigating 12 million acres in the Sacramento and San Joaquin Valleys. A report was authorized by the legislature in 1921, and a series of reports was made in 1923, 1925, 1927, 1929, and 1931. The latter, presented by the state engineer, was called the State Water Plan. Federal agencies were also involved by this time, and in 1931 the Bureau of Reclamation and the State of California issued a joint report. In 1933, the California legislature passed the Central Valley Project Act, in order to implement the initial phases of the State Water Plan. It provided financing through the issuance of $170 million in revenue bonds, approved by the voters in a special election. However, the depression made revenue bonds unmarketable, and financing was arranged through the Bureau of Reclamation, under the Federal Reclamation Act. Construction began in 1935.[4] In 1980 approximately 4.4 maf of CVP water was delivered from the Sacramento River reservoirs to agricultural users in the southern Sacramento and San Joaquin Valleys.[5]

Between 1945 and 1955, the State Water Resources Board continued to investigate the state's water resources. In 1957, preliminary plans for "full practical development of all the water resources of the State to meet its ultimate water needs" were presented in its third and final report, "The California Water Plan." Meanwhile, the Division of Water Resources was developing plans for a multipurpose dam and reservoir on the Feather River, the Delta Cross Channel, and distribution aqueducts. The proposed project was authorized by the legislature in 1951, and a 1955 feasibility report recommended that the legislature appropriate funds for construction, with some modifications. Following devastating floods in 1955-56, the legislature made an emergency appropriation of $25 million to begin construction of the SWP. Appropriations were made in subsequent years, and construction of the South Bay and California Aqueducts began in 1959. However, it was not until 1959 that the legislature enacted the legislation necessary to fully implement authorization of the SWP. Known as the Burns-Porter Act, it authorized the issuance of $1.75 billion in general obligation bonds, subject to ratification by the voters at a 1960 general election.[6]

In order to gain statewide approval, careful attention had to be paid to the requirements of both northern and southern voters. In the 1931 County of Origin Law, and again in the 1933 Central Valley Project Act, priority of right to water was given to areas in which the water originates. The Senate leadership was determined to preserve this provision. Thus, success depended upon ensuring that California had adequate water supplies, including its entitlement to Colorado River water, to meet the needs of both the areas of origin and the areas of deficiency. In addition, the act had to provide sufficient financing for projects to service all areas, including flood control, power production, recreation, and enhancement of fisheries. Provision was made to replenish water supplies available for export from the delta during times of increased withdrawals upstream.[7]

Currently, the SWP delivers 2.3 maf from the northern Sacramento Valley to wholesalers primarily in the San Joaquin Valley and the Los Angeles area.[8] Together the CVP and the SWP operate about 20 reservoirs, providing approximately 45 percent of the annual surface water supply and 25 percent of the total developed water supply in California.[9] Irrigated acreage amounts to some 2 million acres in the Sacramento Valley and 5 million acres in the San Joaquin Valley.[10]

Large amounts of water are also imported into the state from the Colorado River via the Colorado River Aqueduct. The Metropolitan Water District of Southern California, which serves 13 million people, imports approximately 66 percent of its water from the SWP and the Colorado River.[11] The Colorado River Aqueduct also supplies water to the Imperial Valley, which contains approximately 500,000 acres of irrigated farm-land.[12] The importance of this source of water will, however, be reduced as Arizona begins to draw its share of water for the Central Arizona Project. Attempts to reduce the demand for this water, through a cooperative arrangement between these two major users, are discussed in a later section. Such contractual arrangements are likely to become increasingly important as voters withdraw their support for water development projects, as illustrated in a discussion of the Peripheral Canal.

The Peripheral Canal

The San Francisco Bay Delta, formed at the converging mouths of the Sacramento and San Joaquin River systems, is the focal point for water in the state. Originally swampland subject to uncontrolled flooding, the delta has been transformed into numerous reclaimed islands and tracts used for farming. Despite steady urbanization and industrialization, the delta still constitutes an area rich in wildlife and fish, providing a major source of recreational opportunities. However, the delta is also a pool through which northern California water must pass in order for it to be exported to southern California. Diversion of water from the delta affects water quality in the area by reducing the outflow of fresh water to the sea. As a result, the pollution, which results from industrialization, return flows from agricultural drainage, and urbanization of the area, is not effectively flushed into the sea. Also, salt water intrusion during low-flow periods changes the salinity levels. These disturbances have severely affected the migrating salmon and striped bass populations.[13]

All of these problems tend to be exacerbated by subsidence. The peaty soils, which are intensively farmed, are subsiding at an average rate of three inches per year, due to oxidation, wind erosion, and compaction by farm equipment.[14] The area is already below sea level, resulting in inadequate drainage and an accumulation of pollutants. Because of its fragility and marshlike quality, the area has been likened to the Florida Everglades.[15] A series of levees, which protect the area from sea water intrusion, are eroding. According to Legislative Aide Bob Reeb, "fixing the delta is of prime concern for the next few years."[16]

Several suggestions have been proposed to control salt water intrusion into the delta. An interagency committee, consisting of representatives of the DWR, the U.S. Bureau of Reclamation, and the U.S. Army Corps of Engineers, was set up to compare the various costs and benefits of each. They concluded that the interests of fish and wildlife were best served by a canal that would divert water from the Sacramento River at Hood. It would be hydraulically isolated from delta channels, skirting the eastern edge of the delta and transporting water to the intake facilities of the SWP and CVP. Water could be released along the way to meet local needs and control the salinity of the delta.[17] The Peripheral Canal was hailed by officials as "the greatest opportunity for balanced growth of many delta-oriented activities."[18] A cross-delta canal would make more water available to both the SWP and the CVP and would allow for a daily allotment of fresh water to be used as outflow impeding the intrusion of saline water into the delta.

Most of the opposition to the Peripheral Canal came from Contra Costa County officials and county industrial interests, who had never supported diversions of water to southern California. Industrial development advocates in the area contended that sufficient supplies of fresh water should be left in the delta to meet their needs. Others maintained that this would be a waste of fresh water and that county industries could be supplied with canal water diverted further upstream by Contra Costa Water District. The county's position exemplifies nearly all of California's water development issues, focusing on competing economic uses of water. It was felt that the water could be used to enhance and protect Contra Costa's fresh water supply or it could be used to augment southern California's supply, but that there is insufficient supply to satisfy both of these needs without additional water supply development. Officials in Contra Costa County argued that their area, along with northern California, was being sacrificed to overdevelop southern California.[19] Environmental interests joined the issue on the side of Contra Costa County, in an attempt to protect the delta.

Pressure from opposition groups, debate in the California legislature, and problems with funding caused over 15 years of delay to the project. The canal, which was estimated to cost approximately $285 million in the mid-1960s, was finally approved by the legislature in July 1980 at a cost of $5 billion. Opponents of the measure obtained enough signatures to force a statewide referendum in June 1982, at which time it was soundly defeated. Election results showed strong support for development of the canal in southern California, with 61 percent voting for the canal. However, the proposition was overwhelmingly defeated in northern California by an average margin of 92 percent. The largest opposition came from the populous San Francisco-Oakland Bay area.

The Peripheral Canal is a good example of political action in the state because the canal was "a symbol, not the issue."[20] Even though the canal was designed to continuously release water into the delta, flushing out pollutants and keeping out sea water, northern California residents and environmentalists saw the Peripheral Canal as just another attempt to take their water. It is somewhat ironic that environmental groups would oppose the canal, because the idea was adopted partly on the basis that it would enhance the environmental quality of the delta. However, they argued that, aside from the negative impacts of diversion, the clearing of delta water with increased amounts of fresh water would radically change the delicate ecological balance of the delta. They also feared that in times of shortage, southern California's need for water would take precedence over the requirements of the delta.

Critical Issues

Water Supply

The state has already built dams on all of the best sites, and cost estimates for the next major dam that could be built approach $2 to $3 billion. Construction of new projects, in most cases, is no longer as economical as it has been in the past. The focus of present water policy is how to best manage the presently developed resources. This point takes on more significance in light of the nearly completed Central Arizona Project, which will result in a reduction in Colorado River water supply for southern California.[21]

However, there continues to be additional demand for CVP and SWP water. A great deal of this demand results from the low prices for the water, which now appear to many to be inappropriate. Low prices provide little incentive for increased efficiency and reuse. According to Willey, subsidies to water users arise primarily from three sources: (1) use of tax revenues for project development and operation; (2) application of historical average costs to the calculations for repayment rates; and (3) the absence of "price elasticity" as a demand determinant in the planning of future project development.[22] In fact, the U.S. Bureau of Reclamation has in the past determined price based on an ability-to-pay concept, with the result that supply determines demand. Using similar principles, the SWP generates demand by committing the state to contractual entitlements for future water deliveries and then plans supply projects accordingly. "Surplus" water is sold on a spot basis at very low prices--only the variable cost of transporting the water to the user is included in the price; the fixed capital costs are omitted.[23]

In an attempt to reduce the amount of federal subsidy to farmers receiving CVP water, Congress passed the Reclamation Reform Act of 1982. In return for increasing the acreage limit for eligibility for CVP water from 160 to 960 acres, individuals and districts taking advantage of this new acreage limit must renegotiate their contracts so that the full operating and maintenance costs are included in the price of the water. Irrigation districts that do not amend their contracts are required to pay the full cost of water delivered to farmers with more than 160 acres, including interest on unpaid capital. The bureau has been reluctant to implement this latter provision.[24] As of October 1987, a new pricing structure has not been approved by the Secretary of the Interior.[25]

In addition to economic considerations, environmental factors may put constraints on new diversion projects. The Water Quality Control Plan for the Sacramento-San Joaquin Delta, adopted in 1978, requires that the SWP and CVP reduce their withdrawals during part of the year to maintain specified fresh water outflow and salinity levels in the delta. Although it was initially claimed that the CVP, a federal project, was not subject to these restrictions, subsequent federal legislation requires the CVP to cooperate in protecting the delta in accordance with California state law. In addition, the 1968 federal and 1972 California Wild and Scenic Rivers Acts afford some protection to many rivers in northern California. Approximately one-quarter of the state's annual runoff is protected by the state act.[26]

Another example, arising from judicial action, concerns Mono Lake. In 1940, the California water board granted the City of Los Angeles a permit to appropriate the entire flow of four out of five streams flowing into Mono Lake. By 1970, Los Angeles' diversions had resulted in a dramatic drop in the level of the lake, whose surface area was reduced by one third. Following a judgment in the Superior Court against its position, National Audubon Society brought suit in the California Supreme Court. In *National Audubon Society* v. *Superior Court of Alpine County*,[27] the court refused to accept either the plaintiff's position that the public trust doctrine is superior to all appropriated water rights, or the board's position that the public trust doctrine had been subsumed into the appropriative water rights system and no longer had an independent existence. In trying to accommodate both positions, the court concluded that the state has an affirmative duty to take the public trust doctrine into account in planning the allocation of water rights and must continue to supervise the use of appropriated water. However, the legislature may authorize factory licenses that permit an appropriator to take water from a flowing stream in order to ensure the efficient use of the state's waters for population and economic growth, even though this may unavoidably harm the public trust.[28]

Water Quality

The issue of water quality is increasingly becoming a central theme in California, as evidenced by the statement: "never so much has quantity meant quality in California."[29] The state has enough water to meet its needs, but sufficient supply of good quality remains an issue. Since we now have the technical capability to measure potential pollutants in particles per billion (or trillion), there is concern over toxics and other substances never before detected in the water. Irrigated agriculture creates its own water quality problems: both pesticides and natural salts accumulate in agricultural runoff. An inability to solve the problems associated with this problem is threatening the viability of some irrigation projects in the Central Valley.

Despite its low precipitation (5-10 inches per year), the Central Valley is host to some of the most fertile soil in the country and is the heart of California's largest industry, agriculture. The presence of selenium, boron, and sulphur in the soil of the area results in high and potentially toxic concentrations of these elements in the irrigation drainage water. Because of the overly high concentrations of these elements, the drainage water reservoirs and evaporation ponds used to collect these elements have become toxic to the wildlife of the region. In addition, as drainage water is recycled back into the irrigation system, the soil becomes increasingly saline, reducing the yield of many crops. This issue is covered in depth in the Westlands Water District case study.

Ground Water Management
Ground water accounts for approximately 39 percent of the total water used in the state.[30] California also has an abundance of ground water underlying its alluvial valleys. However, statewide total ground water in storage is about 860 maf, of which a substantial portion may not be readily available. Average annual natural replenishment is about 5.8 maf, which is approximately 1.8 maf less than the rate of withdrawal.[31] The most seriously affected areas are in the southern Central Valley region, including the extremely productive agricultural areas on the east side of the valley between Fresno and Bakersfield.

Long-term overdrafting of ground water in the San Joaquin Valley is also evidenced by compaction of deep-lying clay beds and subsidence of the ground surface. In coastal areas, an additional problem is salt water intrusion. In other areas, reliance on surface water supplies for agricultural purposes has resulted in high ground water levels requiring drainage systems to control water levels below crop root zones.[32] All of these factors point to the need for better management of ground water supplies. However, as discussed in the next section, ground water use has never been subject to comprehensive regulation, and attempts to implement a statewide ground water management plan have met with considerable resistance.

STATE INITIATIVES IN WATER RESOURCE MANAGEMENT
Policy Development

Between 1950 and 1970, the population of California doubled (see Table 2.2, Chapter 2), and existing water supplies were seen as inadequate to serve the swelling urban population. However, with changing attitudes toward the environment, the conditions that had previously fostered the development of new water supplies no longer prevailed in the 1970s. The influence of the environmental movement is evidenced by the 1972 Wild and Scenic Rivers Act, which specifically protects many northern rivers from interbasin transfer of their waters. More efficient management of existing supplies was one alternative. However, such policies did not get much attention until the 1976-77 two-year drought, when precipitation was 65 percent (1976) and 45 percent (1977) of average levels. A 20 percent reduction in urban water use, through mandatory conservation programs, realized a savings of 1 maf. The Imperial Irrigation District fined water users when surface runoff exceeded 15 percent of delivered water and allocated $2 million per year for the lining of irrigation canals.[33] Although the development of additional water supplies continues to be a part of the DWR's policy, there is an increased emphasis on conservation and reassignment of existing supplies.

Development of Additional Supplies
The DWR estimates that upstream depletions will reduce the present yield of existing SWP water from 2.3 maf annually to 1.7 maf by 2010. The resulting yield is about 1.5 maf less than projected requirements.[34] Two factors are significant in the planning of new supplies. First, opportunities for additional upstream development projects are restricted by the limited amount of available surface water, the limited number of suitable sites, and financial constraints. In addition, there is continued controversy over the issue of how much additional water can be withdrawn from the Sacramento-San Joaquin Delta without inflicting unacceptable levels of environmental degradation.

In 1978, California passed the Water Quality Control Plan for the delta in an attempt to protect the beneficial uses of water within the delta. As mentioned earlier, the federal CVP did not immediately comply with the regulations, and federal legislation requiring such compliance was introduced into Congress. However, there is still continued pressure to increase the amount of water available from this source. The state Senate recently passed legislation that would require the DWR to build facilities to increase the cross-delta transfer of water and construct three reservoirs for off-stream storage south of the delta.[35] While DWR representatives are neutral on this legislation, they do intend to increase the cross-delta transfer of water, using an incremental approach. The DWR also supports the notion of offstream storage and aquifer recharge.[36] To this end, the legislature in 1984 overwhelmingly approved authorization of Los Banos Grandes Reservoir as a future SWP storage facility.[37] The DWR has also been evaluating two other potential reservoir sites: Kellogg and Los Vaqueros. However, the continued opposition by Contra Costa County residents to additional export of water from the delta is illustrated by the approval, in June 1985, of a subdivision within the proposed Los Vaqueros Reservoir Site by the Contra Costa Country Board of Supervisors.[38]

As in other states, the ability of an agency to utilize underground storage for water reserves may be compromised by inadequate legal protection and lack of clarity in ground water laws. Following the 1976-77 drought, Governor Brown created the Governor's Commission to Review California Water Rights Law. In view of the absence of ground water law and the protracted adjudication procedures that had ensued, ground water was the major issue before the commission. The commission made recommendations in three general areas of ground water law: the establishment of ground water management authority; simplification of judicial procedures for basin adjudication; and establishment of better means for ground water storage. While the recommendations for underground storage were generally accepted, controversy arose over the recommendations for simplification of the adjudication process and for ground water management authority. In an attempt to codify these recommendations, more than nine bills were introduced into the legislature between 1978 and 1981. All failed.[39]

The DWR is basing its water supply and demand projections on the assumption that ground water use will remain largely unrestricted.[40] However, it is the DWR's policy to encourage both better management of ground water and conjunctive use of ground and surface water supplies. A law enacted in 1985 authorizes the inclusion of ground water storage projects south of the delta into the SWP. The DWR is investigating the feasibility of acquiring land in Kern County in order to develop artificial recharge facilities as a means of storing SWP water during years of abundance.[41]

Water Conservation

Several methods for encouraging water conservation have been instituted by the legislature in recent years. These measures have included tax credits on irrigation equipment that saves water; tax credits for water conservation systems, including rainwater and graywater cisterns, the replacement and modification of toilets, and the installation of flow-reducing devices; and tax credits for numerous energy conserving measures, including installation of low-flow shower heads.[42] The state has also made available low-interest bond money for the development of waste water reclamation projects.

The Urban Water Management Planning Act of 1983 requires every urban water supplier providing water for municipal purposes to more than 3,000 customers, or supplying more than 3,000 acre-feet of water annually, to adopt an urban water management plan that meets prescribed requirements.[43] The plans are filed with the Office of Water Conservation of the DWR, which compiles, analyzes, and reports a summary of the status of the plans to the legislature on an annual basis. Each urban water supplier must periodically review its management plan in order to keep in compliance with the prescribed requirements. Violation of the law allows civil suits to be brought against the local agencies, but the state will not initiate legal action itself.

The Agricultural Water Management Planning Act of 1986 was passed as a logical follow-up to the Urban Water Management Planning Act. The laws are essentially the same, applying to agricultural water suppliers supplying more than 50,000 acre-feet of water annually. It also addresses the need for information regarding the opportunity to conserve water or reduce the quantity of highly saline or toxic drainage water. In this case, suppliers do not have to prepare a plan or a report unless funds are appropriated to reimburse the supplier for the costs associated with preparation of the plans. Reimbursement for the costs of these studies will be made for amounts up to $5,000 per report and $25,000 per plan.[44] Other aspects of the bill are the same as the Urban Water Management Planning Act.

Water Marketing

During the 1976-77 drought, some reassignment of water supplies took place. For instance, four southern California water agencies released 0.44 maf of SWP water for use in the Central Valley, in exchange for other supplies. However, other transfers were made difficult by existing water laws and institutional requirements. As a result, the Governor's Commission to Review California Water Rights Law was set up in 1977.[45] Subsequent legislation is aimed at using the marketplace as a forum for the more efficient distribution of water rights.

Water marketing involves setting prices for water that reflect its market value. Richard Katz, a California assemblyman, describes water marketing as "allowing the auctioning of surplus water....Areas with extra water can sell it for a profit and drier areas can purchase it at a large savings compared to the cost of building new water systems."[46] However, it also includes actions such as voluntary transfers, exchanges, and leasing of water, motivated by economic incentives. Innovations in California water policy are being led by the passage of several key laws from the state legislature. Water transfers between users have been promoted by two laws in the 1980s. The Katz-Bates Bill was passed in 1980 in an effort to increase water supply mobility. This measure was designed to meet the growing water needs of the state, by requiring that water be used more efficiently, improving the definition of property rights, and increasing the transferability of such rights. The purpose of this policy was to encourage voluntary transfer of water and water rights, consistent with the public welfare of the places of export and import.[47]

Another bill related to water transfers was passed in 1986. In order to strengthen the state's position, it requires the "Department of Water Resources (DWR) to establish an ongoing program to facilitate the voluntary exchange or transfer of water and implement the various state laws that pertain to water transfers."[48] The bill provides for a water transfer guide containing specific information about water transfers with the proper contracting procedures. It also requires the department to report its findings and recommendations regarding needed changes in existing law or state policies for improvement of water management by the use of voluntary water transfers.

Implementation

Planning
The DWR is the official agency that oversees the daily operation and maintenance of the SWP. Created in 1956, it took over the functions of the Water Project Authority and the Division of Water Resources (in the Department of Public Works), except for those functions relating to appropriative water rights and water quality control, which were vested in the new State Water Resources Control Board. The former State Water Resources Board (now the California Water Commission) was also placed within the DWR.[49] The agency is responsible for technical planning and long-range forecasting for the state's water resources and interacts with local governments and authorities regarding their water needs. It works with the federal government when the federal government is interested in specific water resources plans involving coordination between the SWP and the federally operated CVP.

The DWR also prepares the California Water Plan. The first plan was developed under the direction of the state legislature and was published in 1957. This report was the culmination of ten years of investigations of state water resources and was the follow-up to planning studies done in the late 1920s and early 1930s. The development of this first plan had three phases: identification of the water resources of California; determination of present and potential "ultimate" water requirements; and planning for the orderly development of the state's water resources to meet its potential ultimate requirements.[50] The most notable provision in this plan was the recommendation to construct the SWP. Other notable recommendations were feasibility studies for sea water conversion, waste water reclamation, and weather modification to supplement the water supply.

The California Water Plan has been updated four times: in 1966, 1970, 1974, and 1983. All of the water plans, except for the 1983 update, indicated that the future water needs of the state could be met by existing water developments. The latest version of the plan indicates that, due to growing ground water overdraft, future water shortages can be expected, unless preventative steps are taken. The report places emphasis on nonstructural approaches, such as water conservation, reclamation, and exchanges as ways to curtail total future water needs. The report also points out that these measures will not satisfy the future demands of the system and that some surface water development will be needed to meet future demand.[51]

The State Water Resources Control Board (SWRCB) is an independent agency of the state that is responsible for maintaining and regulating the state's water quality standards and enforcing the state's water rights. It is involved in water supply issues through its Division of Water Rights, which regulates appropriative water rights and most recently focused on the environmental consequences of reduced stream flows. Many restrictions and conditions have been imposed on water rights permits, based on public input, instream needs, and prior appropriations. The SWRCB maintains jurisdiction over the review process for changes in use or changes in point of diversion for existing permits.

Water Distribution

As previously discussed, regional and municipal entities play a key role in the development of water conveyance and distribution systems. Some water districts have partially or completely developed local supplies, while others distribute water supplied by the state or federal systems. In 1975, Kern County Water Agency in the southern part of the Central Valley received over 0.75 maf from the SWP, and the Westlands Water District on the west side of the San Joaquin Valley received over 1.25 maf from the CVP.[52] Together, these two agencies provide irrigation water for more than 1 million acres.

In southern California, three districts--the Palo Verde Irrigation District, the Imperial Irrigation District, and the Coachella Valley Water District--are entitled to the first 3.85 maf of Colorado River water. The Imperial Irrigation District covers 1.1 million acres, of which 500,000 acres are irrigated. Its only source of water is the Colorado River, from which water is transported through the 80-mile-long All-American Canal. Agricultural drainage water from the district is discharged into the Salton Sea. With the completion of the Central Arizona Project, the amount of water available to the next most senior priority holder, the Metropolitan Water District, will be reduced from 1.2 maf per year to 550,000 acre-feet per year. As a result, the irrigation districts have been under pressure to improve irrigation efficiency, in order to reduce their consumption of water. A study completed in 1983 by the U.S. Bureau of Reclamation found that a potential savings of 350,000 acre-feet per year by the Imperial Irrigation District was possible, at an estimated cost of $131 million. An additional savings of 70,000 acre-feet per year could also be realized by lining a portion of the All-American Canal.[53]

The Metropolitan Water District of Southern California was created by the California legislature in 1928, under the Metropolitan Water District Act, as a special district for the purpose of developing, storing, and distributing water. Member agencies receive water at wholesale rates for municipal and domestic use; surplus water is sold for agricultural use.[54] The district serves 27 agencies over portions of six counties of southern California, from Ventura to San Diego. It is governed by a 51-member board of directors that consists of at least one representative from every member agency.[55] The total population of the area is approximately 14 million, and the total annual water consumption is approximately 3.4 maf. The district delivers nearly 60 percent of the water used in this region, obtaining the majority from the SWP and the Colorado River Aqueduct.

The Metropolitan Water District completed the Colorado River Aqueduct in the 1940s in conjunction with the construction of Hoover and Parker Dams. The aqueduct can provide a maximum of approximately 1.3 maf per year. In 1972, the district started to receive water from the SWP, which provided about 50 percent of its supply during the early 1970s. However, during the drought in 1977, in order to alleviate the worsening situation in the Central Valley, the district worked out an arrangement with the DWR to reduce its usage of SWP water and increase its diversion of Colorado River water. The district's board decided that a 10 percent reduction in domestic, municipal, and agricultural demand was needed. To this end, a 100 percent surcharge was added to the domestic and municipal rate for all quantities of water delivered each month in excess of 90 percent of the deliveries made in the corresponding month in 1976. Member districts that had ground water facilities available to them were asked to begin overdrafting as much as possible.[56]

Conservation

Following the 1976-77 California drought, the Office of Water Conservation was set up within the DWR. Its $4 million operating budget is supplemented with $10 million in revolving low-interest loan money for capital investment in water conservation. A major feature of its urban conservation program is increasing public awareness and education of schoolchildren. Agricultural programs focus on improving irrigation techniques. To this end, a cooperative three-year research and development project (the California Irrigation and Management Information System) is being undertaken by the University of California for DWR.[57]

In order to meet the continually increasing demand for water at the lowest possible cost, the Metropolitan Water District is developing a variety of nonstructural means for augmenting its supplies. Currently, it is negotiating with the Imperial Irrigation District for the transfer of 300,000 acre-feet per year. In return, the district would pay for conservation projects, such as improving the efficiency of irrigation techniques. A similar arrangement is also being sought with the Palo Verde Irrigation District. In another effort to enhance supplies during years of low precipitation, an exchange agreement has been negotiated with the Coachella Valley Water District and the Desert Water Agency. Because these two agencies have contracts for SWP water but no delivery system, they use the Metropolitan Water District's entitlement to Colorado River water in exchange for their share of SWP water. In addition, the Metropolitan Water District can store up to 550,000 acre-feet of Colorado River water in their ground water basins during years of surplus. In times of shortage, the irrigation districts will pump the ground water, freeing up their entitlement to surface water.[58]

Both the DWR and SWRCB have programs to facilitate the reuse of waste water as a means of augmenting existing supplies. The 1974 Waste Water Reuse Law directs the DWR to encourage maximum reuse of waste water through three major activities: (1) support of research in waste water reclamation technology; (2) participation in regional waste water reclamation planning and development; and (3) determination of the feasibility of including local projects in the SWP.[59]

In 1977, the SWRCB initiated a major waste water reclamation project designed to conserve 0.4 maf by 1982, with a potential savings of 2.6 maf by the year 2000. California state law has been modified such that the SWRCB must give preference to grant applications for the construction of municipal treatment facilities that would use reclaimed water.[60] Reclaimed water is also used for aquifer recharge, crop irrigation, industrial purposes, and municipal irrigation. The Department of Public Health has set criteria for those uses of reclaimed water that affect public health. Currently, direct injection into ground water is prohibited, and surface water spreading is considered on a case-by-case basis. Waste water reuse in small ground water basins is also discouraged.[61]

The Metropolitan Water District has also encouraged water conservation through a waste water reclamation program, involving a contractual arrangement with each local water agency that it serves. For every acre-foot of water reclaimed by the local agency, the district pays the agency $93--a price that reflects the cost of water from the SWP, its most expensive source.[62] Currently, about 150,000 acre-feet per year of waste water is reclaimed. It is anticipated that this figure will double by the year 2010.

In an attempt to control salt water intrusion, the Orange County Water District uses reclaimed waste water to recharge ground water supplies. However, the high salt content of Colorado River Aqueduct water makes it necessary to desalt a portion of this water by reverse osmosis prior to injection.[63]

Financing

Historically, the public's strong commitment to water development in California resulted in high tax support and bonding programs for project financing. However, the passage of California's Proposition 13 in 1978, limiting property tax rates, denied several billion dollars of tax revenues to local governments. Also, the measure provided deterrents for raising both state and local taxes in the future. Without these measures, however negative they were at the time, the state might not have been prompted to create new, innovative ways of financing vital water programs, including less expensive conservation measures.

Some of the most significant innovations in water policy involve the new financing mechanisms that California has devised. State grants are being replaced by long-term general obligation bonds and low-interest loans, which are financed for shorter periods. These loans are offered at one-half the interest rate of the state's general obligation bonds. Two recent pieces of legislation are significant in the development of these bonds and loans.[64]

The Clean Water Bond Laws of 1970 and 1974, and the Clean Water and Water Conservation Bond Law of 1978 each provide for the issuance of state bonds and for the expenditure of the proceeds on planning, research, development, and construction of waste water treatment works. The most recent Clean Water Bond Law of 1984 was the real impetus for local waste water reclamation projects, providing for the issuance of an additional $325 million in state bonds.[65]

Another new law is the Water Conservation and Water Quality Bond Law of 1986, commonly referred to as Proposition 44. This law provides for the issuance of $150 million in state bonds for purposes of providing loans to local agencies to aid in the acquisition and construction of voluntary, cost-effective, capital outlay water conservation programs and ground water recharge facilities. Also covered by the law is the construction of drainage water management units. This law is vital for addressing the need to develop water conservation projects around the state. "Most of the money will go to the lining of ditches and canals,"[66] and could help to alleviate the agricultural drainage water problems in the Central Valley.

THE ROLE OF WATER RESEARCH
Institutional Arrangements

The University of California system, which is the state's land grant university, is the official research arm for the state government. This relationship began in the 1920s, when state officials foresaw the need for research in the development of state policy. For this reason, the system receives the bulk of the state funding for water research. Of the $15.57 million spent on water-related research projects in 1983-84, approximately one-half was provided through the Agricultural Experiment Station and one-quarter came from federal funds. A breakdown of the projects, according to subject area, is shown in Table 4.2.

TABLE 4.2 Water Research Projects in the University of California System, 1983-84

Major Subject Category	Number of Projects	Annual Value ($ million)
Agriculture	89	6.61
Engineering	44	2.72
Social Sciences and Law	19	0.63
Biological and Physical Sciences	101	5.02
Ground Water	14	0.59
Total	267	15.57

Source: Rex J. Woods and J. Herbert Snyder, *Inventory of Water Research in the University of California*, Report No. 59 (Davis: University of California, June 1984).

The University of California Water Resources Center

The California Water Resources Center, currently located on the university's Riverside campus, was established in 1957 with a special appropriation from the California legislature. It is designated as the state institute to participate under Title I of the original Water Resources Research Act of 1964, the Water Research and Development Act of 1978, and the Water Resources Research Act of 1984. Through the Federal Water Research Institute Program, it receives an annual federal allocation of approximately $105,000. However, over 90 percent of its annual budget of $1.2 million is provided through state funds. The center supports an average of 35 relatively modestly sized basic and applied water research projects on eight campuses of the university and the various campuses of the California State University system.[67]

Through its Citizens Advisory Council and Public Agency Research Review Committee, the center strives to keep the overall research program responsive and relevant to California's water research needs, while maintaining the basic tenets of academic research.

The center maintains a comprehensive information dissemination and public service program consisting of various types of publications, conferences, symposia, and programmatic research initiative task forces, composed of both faculty and practitioners. Currently, center-sponsored task forces are developing research initiatives related to the quality of California's drinking water, the management of the state's watersheds, and the San Francisco Bay Estuary.

The Water Resources Center Archives are considered the premier collection of materials relating to water resources in California and the West. With over 100,000 titles in the collection, the archives serve the entire university water research community and the interested public.[68]

San Francisco Bay Aquatic Habitat Institute

One example illustrating public and private cooperative research efforts is the development of the San Francisco Bay Aquatic Habitat Institute (AHI). The AHI was created in accordance with recommendations of a policy task force created by the SWRCB to look into public concern over the impacts on the San Francisco Bay-Delta by waste water pollutants. The formation of the AHI was approved in October 1982. Legal concerns delayed incorporation of the institute until May 1983, with limited operations beginning in the fall of 1984.[69]

The AHI is an independent nonprofit corporation, whose purpose is "to implement a scientific program to monitor and evaluate the present and potential effects on beneficial uses" of the San Francisco Bay-Delta. It will coordinate monitoring and research activities of the bay-delta through relationships with various private, academic, and government organizations. It will make the data from those efforts available to regulatory agencies and other interested parties, and will act as a facilitator for the exchange of information related to water quality and ecology of the bay-delta area. The AHI will carry out the aquatic habitat program goals of: (1) assessing the health of the aquatic organisms in the bay related to the effects of pollutants; (2) determining the specific causes of any changes in the health of the bay that appear to be pollutant-related; and (3) getting maximum use of available funds, by coordinating the activities of this program with all other monitoring and research activities around the bay. The AHI does not have laboratory or fieldwork logistics capabilities, nor will it make recommendations for water quality policy.[70]

It was decided to make the AHI an independent, nonprofit organization, in order to facilitate cooperation between the various levels of government, while maintaining public confidence. Funding for the institute comes from industrial and municipal dischargers of waste water pollutants, the SWRCB and federal agencies (including the EPA). Its nonprofit status allows it to accept government and private grants to supplement scarce state and local agency funds for regional research and monitoring. A plan is being devised for long-term funding from local sources.

The AHI represents a significant step in the development of cooperative efforts to solve water problems in this region of the state. It has the first integrated and completely usable data base for the bay-delta and the first coordinated, permanent, long-term monitoring program. Its efforts will complement ongoing studies on the currents, chemistry, and biology of the bay-delta system. The institute is an example of an innovative means of developing a viable research program, despite decreasing research funds.

Research Activities

Technical Research Areas

A great deal of the research being conducted by California academics continues to emphasize technical advances, especially in the area of water quality. Advances in sampling, monitoring, and removal techniques are being sought in order to control pollutants in both water supply and waste water effluent. Monitoring of ground water is used to detect sources of contamination and to analyze movement and decay of chemical pollutants. Other research activities include investigations of precipitation and stream flow relationships, weather forecasting, and climate modification. Research is also needed on salt pickup and deposition problems associated with irrigated agriculture.

Policy Research Areas

While technical research continues to be the foundation of water resources advances, policy research areas are receiving most of the attention of state officials and administrators. Policy research activities include studies on water conservation policies (including water pricing); modeling procedures as a tool for planning and operating supply systems; the energy needs of various development and management alternatives; and the evolution of past water planning policy. Other research relates to potential institutional conflicts associated with specific development and management alternatives, including barriers to increased cooperation, changing attitudes toward water rights, and increased public education programs. Efforts are also being made to improve research coordination and information dissemination systems.

One entity that deals with water policy research is the California Policy Seminar (CPS), which is hosted by the Institute of Governmental Studies at the University of California at Berkeley. It was created in 1977 to better link the intellectual resources of the University of California system with the needs of the state's decision makers on a variety of policy issues. Since 1982, the CPS has grown in importance, successfully creating more contact between academic researchers and policymakers. Many of the CPS projects are supported by the Senate and Assembly Office of Research and the Governor's Office.

Currently, the CPS is working on several different policy research programs involving water. One of these concerns agriculture and fishery enhancement in the Sacramento-San Joaquin Delta, in response to an Assembly Office of Research request. The University of California at Davis faculty is exploring alternative uses for inundated portions of land in the Sacramento-San Joaquin Delta region, including the feasibility of instituting aquaculture and fisheries-enhancement projects in the delta.

Another program, titled "The Implications of the San Joaquin River Pollution for Southern California Water Quality," was supported by the CPS and the Senate Office of Research. In addition, working with the support of the Assembly Office of Research, the CPS developed criteria that policymakers, agency administrators, and the general public could use to evaluate decision making on decontaminating toxic ground water. The CPS also held a symposium on problems of water quality, cosponsored by the University of California at Berkeley School of Public Health and attended by senators, assembly members, and their legislative staff.

CASE STUDY: AGRICULTURAL DRAINAGE WATER PROBLEMS IN THE WESTLANDS WATER DISTRICT

Agricultural drainage water problems have been an issue in California since irrigation methods were introduced in the late 1800s. The focus of this case study is on the innovative methods being employed by the Westlands Water District (WWD) in Fresno, California, to combat the problems associated with high salinity and high concentrations of toxic substances in the drainage water of the local agriculture industry.

History of the Westlands Water District

The Central Valley, situated on the west side of the San Joaquin Valley between the Coastal Range and the Sierra Nevada Mountains, is extremely fertile as a result of sediment washed down off the Coastal Range.

However, with an annual rainfall of less than ten inches, the potential for agricultural development of the area could not be realized without extensive irrigation.

Irrigated agriculture began in the 1880s with water diverted from the San Joaquin River, and was augmented by ground water pumping from the 1920s through the 1960s.[71] The Westlands Water District was created in 1952, at a time when ground water levels were dropping rapidly. The largest agricultural delivery agency in California, covering 942 square miles,[72] it is governed by a board of nine directors elected by the landowners of the district. In 1960, the San Luis Unit of the CVP was authorized in order to convey water from northern California to the valley. The sale and delivery of CVP water, purchased from the U.S. Bureau of Reclamation, is administered by the WWD. In 1955, ground water was used to irrigate an area of 450,000 acres (not all intensively). Utilizing the additional surface water, the irrigated acreage had grown to 504,000 in 1985. Total water deliveries for 1985 were 1.15 maf.[73]

Agricultural Drainage Problems

Subsurface drainage water from soils once covered by the Pacific Ocean contain high levels of natural salts. Problems regarding the management and disposal of this drainage water are immense. Various groups have attempted to solve these problems in the Central Valley, but solutions have been partial and somewhat temporary. Recent analytical improvements enable elements in water to be measured at the level of parts per billion instead of parts per million, heightening awareness and concern over the quality of the water being discharged into the state's water courses. Because agriculture of the area is vital to California's economy, and because the rivers of the region flow into the San Francisco Bay Delta, any problems that develop have an impact on the economic and ecological system of the state as a whole.

The San Luis Drain is a part of a canal that was designed to service the drainage needs of the San Luis Unit served with CVP water. Because of political considerations, funding problems, and the ecological sensitivity of the San Francisco Bay Delta, the drain was never completed. A segment of the drain, reaching only 82 miles from Westlands north to Kesterson Regulating Reservoir, was completed in 1975 and operated until February 1985, when the State Water Resources Control Board (SWRCB) issued a cleanup and abatement order to the U.S. Bureau of Reclamation, the agency that operates the CVP.

The order was issued because of health problems and abnormalities among fish and waterfowl at Kesterson, resulting from high levels of selenium (a naturally occurring element) in the drainage water that collected in Kesterson. Selenium exists in several forms, and the high concentrations of the element found in the Central Valley are toxic to some plants and animals. In March 1985, the U.S. Department of the Interior announced plans to immediately close Kesterson and the drain because of possible violations of the Migratory Bird Treaty Act. In addition, the department announced plans to terminate irrigation flows to the 42,000-acre problem drainage area.

An agreement was subsequently reached between the U.S. Department of the Interior and the WWD to continue irrigation deliveries, saving an estimated $180 million in crops and related industry. Under the agreement, the WWD was responsible for devising and implementing a method to reduce the flow of drainage water to the San Luis Drain to Kesterson and to plug the district's drainage collector system by June 30, 1986.

In addition to the wildlife problem, selenium and other trace elements (boron and other heavy metals) were known to be in high concentrations in the perched underground water table. There was a great deal of concern that, without drainage, the saline water table would encroach upon the crop root zone and reduce crop yields. There was considerable debate that continued irrigation of such land, while decreasing the drainage flow by plugging the drainage system, would make a threatening situation worse. The WWD enacted some short-term solutions to minimize the contribution of applied water to the water table and subsequently plugged the drainage system a month ahead of schedule. The district also devised a plan to address the problem.

One possible solution is simply to stop irrigating, either by retiring the land altogether or converting it to dryland farming. Unfortunately, this would not solve the problem, as neither the high water table nor the toxic elements would go away. In fact, if low-lying farmlands were abandoned, water tables would probably rise as a result of lateral flows from upslope irrigated lands. This would create a toxic swamp along the valley trough, and the salts and selenium in the perched water tables would concentrate in these lands. The present solution aims to reduce the quantity of applied water going to the water table (by improving irrigation efficiency), while developing a means of disposing of a smaller amount of more concentrated toxic constituents at an affordable cost.[74]

Development of the WWD Projects

Between May 1985 and May 1986, while the short-term drainage-flow-reduction solutions were being implemented, the WWD was formulating plans for a long-term solution. The first possible solution discussed was to build a series of evaporation ponds on 366 acres of the district's land. The initial estimated cost of this project was about $20 million. Different regulatory agencies, including the SWRCB and the U.S. Department of the Interior, continually added requirements and restrictions to the project, increasing the estimated cost to nearly $80 million. The project became much too costly and too bureaucratically complex to implement.

During the same period, the WWD was also conducting research on two other projects. The projects involved a biological processing plant that removes selenium and a deep-well injection program. In August 1986, the WWD Board of Directors approved a two-part program based upon these projects. The district, at its own expense, has taken the lead in addressing the growing drainage water problem of the Central Valley, instead of depending on the state or federal government. In fact, even though the salinity problem affects the economy and ecology of the entire west side of the San Joaquin Valley, the state has left the responsibility for the development of measures to combat this potentially serious situation to the local governmental authorities, hoping that the WWD's solutions can be implemented on a statewide basis.

Selenium Removal Project

The selenium removal project, a biological treatment process, was developed by a London-based engineering firm, Binnie & Partners, Ltd. The firm has been operating a pilot plant in the WWD since 1985, with considerable success. The process removes up to 98 percent of the selenium and boron, as well as some heavy metals, from the drainage water. The WWD approved a 1 million gallon per day (mgd) prototype plant with associated evaporation ponds to dispose of the treated water. The plant is scheduled to be commissioned in late 1987, after the necessary permits are obtained from the SWRCB. The plant should begin operation in early 1988 and will be monitored until the beginning of 1990, when a decision will be made to proceed with further operations, including the construction of a ten-mgd treatment plant.

An interesting and innovative part of the WWD's program is to treat the elements in such a way as to produce salable by-products. Considerable research has been conducted to determine how to extract these products and use them to offset the costs of the plant's production. Sulfur can be extracted and converted for use as a dusting fungicide. Selenium can be extracted and converted for use as sodium selenite for the animal feed industry, and boron is recovered as boric acid crystals, which are used in the plant itself. The potential revenues from the recovery of these elements are discussed in the "Financing Mechanisms" section of this chapter.

Deep-Well Injection Program

The deep-well injection project will be operated by URS Corporation, an international professional services organization. The company has conducted an investigation of the process under contract to the U.S. Bureau of Reclamation. The company's investigations show that the process is possibly suitable for the disposal of subsurface agricultural drainage water. The waste would be injected through a well into the earth to depths ranging from 5,000 to 7,000 feet, far below any usable ground water. Some pretreatment of the waste water is necessary to filter and remove suspended solids, reduce the pH level, and kill any bacteria. A 1-mgd prototype well may be built and tested by the spring of 1988. After about nine months to a year of monitoring, the WWD Board will decide whether to expand the deep-well project or to plug and abandon the prototype well.

Financing Mechanisms

The financing mechanisms for the selenium removal and deep-well injection programs are also quite innovative. Compared with the possible $80 million cost of the initial long-term program, this two-part program represents an impressive savings. Cost estimates as of January 1987 projected the total cost of the program to be $6.85 million. The selenium removal project cost is estimated at $4.9 million and the deep-well injection project at $1.7 million. The remaining $250,000 are general overhead costs to the district. The WWD has costs distributed over a four-year period, with most of the expenditure to occur in 1987 and 1988.[75]

The district is making full use of a state low-interest funding source and a combination of short- and long-term borrowing on the open market. Start-up funds depend upon short-term borrowing, and the costs will be built into the WWD rates over the next five to six years. The most interesting financing is related to the long-term plan and includes a drainage trust fund to be built to $100 million over the next five years with a two to one federal to WWD matching fund program.

As was mentioned in the previous section, the WWD is also conducting research on the possibility of recovering the costs of the selenium removal project from the sale of certain by-products of the process. The value of sulfur as a dusting fungicide could be $186 per acre-foot of drainage water processed. The potential revenue in each acre-foot of water from recovered selenium, for use in the animal feed industry, is $33, and the value of boron is $10 per acre-foot of water. The estimated profit from the sale of these by-products is $30 per acre-foot of drainage water processed, or $30 million total.[76] If some of these returns from the selenium removal project are realized, it would help tremendously in the project financing.

CONCLUSIONS

1. Availability of water has always been a concern in California, shaping its economic development. As a result, it has always been a high-profile public policy issue. As water development projects have become less feasible and more expensive, more emphasis on better management of existing supplies is the predominant approach. The withdrawal of the federal government from water resource issues has forced the state to address these issues and to focus on innovative ways to (re)distribute limited supplies.

2. As in other western states, water policy initially centered around water supply issues, with the federal government subsidizing water development projects. In California, a great deal of the emphasis derived from a need to divert water from the water-rich northern half of the state to more populous, dry southern regions. Irrigated agriculture became the major industry in the Central Valley.

3. With water development projects becoming increasingly expensive, and the federal government withdrawing its financial support, the focus has

changed. The development of an effective water management policy, incorporating "nonstructural" elements, is a top priority among government officials and the general public. Today, issues of primary concern to Californians include water quality, conservation, reclamation, and redistribution of water and review of water rights. The Office of Water Conservation was set up within the Department of Water Resources to address the issue of better management of existing water supplies.

4. Some serious water quality problems have arisen as a result of the irrigated agriculture in the Central Valley. Natural salts in irrigation water have caused the encroachment of saline water upon the crop root zone and the deposition of naturally occurring selenium. As a result of a court order to solve the environmental problems, the viability of this irrigation project could be in jeopardy.

5. California's long history of concern for water management is reflected in its commitment to water research. Nearly $30 million annually is funnelled through the university system for water research. Other local initiatives include such projects as the experimental selenium removal project undertaken by the WWD and the AHI, an independent, nonprofit organization, funded by industrial and municipal dischargers of waste water pollutants. This combined effort has made California less sensitive to cuts in federal funds for water research.

6. Although attempts have been made to coordinate water research efforts statewide, more coordination is needed. Along this line, the CPS has, in recent years, facilitated interaction between academic research and state government. Under the short-term initiatives program, officials in Sacramento have been able to get specific issues addressed, such as the legal and economic feasibility of selling, leasing, or exchanging conserved water.

Material for this chapter was provided by J. Scott DeFife and Carlos J. Gonzalez-Pena.

NOTES

1. Department of Water Resources (DWR), *The California Water Plan: Projected Uses and Available Water Supply to 2010*, Bulletin 160-83 (Sacramento: DWR, December 1983), p. 2 (hereafter cited as *California Water Plan*).

2. DWR, *California Water Plan*, pp. 8-9.

3. Zach Willey, *Economic Development and Environmental Quality in California's Water System* (Berkeley: Institute of Government Studies, University of California, 1985), p. 41 (hereafter cited as *Economic Development*).

4. Department of Water Resources (DWR), *California State Water Project, Volume 1: History, Planning and Early Progress,* Bulletin 200

(Sacramento: DWR, November 1974), pp. 5-6 (hereafter cited as *California State Water Project*).

5. John Gronouski and Ernest Smerdon, eds., *Texas Water Management Issues*, Lyndon B. Johnson School of Public Affairs, Policy Research Project, no. 77 (Austin: University of Texas, 1987), p. 186.

6. DWR, *California State Water Project*, pp. 7-8.

7. DWR, *California State Water Project*, pp. 12-13.

8. Gronouski and Smerdon, *Texas Water Management Issues*, p. 186.

9. Willey, *Economic Development* , p. 43.

10. Department of Water Resources (DWR), *Water Conservation in California*, Bulletin 198-84 (Sacramento: DWR, July 1984), p. 59.

11. Metropolitan Water District of Southern California, *Focus* 7, (1985), p. 8.

12. DWR, *Water Conservation in California*, p. 59.

13. Department of Water Resources, *Phase II: Alternative Courses of Action to Provide Delta Protection and Adequate Water Supplies for California* (Sacramento: DWR, March 1976), pp. 5-6.

14. DWR, *California State Water Project*, p. 40.

15. Interview with Clyde MacDonald, principal water consultant for Assemblyman Jim Costra of Fresno, California, January 1987.

16. Interview with Bob Reeb, water consultant for Assemblyman Jim Costra of Fresno, California, January 1987.

17. DWR, *California State Water Project*, pp. 41-42.

18. W. Jackson and Alan Paterson, *The Sacramento-San Joaquin Delta: The Evolution and Implementation of Water Policy* (Davis: Water Resources Center, University of California, June 1977), p. 93 (hereafter cited as *Sacramento-San Joaquin Delta*).

19. Jackson and Paterson, *Sacramento-San Joaquin Delta*, p. 143.

20. Interview with Clyde MacDonald, January 1987.

21. DWR, *California Water Plan*, p. 188.

22. Willey, *Economic Development*, pp. 6-7.

23. Willey, *Economic Development*, pp. 11-13.

24. Mohamed T. El-Ashry and Diana C. Gibbons, *Troubled Waters: New Policies for Managing Water in the American West* (Washington, D.C.: World Resources Institute, 1986), p. 62.

25. Correspondence with Ernest Sartelle, Public Affairs Office, U.S. Bureau of Reclamation, Sacramento, California, October 1987.

26. Western Water Education Foundation (WWEF), "California Water Resources Development," mimeographed (Sacramento, Calif.: WWEF, 1983).

27. National Audubon Society v. Superior Court of Alpine County, 33 Cal. 3d 419, 658 P. 2d 709, 189 Ca Rptr. 346 (1983).

28. Jacqueline Weaver, "The Public Trust Doctrine and Texas Water Rights Administration: Common Law Protection for Texas Bays and Estuaries?" *State Bar of Texas Environmental Law Journal* 15 (1985), p. 1.

29. Interview with Clyde MacDonald, January 1987.

30. DWR, *California Water Plan*, p. 12.

31. DWR, *California Water Plan*, p. 9.

32. State Water Resources Control Board (SWRCB) and the California Department of Water Resources (CDWR), *Policies and Goals for California Water Management: The Next 20 Years* (Sacramento: SWRCB and CDWR, January 1982).

33. John Dracup and Pamela Painter, "Drought Planning and Management," in *California Water Planning and Policy, Selected Issues,* Ernest Engelbert, ed. (Davis: Water Resources Center, University of California, 1979).

34. DWR, *California Water Plan*, p. 4.

35. "State Water Legislation is Bad News," *The Sierra Club Yodeler*, July 1987.

36. Interview with Arthur Gooch, Division of Planning, DWR, August 1987.

37. Department of Water Resources (DWR), *Management of the California State Water Project,* Bulletin 132-86 (Sacramento: DWR, September 1986), p. 88 (hereafter cited as *Management of California*).

38. DWR, *Management of California* p. 90.

39. Arthur Littleworth, "New Legislation in California and its Effects," in *Proceedings of the Thirteenth Biennial Conference on Ground Water,* Irvine, Report No. 53 (Davis: University of California, September 1981).

40. DWR, *California Water Plan*, p. 137.

41. DWR, *Management of California,* pp. 96-97.

42. DWR, *Water Conservation in California*, p. 128.

43. California State Legislature, Assembly Bill 797, Klehs.

44. California State Legislature, Assembly Bill 1658, Isenberg.

45. Dracup and Painter, "Drought Planning and Management."

46. "Can Water Marketing Answer California's Water Needs?" *Sacramento County Alert*, May 23, 1986.

47. California State Legislature, Assembly Bill 2736, Katz.

48. California State Legislature, Assembly Bill 3722, Costa and Isenberg.

49. DWR, *California State Water Project,* p. 9.

50. DWR, *California Water Plan*, pp. 15-16.

51. DWR, *California Water Plan*, p. 2.

52. Robert Hinks and J. Herbert Snyder, *Five Year Water Resources Research Plan for the State of California*, Report No. 49 (Davis: University of California, 1980), p. 29.

53. DWR, *Water Conservation in California*, p. 84.

54. Metropolitan Water District of Southern California (MWDSC), *1985 Annual Financial Report* (Los Angeles: MWDSC, 1985), p. 11 (hereafter cited as *1985 Annual Report*).

55. MWDSC, *1985 Annual Report*, p. 12.

56. The Metropolitan Water District state legislation and federal (EPA) guidelines.

57. DWR, *Water Conservation in California*, p. 109.

58. Interview with Jay Malinowski, Metropolitan Water District, Los Angeles, California, November 3, 1987.

59. DWR, *California Water Plan*, pp. 189-190.

60. Ernest Engelbert, "Policies and Strategies for Water Conservation in California," in *California Water Planning and Policy, Selected Issues,* Ernest Engelbert, ed. (Davis, Calif.: Water Resources Center, University of California, 1979) (hereafter cited as "Policies and Strategies ").

61. Engelbert, "Policies and Strategies," p. 189.

62. Interview with Bob Gomperz, California Department of Public Information, Metropolitan Water District of Southern California, Los Angeles, California, January 1987.

63. DWR, *California Water Plan*, p. 253.

64. Interview with Kurt Wasserman, State Water Resources Control Board, Sacramento, California, January 1987.

65. California State Legislature, Assembly Bill 1732.

66. Interview with Suzanne Butterfield, chief, DWR, Office of Water Conservation, Sacramento, California, January 1987.

67. Correspondence with Rex Woods, assistant director, Water Resources Center, University of California, Davis, October 1987.

68. Correspondence with Rex Woods, October 1987.

69. The San Francisco Bay Aquatic Habitat Institute, Background Report.

70. The San Francisco Bay Aquatic Habitat Institute (AHI), "Bylaws" (March 12, 1986).

71. William Johnston and Michael G. Heaton, "Legal, Economic, and Political Constraints on Managing Agricultural Drainage Water in California," in *National Symposium on Water Resource Law Proceedings* (American Society of Agricultural Engineers, December 1986), pp. 188-195.

72. Ed Simmons, *Westlands Water District: The First 25 Years, 1952-1977* (Fresno, Calif.: Westlands Water District, 1983), p. 1.

73. Westlands Water District (WWD), *Facts and Figures* (Fresno, Calif.: WWD, 1986).

74. Ray Coppock, *Resources at Risk: Agricultural Drainage in the San Joaquin Valley* (Davis, Calif.: Water Resources Center, University of California, 1987).

75. Westlands Water District (WWD), *Cash Flow: Drainage Projects* (Fresno, Calif.: WWD, January 1987).

76. Rodney Squires and William Johnston, "Agricultural Drainage Water Treatment: Are Toxic Elements Useful?" unpublished manuscript, 1986.

FLORIDA

BACKGROUND
Historical Factors

The pressures of growth and development experienced in Florida are more intense than those felt in other states. Florida's peninsular environment is extraordinarily delicate and susceptible to upset. Increased demands for housing, water, waste disposal, transportation, boating facilities, and flood control compound the stress placed on coastal estuarine systems and threaten to overwhelm their assimilative and recuperative capabilities. Increased inland development, both domestic and industrial, has placed environmental stress upon fresh water and wetland systems needed to support the environmental health of the estuaries.[1]

Florida's abundant surface water resources have historically presented its settlers with a formidable challenge for development. The state's unusually low relief has given to the formation of thousands of natural lakes and channels. The many water passageways served as natural channels of communication for early settlers. From the time of its admission to the union, Florida's goal has been drainage of the wetlands in order to establish a strong agricultural base. In 1856, the first of a series of laws was passed encouraging riparian landowners to build wharves and to fill in submerged lands. Post-Civil War policy was to sell lands on the condition that they be drained.[2]

In the early 1880s, 4 million acres were sold for $1 million to Hamilton Disston, who cut several major channels, including an outlet from Lake Okeechobee to the Gulf of Mexico. Drainage and navigation projects were followed by development of the railroads. The economic development of south Florida was under way. In 1899, in accordance with the Rivers and Harbors Act, the U.S. Army Corps of Engineers began a survey of the Kissimmee-Okeechobee-Caloosahatchee water system. They concluded that private concerns would not act in the best interests of the overall development of the area and that the public should have more input into the process. This sentiment was echoed by Governor Napoleon Bonaparte Broward, elected in 1905. However, subsequent attempts by the Florida legislature to oversee water management and land development on a statewide basis were found to be unconstitutional by the U.S. Supreme Court, and the legislation was amended to create an agency responsible for the drainage of the Everglades.[3]

Construction efforts between 1913 and 1927 resulted in six major drainage canals with 440 miles of levees and 16 locks and dams. Although such drainage efforts were successful in opening up the land for agricultural development, they did not prove to be adequate in the event of severe flooding. Hurricanes in 1926 and 1928 caused devastating flood damage, and the Okeechobee Drainage District was formed. Working with the Corps of Engineers, additional floodway channels were constructed. The state was expected to share the cost, provide land, and maintain the works on completion of the project. Flood control in other areas was considered a local problem until 1936, when the federal government passed the Flood Control Act. The extreme weather conditions that were characterized by floods in the 1920s resulted in drought in the 1930s and 1940s. Ground water levels were so low that salt water contamination threatened municipal wells in coastal areas and the dessicated muck soils ignited.[4]

The hurricane of 1947 emphasized the need for more comprehensive planning. In 1948, Congress adopted the Central and Southern Florida Flood Control Project. The Florida legislature created the Central and Southern Florida Flood Control District to act as the local sponsor for the federally authorized project. Again, flood control became the primary goal. However, salt water intrusion increasingly became a concern, and three water conservation areas were formed to supplement the storage available in Lake Okeechobee. This permitted retention of water from the canal system, thereby allowing recharge of underlying aquifer formations. Structural solutions prevailed from 1949 to 1969, when Congress passed the National Environmental Protection Act. From then on, environmental damage had to be considered as part of water management decisions.[5]

Critical Issues

Water Supply
More than 7.3 billion gallons of fresh water are withdrawn from surface and ground water each day for public supply and industrial, agricultural, and thermoelectric needs.[6] The greatest consumer of fresh water in the state is the agricultural sector, with irrigation accounting for 41 percent of the total. By contrast, public withdrawals amount to only 18 percent of the total, of which 87 percent comes from ground water sources (Table 5.1).

Overall, Florida has abundant surface and ground water, although not necessarily in those areas that are destined for the most rapid growth. This is particularly true along the state's extensive coast, especially in central and southern areas. By 1990, Florida will have more than 12 million residents--twice its 1970 level. Over 80 percent of this growth will have occurred in coastal regions. Water supply in these coastal areas is limited by shallow aquifers and the need to restrict water withdrawals to control salt water intrusion. Florida, however, is not expected in the foreseeable future to encounter water supply problems requiring drastic legislative and regulatory remedies.[7]

TABLE 5.1   Estimated Water Use in Florida, 1965-80

	1965	1970	1975	1980
Population (millions)	5.80	6.79	8.49	9.74
Consumption by use (offstream)				
Total (mgd)	1,673	1,850	2,290	2,480
Public supply	160	230	590	330
Rural use	83	160	110	100
Irrigation	1,300	1,300	1,300	1,500
Industrial	130	160	290	550
Per capita (gpd)				
all uses	288	272	270	255
excl. irrigation	64	81	117	101
Withdrawals by source				
Total (mgd)	6,800	5,900	6,900	7,400
Ground water	2,700	2,900	3,300	3,800
Surface water	4,100	3,000	3,600	3,600

Source: U.S. Geological Survey, *Estimated Use of Water in the United States, 1965; Estimated Use of Water in the United States, 1970; Estimated Use of Water in the United States, 1975; Estimated Use of Water in the United States, 1980*, Geological Survey Circulars 556, 676, 765, and 1001 (Reston, Va.: U.S. Department of the Interior, 1968, 1972, 1977, and 1983).

In 1974 and 1975, during the so-called "water wars" in the Tampa area, the densely populated county of Pinellas in southwestern Florida sought to augment inadequate supplies by developing inland water-well fields.[8] This area had been experiencing water shortages and salt water intrusion into its wells since the 1930s. Inland interests objected strongly, partially out of fear that their own water supplies would be dangerously drawn down and partially out of a sense of helplessness in the face of a Florida law that allows counties to take, by imminent domain, land outside their political boundaries as a source of water. The conflict led to legal battles and sometimes emotional confrontations among the participants. It was ultimately resolved, principally through the creation of a three-county supply authority called the West Coast Regional Water Supply Authority.

The problem of water shortages poses a number of important questions for the future of water allocation in Florida. Can future water wars be avoided given the fast pace of population growth, particularly in the water-poor coastal regions? Should inland areas subsidize, or be forced to subsidize, the water needs of coastal areas? The water management districts, through their consumptive use permitting programs, will play a very important role in deciding the existence and extent of future water transfers.[9]

Water Quality

Water quality problems in Florida are associated with population concentration and industrial and agricultural activity. In most states, including Florida, agricultural sources, such as pesticides and fertilizers are a cause of ground water pollution. In recent years, Florida's water officials have discovered that a great number of contaminants from waste-disposal sites, as well as pesticides, used to protect citrus trees, find their way into large, shallow, limestone aquifers.

Mineral extraction is a major economic activity in Florida. Mining of phosphate, oil, gas, peat, limerock, gravel, clay, and titanium contributes to the state economy. However, these benefits are diminished by the adverse environmental impacts associated with mining activities. "According to a 1979 United States Department of Agriculture study, only three states have had more acreage disturbed by surface mining than Florida. Improper mining techniques result in surface drainage patterns, the loss of topsoil, and the loss of important, environmentally sensitive resources."[10]

According to the Florida Department of Environmental Regulation (DER), resource extraction must be prohibited from environmentally sensitive areas that cannot be restored, such as river- and streambeds and basins, mature and pristine wetland areas, and endangered plant and animal habitats.[11] Mining can also alter the hydrology in such a way that the quantity of water in a shallow aquifer is reduced to the point that it affects streams and other bodies of water dependent on ground water levels.

Perhaps the most important water quality issue that Florida needs to address in the next twenty years is storm water, which accounts for as much as 60 percent of the pollution that enters Florida's surface water. In many water bodies nearly all the pollution is from storm water sources, which include urban storm water, agricultural runoff, construction site runoff, drainage from mined areas, and leachate from landfills. Storm water pollution is responsible for 80 to 95 percent of the heavy metals in water, and reportedly contributes as much nutrient as treated sewage.[12]

The northeast and central regions of Florida experience water quality problems for all of these reasons. Virtually the entire stretch of the St. Johns River has water quality problems associated with agricultural runoff. Southwest Florida suffers from pollution caused by phosphate mining, chemical plants, and urbanization. In southeast Florida, there are problems with the upper reaches of the Kissimmee River and from the development of areas that were the original floodplain of the river before it was channelized. The south Florida area, particularly the Miami and Tamiami canals, show "severe dissolved solids problems." Areas around Ft. Lauderdale have suffered "extreme degradation," resulting from treated sewage effluent. Nonetheless, the overall quality of water in the Everglades region is generally good.[13]

Numerous federal, state, and local agencies monitor Florida's surface water quality. There are over 1,000 surface water sampling sites in Florida, but sampling is routine on only a fraction. Fifty-seven of these sites are part of a national water quality monitoring network carried out in cooperation with the U.S. Geological Survey and the U.S. Environmental Protection Agency (EPA).[14] The data gathered at these sites are used to measure three constituents: phosphorus, nitrogen, and dissolved solids. These give a rough idea of the amounts of organic and inorganic pollutants present in surface waters.

Ground Water. There is a close relationship between surface and ground water quality as a result of Florida's low water table. However, monitoring operations for ground water are not nearly as well developed as for surface water. Despite provisions for systematic analysis of ground water quality in the Water Quality Assurance Act of 1983, lack of data contributes to the absence of a clear understanding of the degree to which contamination may be taking place.[15]

Salt water intrusion from the ocean or from underlying saline aquifers has been one of the major problems of water management. It is also one of the major threats to the ground water supplies of many coastal areas. According to Florida water experts, several factors contribute to salt water encroachment:

-- Loss of [hydrostatic] head through increased demands by municipalities;
-- Excessive drainage, especially in the Everglades and under the Atlantic coastal ridge;
-- Lack of protective works against tidewater in bayous, canals, and rivers;
-- Improper location of wells;
-- Highly variable annual rainfall with insufficient surface storage during droughts; and
-- Uncapped [artesian] wells and leakage.[16]

In addition, in most of the aquifers in Florida, fresh water is stored at great pressure. When pressure in these aquifers decreases, because of overdrafting or lack of rainfall and recharge, the reservoir pressure drops, permitting salt water from the Atlantic or the Gulf of Mexico to enter the ground water system along the coastal regions.

Victoria Tschinkel, former Secretary of the Florida Department of Environmental Regulation (DER), notes that there are an estimated 60,000 petroleum storage tanks at 18,000 operating sites that are a serious threat to Florida's ground water.[17] The DER has identified nearly 400 active petroleum contamination cases, but there may be as many as 6,000 leaking tanks in the state. According to the DER, estimates of the cost for investigation and cleanup at these sites range from $150,000 to $250,000 per site. This could increase significantly at sites with complicated geology or where contamination has spread extensively.

Degradation of Natural Systems

One of the most important sectors of Florida's economy, amounting to $22 billion in 1983, is the tourist industry. A great deal of this activity revolves around Florida's water resources: its beaches, lakes, and rivers, which provide fishing, boating, and swimming. Tourists also come to Florida to see its unique natural ecosystems, such as the Everglades. If water quality and quantity are not protected, these natural settings may be degraded, resulting in a loss of recreational opportunities and wildlife populations.

Drainage of Florida's wetlands has been an integral part of its economic development. However, as the organic peat soils dry out and are exposed to air, they are lost through oxidation and occasional wind erosion. Drainage also causes a lowering of water tables, salination of estuaries, subsidence, and loss of wildlife. In the Everglades, a year-long drought in 1980-81 brought the situation to crisis proportions as the muck caught fire, and salt water intrusion resulted in water rationing and an increase in water-borne diseases. In February 1983, Everglades National Park Research Director Gary Hendrix told the board of the South Florida Water Management District (WMD) that the park's wildlife population had sunk to levels so low that only swift, emergency action to restore the natural drainage patterns would enable recovery. Governor Bob Graham launched his Save the Everglades Program the same year (see case study for details).[18]

STATE INITIATIVES IN WATER RESOURCE MANAGEMENT
Policy Development

The unprecedented growth of the early 1970s made Florida the fastest growing state in the nation. Increasing public awareness of the potentially devastating effects of uncontrolled growth, together with a severe water

shortage in south Florida in 1971, provided the impetus for legislative reform of the state's land-use regulatory system. In 1972, Florida became the first state to adopt Article 7 of the Model Code, developed by the American Law Institute, in an attempt to increase state participation in land-use decision making. The Florida Environmental Land and Water Management Act of 1972 incorporated two techniques for injecting a state and regional perspective into local land-use decision making. The act provides for review of developments of regional impact by regional planning councils and authorizes the Administration Commission (consisting of the governor and six elected state officers) to designate areas of critical state concern.[19]

Although enacted in the same year, the Florida State Comprehensive Planning Act was not implemented until 1978. It therefore had no impact on the critical areas program prior to that time. Moreover, given the ill-defined goals of the planning process, it is not surprising that the document that emerged was highly generalized in nature. Conceived primarily as a state land-planning document, it evolved to include a broad range of social and economic issues. Overwhelmed by the magnitude and implications of the document, the legislature amended the original statute, which would have made the recommendations official state policy, to provide that the plan would be limited to an advisory role.[20]

Two other pieces of legislation enacted in the 1970s also relate to planning and water resource management. The 1972 Water Resources Act established five water management districts to be responsible, under state supervision, for water supply, water consumption, and flood control. The act called for unified planning and management of the state's water resources. In 1975, the Local Government Comprehensive Planning Act was passed. It required all local governments to prepare and adopt a plan consistent with the goals of the comprehensive plan, no later than July 1, 1979.[21] However, a policy base was lacking to support the new programs.[22]

The Resource Management Task Force, appointed by the governor in January 1980, recognized these limitations and made a number of recommendations aimed at strengthening the planning process. These included consolidation of water quality planning with water quantity planning at the district or regional level, with the Department of Environmental Regulation retaining supervisory responsibilities. It also proposed strengthening of the regional councils, with a long-term goal of consolidating them with the water districts. As a result of these recommendations, the legislature amended the State Comprehensive Planning Act. The 11 regional councils were restructured by requiring that one-third of their members be appointed by the governor. The adoption of comprehensive regional policy plans was also required. In addition, revision of the Environmental Land and Water Management Act gave the regional councils a more prominent role in the review of developments of regional impact.[23]

With passage of the Florida State and Regional Planning Act of 1984, the legislature established the blueprint, or framework, for an integrated statewide planning process to guide Florida into the next century. It authorized the Department of Community Affairs to prepare the State Land Development Plan, a policy framework for all state agencies and regional planning councils. The following year, the legislature adopted the State Comprehensive Plan (SCP),[24] derived from the State Land Development Plan, the State Water Use Plan, and the Florida Transportation Plan. The SCP represents Florida's aspirations for the future management of its natural resources, through 25 goals and 362 policies.[25]

With the adoption of the SCP in 1985, Florida took the first step in instituting a three-step approach consisting of:

-- A state plan that provides broad-ranging goals and policy directions;
-- A set of agency functional plans that will guide the operations of agency programs and set priorities to be reflected in agency budgets; and
-- A set of comprehensive regional policy plans and revised local comprehensive plans that will guide local programs.

Florida's revised planning process is characterized by an attempt to directly link the short-term policies of the state's budget and permitting programs with longer-range policies necessary to guide the state's future. It also begins to break down the traditional definition of "top-down" planning efforts, where direction is set at a higher level and participants must respond solely to those policies. The functional plans of three agencies received high-priority status under the new planning process: the State Land Development Plan, the State Water Use Plan, and the Florida Transportation Plan. Here, we will focus on the State Water Use Plan, which was prepared by the DER.

A fundamental concern throughout the State Water Use Plan (SWUP) is the relationship of water to growth management. The plan states that:

Florida is blessed with large amounts of clean water that should more than adequately meet anticipated uses for the foreseeable future. The critical issues to be addressed over that period relate to determining how, where, and under what conditions water resources will be distributed to accommodate growth and to protecting the water resource itself from the impacts of growth. The issue of the distribution of water is only now being seriously addressed; the issue of the protection of the resource is a key element of state policy and programs, and is reflected in numerous regulatory, management, and acquisition programs. Actions to protect the quality of the resource can continue to be a major constraint on growth and will continue to influence the choice of areas most suitable for growth.[26]

Key Elements of the State Water Use Plan

Storm water. Storm water accounts for as much as 60 percent of the pollution that enters Florida's surface water. Accordingly, the State Water Use Plan lists management of storm water as one of the most important issues that it addresses. The plan establishes three objectives for reducing the effects of stormwater pollution. They are:

-- By 1987, each new development in Florida will treat its storm water runoff so that at least 80 percent of the pollutants are removed;
-- By 2005, reduce storm water pollution resulting from existing development into natural surface water systems by 30 percent; and
-- By 2005, reduce the amount of untreated storm water entering into estuarine systems by 50 percent.[27]

Preliminary estimates by the department indicate that the total costs of managing Florida's storm water to achieve these targets over the next 20 years will be approximately $32 billion, more than 65 percent of the total estimated costs of the water-use plan.[28]

Restoration of Natural Systems. Many of Florida's natural water resources have been damaged as a result of unwise past decisions and practices. The State Water Use Plan addresses this need by setting a number of objectives. By 2005, Florida will achieve the following:

-- Restore 62,000 acres of degraded lakes;
-- Restore or reclaim 220,000 acres of degraded wetlands;
-- Restore 98 miles and upgrade 2,720 miles of degraded rivers;
-- Upgrade the overall pollution climate of 600 square miles of degraded estuaries;
-- Restore 19 miles of chemically polluted estuaries;
-- Increase the number of functioning wetlands in Florida over those in 1985; and
-- By the year 2000, the Everglades will look and function more as it did in 1900 than when the Save Our Everglades Program was started in August 1983.[29]

A comprehensive study of the water resources of the state concludes that one of the objectives for improving Florida's water laws and policies should be a program to "maximize public acquisition of lands for the protection of our important water resources."[30] The first acquisition program was created by the Land Conservation Act of 1972. The act authorized issuance of $240 million in state bonds, of which $200 million was destined for the purchase of environmentally endangered lands and the remaining $40 million for outdoor recreation lands. The second land acquisition program was created by the Conservation and Recreation Lands Trust Fund, usually referred to as CARL. Considered to be one of the oldest, active, land purchase programs, it is financed by severance taxes from the phosphate and oil industries. Up to $20 million is collected each year for the protection of environmentally endangered lands, natural floodplains, marshes, estuaries, or wilderness areas and wildlife management. High priority is given to land in or near counties with highly concentrated populations and within designated areas of critical state concern that cannot be adequately protected by development regulations alone.[31]

A third acquisition program, aimed at preserving some of the remaining riverine ecosystems, is the Save Our Rivers Program. Created during an "unparalleled" water crisis, caused by a dry summer, the Save Our Rivers program stresses the protection of the resource and how it will contribute to the overall water system. It is intended to buy land necessary for water management, water supply, and the conservation and protection of water resources. Authorized by the 1981 Resources Rivers Act, it provides land acquisition funds, through a surcharge placed on Florida's documentary stamp tax. It is part of Florida's strategy to preserve some of the state's natural systems, by transferring them from the private domain to public ownership and management.[32] The act specifies that money, collected at the county level and deposited in the Water Management Lands Trust, will be available to the five water management districts for the purpose of acquiring environmentally sensitive lands adjacent to rivers, streams, and other water supply areas. Some of the more significant purchases made in 1986 are shown in Table 5.2.

Leaking Underground Storage Tanks. John Svec, an engineer with the DER, confirms that gasoline leakage can create an immediate problem: "at many facilities, owners are not reporting their leaks for fear of going out of business." Svec mentioned that the DER is concerned by this trend, especially since ground water is the source of drinking water for over 90 percent of Florida's population. As part of an effort to protect this resource, the state has developed comprehensive rules regarding underground tanks and a fund to provide speedy cleanup and replacement of drinking water supplies that have been contaminated. Among other measures, the program guarantees that operators who report leaks before October 1987 will be reimbursed for cleanup costs barring gross negligence, evidence of a concealed leak, or failure to keep a written record of the gasoline that was stored and sold.[33] The DER is also supporting legislation that would levy 10 cents per barrel tax on petroleum products entering Florida. A $50 million fund would be established to protect well owners, by improving regulatory efforts and covering cleanup costs.[34]

TABLE 5.2 Most Important Land Purchases Made in 1986 Through the Save Our Rivers Program

Water Management District	Land Purchased	Acres
Northwest Florida	Wakulla Springs	2,888
	Escambia River floodplain	17,998
	Choctawhatchee River floodplain	35,198
	Apalachicola River floodplain	35,509
Suwannee River	Santa Fe Swamp (donated)	5,358
	Andrews Tract	576
	Baynard-Zeisse Tract	1,063
	Sunbelt Tract	578
	Brown Tract	600
	Christian Tract	27
	Chotiner Tract (donated)	63
St Johns River	Seminole Ranch	14,000
	Latt Maxcy	9,800
	Lake Miami Ranch	2,800
	Greenbaum	3,970
	D.C. Scott	4,100
	Fellsmere	8,000
	Silver River	1,100
South Florida	Loxahatchee River floodplain	451
	Water Conservation Areas	217,429
	East Everglades Canal 111	38,000
	Kissimmee River floodplain	17,900
	Hidden Lake	589
	Sawgrass Lake	51
	Cypress Creek	427
	Anclote Water Storage Lands	2,528
	Green Swamp River Systems	8,845

Source: Office of the Governor, *Save Our Rivers: Celebrating Five Years of Progress* (October 1986).

Water Reuse. A key issue in ensuring the efficient use of Florida's water resources is reuse. Florida now reuses approximately 3 percent of its waste water, an amount that can be increased, according to DER officials. The State Water Use Plan establishes the objective that by 1995 Florida will reuse 9 percent of its waste water. The DER does not have the authority to impose waste water reuse as a condition of a permit, but it will encourage reuse wherever possible.[35]

Implementation

The Florida Environmental Land and Water Management Act
Not surprisingly, the development of land-use controls was not easy. Even after legislation was enacted, it was often subject to judicial review, as private landowners resisted attempts to limit development of their property. A review of the critical areas technique illustrates the point. It is a time-consuming process and, in most cases, has been used as a natural resource management tool in primarily rural, environmentally sensitive areas. Although designed to proceed by an administrative review process, the first area to be protected--the Big Cypress--was treated as an emergency situation. Consisting of 1.5 million acres in southwest Florida, it is underlain by a shallow aquifer that serves the fresh water needs of Florida's southwest coast, agriculture, and the Everglades National Park. It also contains important wildlife habitats. In 1973, the legislature partially bypassed the administrative process by directly conferring critical area status on the Big Cypress. Bowing to political pressure, all urbanized areas were excluded from the designated area.[36]

This opposition provided a greater challenge to the process when the Green Swamp and the Florida Keys were designated as critical areas by the Administration Commission. Located in the central highlands of Florida, the Green Swamp is a major recharge area for the Florida aquifer, which supplies about 70 percent of all ground water consumed in the state. The area also contained valuable wetlands, the headwaters of five rivers, wildlife habitats, and recreational facilities. Administrative delays were successful in killing the designation.[37] In the case of the Florida Keys, the designation was reversed by judicial review. The Florida Supreme Court held that the legislature could not delegate legislative power to regulate land use to an administrative agency, not to mention the reallocation of power between state and local governments. In a special session, the Florida legislature provided temporary protection to these two areas, which were later given critical area status, subject to repeal by the Administration Commission no later than July 1, 1982. Although these two areas were insulated from further constitutional attacks based on the nondelegation doctrine, the legislature failed to remove this potential barrier to future critical area designations.[38]

The Florida version of the Development of Regional Impact Review Procedure, enacted as part of the Florida Environmental Land and Water Management Act of 1972, did not realize its full potential. Responsibility for presenting evidence of regional impact was vested in a series of voluntary regional planning councils controlled by local governments, rather than an independent state planning agency, as proposed by the Model Code. In the absence of established priorities among the factors to be considered, development could be denied on the basis of a few adverse impacts, rather than the overall unreasonableness of the proposal.[39]

Realizing these limitations, the Resource Management Task Force, appointed by the governor in January 1980, made a number of recommendations aimed at strengthening the planning process. Now one-third of the council is appointed by the governor, and the council is responsible for coordinating the review of the development of regional impact with state permitting procedures. Although the local jurisdiction still retains the authority to approve or disapprove a project, it does so in light of recommendations made by the regional planning council. Decisions may be appealed to a state adjudicatory commission and ultimately to the courts.[40]

The Water Resources Act

The Water Resources Act of 1972 governs water management throughout the state. The legislation mandated unified planning and management of water resources. It established five regional water management districts responsible, under state supervision, for water supply, water consumption, and flood control functions. The districts are governed by boards, whose members are appointed by the governor. Overall responsibility for integrated, comprehensive water planning and management is assigned to the Department of Environmental Regulation.[41]

South Florida WMD. Despite its level terrain and abundant rainfall, which produce a continually swampy, flooded condition, the South Florida WMD's 16 counties include 31 percent of the land area of the state and 40 percent of the population. The South Florida WMD, formerly the Central and Southern Florida Flood Control District, has the authority to levy local property taxes to fund its programs. In addition, it has purchased nearly 9,000 acres of floodplain under the Save Our Rivers Program, and some 19,000 acres of Kissimmee River floodplain now are under public ownership.[42,43]

Southwest Florida WMD. The Southwest Florida WMD is a regional flood control and water management regulatory agency. Dr. Warren Viessman of the University of Florida described the Southwest Florida WMD as an example of new authority having capabilities for managing some aspects of water over an intergovernmental region.

> The Southwest Florida WMD is a regional flood control and water management regulatory agency. It covers about 10,000 square miles centered around the Tampa-St. Petersburg metropolitan region. The district was created in 1961. Its responsibilities have progressed from sponsorship of flood control projects to ground water regulation, issuance of consumptive use permits, and management, and storage of surface water....The taxing authority of the Southwest Florida WMD is substantial. Based on 1980 figures, tax revenues could have totaled about $28 million, although this level of assessment was not considered necessary and the income was closer to $7 million.[44]

St. Johns River WMD. The St. Johns River WMD is responsible for researching, planning, regulating, and managing all the ground and surface waters within its 19-county area in northeast and east central Florida. The district's major surface water basin is the 9,574 square miles of St. John's River watershed, which is the longest in the state. Most of the population of the district is concentrated in coastal cities, including Gainesville, Ocala, Leesburg, Orlando, DeLand, Daytona Beach, St. Augustine, and Jacksonville.[45]

The legislature increased the *ad valorem* tax limit for the district to a maximum of 60.0 cents per $1,000 of assessed property valuation. The increase is for land acquisition and related capital projects. Furthermore, the previous district-basin *ad valorem* apportionment was changed in order to provide a more effective distribution of funds and better management of the resources of the Oklawaha Basin.[46]

Suwannee River WMD. The Suwannee River WMD is located in north central Florida. The district has jurisdiction over 15 counties, which are mostly rural, with an average population density of 25 persons per square mile.[47] Over 75 percent of the land is in agriculture and timber production, while phosphate mining is the major industry.[48] The district has its headquarters in the small city of Live Oak and is composed of three organizational units: the Executive Office, the Department of Surface Water Management, and the Department of Groundwater Management. The single major source of funding for the district has been the state general fund.

Northwest Florida WMD. The Northwest Florida WMD encompasses 16 counties from the St. Marks River basin in Jefferson County to the Perdido River in Escambia County.[49] The district has the responsibility to purchase and manage lands, implement flood and aquatic weed control, engage in technical investigations, develop water resources plans, regulate surface water management facilities, and regulate consumptive use of water, artificial recharge, and well construction.

The Northwest Florida WMD has jurisdiction over 19 percent of the total land area of the state and almost 10 percent of the state's population. The district includes the watercourse of the Apalachicola River, the largest river by flow rate in the state.[50]

Cooperation among WMDs. The five water management districts hold annual conferences, which are attended by the governor, the pertinent state agency officials, and members of the Florida legislature. These conferences serve as a forum for coordinating activities and establishing long-term goals and direction. One of the salient problems that is reinforced by these gatherings is the disparity that exists among the various WMDs in terms of financial resources. This is principally a function of population density or tax base, as the revenues of WMDs are obtained in large measure from *ad valorem* taxes. The Northwest Florida and Suwannee River WMDs are particularly underfunded. In the case of the Northwest Florida WMD, the district has a millage cap of .05 mill, compared with one mill for the remaining four WMDs. This discrepancy came about during the 1975 legislative session, when legislators from northwest Florida threatened to withdraw support for a proposed constitutional amendment to establish the *ad valorem* taxing authority for all districts at one mill. In order to gain the support of those legislators, a smaller millage cap was put on the Northwest Florida WMD.[51]

State Comprehensive Planning

The 1972, State Comprehensive Planning Act directed the Division of State Planning to prepare a state comprehensive plan to be approved by the governor and state legislature. The division spent two years devising a process for preparing the plan. "Working papers" were prepared by agency officials with the assistance of interested citizens. Following periodic review at all levels of government, they were subjected to two series of public hearings. On February 9, 1978, the governor approved the plan and forwarded it to the legislature, which approved it as an advisory document in June 1978. It contained a compilation of goals, objectives, and policies, with its original goal of a land-use development plan being replaced by a policy-oriented approach.[52]

The success of comprehensive statewide planning depends upon the coordination of local plans with the state plan. Florida tried to address this issue by passage of the 1975 Local Government Comprehensive Planning Act. It required local governments to develop plans consistent with the comprehensive plan and coordinated with the plans of adjoining local governments. The local plans must then be submitted to the Division of State Planning for review and comment, and implemented through the adoption of development regulations and orders consistent with the plan. With the comprehensive plan not being approved until June 1978, the July 1, 1979, deadline for submission of local plans was not realistic, especially since only one staff person was available to review these plans. In addition, in view of the highly generalized nature of the state comprehensive plan, state review of local plans appeared to be a highly perfunctory process.[53] The act was strengthened in 1982.[54]

The State Comprehensive Plan, developed as a result of legislation enacted in 1984 and adopted by the legislature in 1985, provided the framework for statewide planning. The 1984 act placed a high priority on developing goals and policies--something that was lacking previously. The legislature required that the State Land Development Plan and the State Water Use Plan be completed within six months of the adoption of the State Comprehensive Plan, well before the deadline for other agency plans. Subsequently, the Transportation Plan was also required to meet this deadline, emphasizing the fundamental importance of these three elements in planning activities. It is too early to evaluate the effects of the State Comprehensive Plan. However, at the Tenth Annual Conference on Water Management in Florida, it received a mixed review. Jim Wolf, of the Florida League of Cities, claimed that it "is not a clear statement of legislative policy because most of the policymaking is delegated to administrative agencies, most of which are not sure what the others are doing." He and others also criticized the lack of a funding mechanism.[55]

Financing

The major federal funding programs for Florida are administered through the Corps of Engineers, the U.S. Geological Survey, the U.S. Department of Agriculture (Soil Conservation Service), and the U.S. Environmental Protection Agency. It is likely that some or all of these areas will experience continued funding cutbacks, given the present federal budgetary crisis. The level of funding to Florida's water resource agencies from the EPA and the Corps of Engineers has decreased over the past few years.[56] Figures 5.1 and 5.2 show the most recent budget requests by the DER. These figures show both the federal contribution to Florida's environmental programs and the importance of water issues.

FIGURE 5.1 Legislative Budget Request by Source of Funds, FY 1987-88

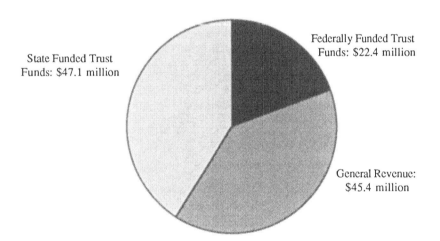

State Funded Trust Funds: $47.1 million

Federally Funded Trust Funds: $22.4 million

General Revenue: $45.4 million

Source: DER, Program Overview

Because of the importance of water resources for the economic viability of Florida, there are sufficient state funding mechanisms to sustain the requirements of existing programs. When settlers first came to Florida, a great deal of effort was given to drainage and flood control, just to make the land usable. Eventually, flood control and drainage districts were formed, and they were locally financed through a variety of taxing instruments. The taxing authorities eventually evolved into the WMDs that operate today. The people of Florida have been willing to fund water programs, in spite of their general reluctance to approve tax increases. Despite a proposed constitutional amendment in 1984 to put a cap on annual increases in local and state government revenues, spending on water programs has increased by almost threefold from $5.71 per capita in 1975 to $15.81 in 1981.[57]

FIGURE 5.2 Legislative Budget Request by Program, FY 1987-88

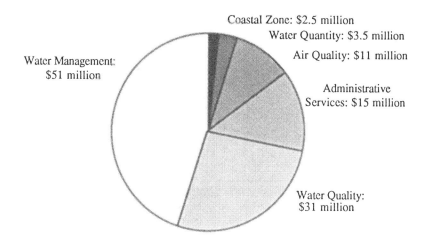

Coastal Zone: $2.5 million
Water Quantity: $3.5 million
Air Quality: $11 million
Administrative Services: $15 million
Water Quality: $31 million
Water Management: $51 million

Source: DER, Program Overview

Documentary Stamp Tax

Under the state's Documentary Stamp Tax, for each $100 worth of property sold, a 50-cent tax is levied. Of this, 45 cents buys environmental and coastal lands or contributes to the general revenue fund. Five cents is transferred to the DER for deposit into a Water Management Lands Trust Fund. During the 1985 legislative session, the various districts were given the ability to issue revenue bonds to be repaid from receipts to the Water Management Lands Trust Fund. This fund enables the state's water management district to acquire environmentally sensitive lands adjacent to rivers, streams, and other water supply areas, as authorized by the Save Our Rivers Act. The $300 million raised from the bond issue has been allocated solely for the purchase of lands that have water resource value and have created an impact on the state economy.

The 1985 legislature boosted the Save Our Rivers land acquisition program by increasing the stamp tax. In his address before the Tenth Conference on Water Management in Florida, Governor Graham told his audience, comprised of water management district officials: "With the increase in the documentary stamp tax, the lifting of the 'sunset' on the existing documentary stamp tax for Save Our Rivers purposes, and the bonding capacity, you will have over the next 20-25 years, almost a billion dollars to help us protect some of the most critical areas in our State."[58]

Table 5.3 shows the distribution of these funds among the WMDs for December 1986.

TABLE 5.3 Transfers for Documentary Stamp Taxes Collected during December 1986

Water Management District	Revenue	Percentage of Total
Northwest Florida	410,144.16	10
Suwannee River	410,422.15	10
St. Johns River	1,026,055.40	25
South Florida	1,026,055.40	25
Southwest Florida	1,231,266.47	30
Total	$4,104,221.58	100

Source: Office of the Governor, *Save Our Rivers: Celebrating Five Years of Progress* (October 1986).

THE ROLE OF WATER RESEARCH

The Florida University system is the primary center of water resources research activities.[59] The University of Florida at Gainesville conducts research through the Water Resources Research Center and several departments, particularly the Department of Environmental Engineering. The universities receive research contracts from a number of sources, including federal and state agencies and local water management districts. The state does not allocate funds specifically for water research; the Water Resources Research Center receives its support through the university.[60]

At the state level, there are funds available for "problemsolving," that is, applied research, including approximately $2 million per year for water-related research in agriculture.[61] Currently, there is a proposal at the DER to establish an office to coordinate agency research activities, as well as to seek sources of support for research activities throughout the state.[62]

Water management districts conduct research activities, both in-house and on a contract basis. The majority of the contracts are let to Florida university research units, but some are out-of-state contracts, such as the

Kissimmee River Physical Model Study with the University of California at Berkeley, discussed in the case study. There is a proposal to establish a water resources research program in the Lake Okeechobee District of the South Florida WMD, possibly including a center site.

Some research--primarily applied research--is carried out by private and industry sources. The Florida Institute for Phosphate Research is funded from severance taxes. The investigations are typically contracted out. Available funds are about $4 to $5 million, of which about $300,000 to $400,000 go to water research.[63] Some chemical companies fund research in agriculture, particularly on the effects of pesticides on water supply. Hazardous waste research has been funded by companies that have been pressured to do so by the state.[64]

CASE STUDY: KISSIMMEE RIVER RESTORATION PROJECT

This case study will explore the role that water resources research can play in the development of water policy, by focusing on an ambitious program to restore the Kissimmee River. The Kissimmee River restoration project represents the first known case of a channelized river being restored to its former natural state. We provide a brief overview of the Kissimmee River's historical development, in order to lay out the scope of this case study, and then follow with a detailed treatment of the various stages of its development. We conclude with a look at a major research effort, involving the use of a physical simulation model, aimed at determining the feasibility of the project.

Channelization of the Kissimmee River System

The Kissimmee River falls within the jurisdiction of the South Florida WMD and is a major source of surface water flow into Lake Okeechobee.[65] The watershed occupies a major portion of the district, including Orange, Polk, Osceola, Highlands, and Okeechobee Counties.

As early as the 1880s, initial work was performed by the Corps of Engineers, to connect the lakes of the Kissimmee chain by channels, primarily for navigation purposes.[66] Prior to Corps' involvement, water projects in Florida, principally drainage, were carried out by private concerns.[67] Repeated natural disasters including hurricanes, droughts, and floods ravaged the south and central Florida region during the 1920s. Reclamation of rich muck lands along Lake Okeechobee and the Kissimmee River floodplains attracted agricultural and land development interest. However, two great hurricanes, in 1926 and 1928, devastated containment structures and caused the drowning of at least 250 persons.[68] Some 600,000 acres in the Kissimmee Basin were flooded in the major flood of 1947. Heavy summer rains, followed by hurricanes in September and October, brought torrential downpours. Although there was no loss of life, total property damage was estimated at $9 million by the Corps of Engineers.[69]

Components of the Project

A general plan for flood protection in the Kissimmee Basin was incorporated in the comprehensive plan for central and southern Florida presented to the U.S. Congress in 1948. The general plan contemplated: (1) use of the major lakes as storage for flood control and reduction of runoff rates; (2) use of the major lakes as water conservation reservoirs; (3) connecting channels between the major lakes and provision of control structures; and (4) channel and control structures in the Kissimmee River portion of the basin.[70]

In 1954, the Kissimmee River Waterway Project was authorized by Congress for construction by the U.S. Army Corps of Engineers, at an estimated cost of $34 million. Prior to its channelization, the Kissimmee River meandered southward for 98 miles back and forth across the Kissimmee Valley from Lake Kissimmee to Lake Okeechobee.[71] To provide flood protection in the lower Kissimmee River Basin, beginning in 1964, the natural curves of the river were straightened into a canal, designated C-38. Canal C-38 runs along a straight-line route 52 miles long, 200 feet wide, and 30 feet deep, with six water control structures and navigational locks.

Regulation of the lake levels started in 1964, and channel excavation was completed in late 1970.[72] By 1965, it was considered that "some degree of man-made control" of flows and water levels in the Kissimmee Basin had started. Canal C-38 functions as a huge drainage ditch for the lower Kissimmee Basin, resulting in the drainage of almost 200,000 acres of river marsh and other wetlands.[73] Ground water levels in large areas of the basin have been significantly lowered. As a result of channelization, water recedes from the river valley up to 11 times faster than before.

The natural fall of the land from Lake Kissimmee to Lake Okeechobee is about 36 feet. Five water control structures, which act as dams, were placed in strategic locations to terrace the water level in the canal in increments of about six feet. In doing so, the natural slope of the river was removed, and flat pools (impoundments), resembling stairsteps, were created in its place. The water level of each pool is held constant, with no fluctuation or slope. The result has been a permanent draining of the marshes in the northern reach of each pool, and permanent flooding of the marsh in the southern end of the each pool.[74]

The Consequences

Although channelization enhanced flood control and created additional pasture land, some water quality and environmental values were compromised. Under the natural hydrologic period, the marshes helped maintain water quality by absorbing agricultural nutrients and functioning as a natural filter for storm runoff. With channelization, the river's increased flow transports large amounts of phosphates and nitrates, discharging them into Lake Okeechobee.[75]

The value and impacts of the Kissimmee River Waterway Project were questioned in the early 1970s. The project, once heralded by the South and Central Florida Flood Control District as a "wide, broad superhighway" in 1964, was being referred to as the "Kissimmee ditch" less than a decade later.[76] Inspired by the nation's increased awareness of ecology and aided by new federal environmental protection legislation, the state of Florida focused its attention on the natural resources of the Kissimmee River-Lake Okeechobee-Everglades ecosystems.

Channelization of the Kissimmee River Basin presented south Florida water resources planners with a dilemma: major conflicts in management occur because lake stages have to be maintained high enough to provide adequate water for irrigation and navigation, yet low enough prior to the wet season to provide flood protection.[77] The artificial regulation of the river's levels, while alleviating the drainage and water supply problems, posed a potential threat to the ecosystems.

The Kissimmee River Restoration

In 1969, the National Environmental Protection Act was passed, re-quiring that the flood control district consider damage to the environment when making water management decisions. Growing concern for preservation of the environment prompted the governor's conference on water management to ask for restoration of lakes and marshes.[78] It recommended development of a comprehensive water-use plan for the state and reinforced the importance of establishing environmental and water quality controls.

Florida's Evaluation of the Situation
A number of studies were carried out to evaluate the effects of the artificial setting on the local environment. One such study notes:

The lack of significant water fluctuations is of decided detriment to fish and wildlife values in the impoundments. There is no explosively reproductive expansion of the small aquatic animal species into annually reflooded marsh. In the dry season, there is no concentration of forage to feed game and pan fish and attract wading birds and waterfowl. There is no alternating hydro period to stimulate and maintain growth of aquatic vegetation types highly prized by waterfowl. There is, in summation, no rejuvenation of the typical Florida marsh ecosystem.[79]

Studies conducted by the South and Central Florida Flood Control District (precursor of the South Florida WMD) of the Kissimmee lakes during the 1970s have shown that the productivity of these lakes has been steadily increasing because of the influx of excessive nutrients from adjacent agricultural and urban areas. Nutrients in the water cause algae to bloom until the lake is filled with silt and vegetation--a process called eutrophication. Although it is a natural process, the rate of eutrophication can be drastically accelerated by man's activities, resulting in overproduction of algae and other aquatic plants, deterioration of fisheries, and degradation of water quality.[80]

Even before concerns were expressed by the state and the public in the 1970s, the flood control district had initiated a series of research projects to address the environmental problems of the Kissimmee system. This resulted in a series of technical studies, including surveys of biological conditions in the system, as well as studies of management methods that can be used to improve environmental conditions in the Kissimmee lakes and floodplain. Those studies have shown that problems of the Kissimmee River result primarily from the "effects of overdrainage and water level stabilization on the marshes of the floodplain, which occurred as the result of construction of impoundments."[81] These studies showed that if water levels in the impoundments fluctuated on a seasonal basis, growth of desirable wetland vegetation, small fishes, and macroinvertebrates was stimulated in the marshes.

The Corps of Engineers' Response
In response to study results and public concern, the Corps of Engineers, which had build the waterway project, was asked to restudy the situation and evaluate methods for alleviating the adverse impacts of the channel. In October 1985, the Jacksonville District of the Army Corps of Engineers submitted the Final Environmental Statement and Feasibility Report on the Kissimmee River for review by the Corps' Board of Engineers for Rivers and Harbors. The report recommended several measures to ameliorate the state of the Kissimmee River, including pool state manipulation and implementation of best management practices. However, the report stated that "these plans of action do not qualify for federal implementation under current guidelines for federal water and land resource planning." The report recommended no federal funding of the Kissimmee restoration program, because the Corps concluded that none of the restoration plans makes a net contribution to national economic development.[82] On June 4, 1986, the Board of Engineers for Rivers and Harbors concurred with the Jacksonville District of the Corps.[83]

The Kissimmee report is now being reviewed by the Corps' chief of engineers, who will submit his recommendations to the Army's assistant secretary for civil works.[84] The assistant secretary will subsequently make a recommendation to the Office of Management and Budget, which will make final recommendations to Congress.

Save Our Everglades Program
In *Save Our Everglades: Third Anniversary Report Card*, issued August 22, 1986, Governor Graham stated that "Florida should not have to pay the

entire cost of correcting environmental damage caused by a Corps project. If the Corps is unable or unwilling to find economic values in clean water, wetlands, fish and wildlife, and recreation, then Congress should direct it to participate with Florida in restoring the values of the Kissimmee."[85]

The state of Florida had already decided to undertake the restoration of the Kissimmee River and had instituted several programs to carry out the project. As part of his Save Our Everglades Program, Governor Bob Graham created the Kissimmee River Resource Planning and Management Committee in September 1984. The committee is chaired by a member of the South Florida WMD Governing Board and includes its executive director, John Wodraska. It is charged with devising a management plan to ensure proper land development and environmental protection in the lower Kissimmee River Basin.[86] In August 1985, the committee completed and adopted the Resource Management Plan for the Lower Kissimmee River and Taylor Creek Drainage Basins.

The management plan addresses five major elements that Governor Graham stipulated were to be addressed by the committee:

-- Protection of the Kissimmee River's unique "riverine system" to ensure the continuation of indigenous fish and wildlife, the river's aesthetic appeal, and other benefits;
-- Maintenance and improvement of the basin's water quality;
-- Development of a land acquisition strategy for areas that cannot be managed through planning and regulatory programs and that should, as an exception, be brought into public ownership;
-- Development of land-use management plans that will ensure compatibility with the protection of critical resources in the area; and
-- Action to encourage economic development in the study area.[87]

Implementation actions, with accompanying timetables, were assigned by the committee to appropriate federal, state, regional, and local governments and agencies. As a component of the restoration plan, the South Florida WMD is in the process of purchasing the original Kissimmee River floodplain (50,000 acres), under the Save Our Rivers land acquisition program. Since January 1985, the district has purchased 9,000 acres in the floodplain, bringing public ownership to 19,000 acres.[88]

Kissimmee River Demonstration Project
As part of the investigations for evaluating restoration measures, the South Florida WMD has built a demonstration project for full-scale testing of one means to dechannelize the Kissimmee (C-38). The South Florida WMD is attempting to partially fill in portions of Canal C-38 and direct flows of water back into the Kissimmee River oxbows.[89] According to South Florida WMD projections, evaluation of this undertaking should be completed between 1987 and 1989, at which time a plan may be developed for restoration of the river.

The Kissimmee River Demonstration Project is being conducted in pool B of the Kissimmee River, between S-65A and S-65B, in Osceola, Okeechobee, and Highland Counties. The aim is to restore the flow-through sections of the historic Kissimmee River channel and recreate the floodplain wetland habitat. The structural components of the project include:

- -- Construction of three sheet pile weirs across C-38 (begun in September 1984; the third weir was completed in August 1985);
- -- Implementation of an annual pool-stage-fluctuation schedule 39-42 feet above mean sea level (initiated in October 1985);
- -- Construction of a berm along a section of the east bank of C-38 (finished in the early summer of 1986);
- -- Installation of culverts adjacent to S-65A and along the west side of C-38; and
- -- Removal of a dike from the floodplain in the lower portion of pool B.

The pool-stage-fluctuation schedule is intended to reestablish former floodplain wetlands that have been eliminated as a result of adherence to a constant pool stage, as well as to provide more natural wet and dry cycles for existing floodplain marshes. Removal of the dike in the lower portion of the pool will allow water stages in an existing marsh to fluctuate according to the pool-stage schedule. The weirs are designed to divert water into three adjacent oxbows, thereby reestablishing flow in these sections of the historic river channel. The culvert and berm in the northeast section of the pool are intended to create a flow-through marsh in a drained section of floodplain, while the culvert on the west side will reestablish a similar system in an existing marsh.[90]

The demonstration project was constructed at a cost of $1.3 million.[91] The South Florida WMD and the DER are monitoring the effects of the demonstration project on water quality, wildlife populations, vegetation, and reestablishment of wetlands. Monitoring, which began in July 1984, will continue through 1988 and will serve as a basis for designing further restoration plans. The South Florida WMD has contracted with the University of California at Berkeley to develop a large-scale physical model of the Kissimmee River Basin to facilitate the design and testing of the next phase.

Kissimmee River Modeling Study

On August 15, 1986, The University of California at Berkeley was awarded an $800,000 contract by the South Florida WMD to construct and conduct a physical model of the Kissimmee River. The principal investigator and manager of the project is Dr. H. W. Shen, professor of civil engineering at the University of California.

The study will include three components: field measurements, physical modeling, and mathematical modeling. The main effort will be concentrated on pool B, the 12-mile reach between structures S-65A and S-65B in Canal C-38. According to the language of the contract, "the results will be extrapolated and interpreted for the entire river and suggestions will be given accordingly for the restoration approach."

According to the proposal submitted by Dr. Shen, the study's principal objectives are:

-- To construct and conduct a physical model study (with a horizontal scale on the order of 1:10) to study the flow and sediment distributions and movements from five to six dechannelization approaches for a 12-mile reach of the Kissimmee River;
-- To construct a mathematical model or models for supplementing and completing the analysis of results from physical models;
-- To construct and conduct separate physical models to test localized scour and deposition problems in the channel and/or adjacent to hydraulic structures. The needs of these separate models will be discussed and determined with staff from South Florida WMD;
-- To use both physical and mathematical models to demonstrate to the public the effects of various flow distribution schemes; and
-- To establish design criteria for hydraulic structures, if needed.

This proposed model study will be conducted at the Richmond Field Station of the University of California, which has a building with a length of 1,028 feet and a width of 32.3 feet. The research group proposes modifying this building to fit the model. In addition, they have two 1,000-foot-long concrete channels, which can be used to feed flows into the river model. A pump has already been installed in these two long concrete flumes. The discharge from this pump should be sufficient to supply adequate flow through the river model.

CONCLUSIONS

1. A great deal of Florida's early development depended upon massive draining and flood control projects. Land reclamation projects, first privately organized and then funded through federal and state sources, have been imperative to the economic development of the state. This has contributed to the perception among government officials and the public that water issues should have a high priority, and are deserving of financial support.

2. Starting with the passage of the 1969 Environmental Protection Act, Florida (along with the rest of the nation) developed a sense of urgency in putting in place programs to safeguard the state's natural resources. Throughout the 1970s and early 1980s, an integrated, comprehensive, planning mechanism was developed in order to link long-term goals with

specific regional needs. The 1985 State Comprehensive Plan is the basis for future development and management of Florida's resources.

3. As in other states, institutional changes have been necessary as a means to implement water management plans. In Florida, five WMDs serve as regional agencies that are responsible to the DER. Annual conferences, attended by a representative of each WMD, allow for the coordination of programs and delineation of overall goals.

4. The realization that massive drainage projects have jeopardized valuable ecosystems, threatening much of Florida's wildlife, resulted in the inclusion in the SCP of a restoration program for some of the more critical habitats. Through a surcharge on the documentary stamp tax, it provides funds to the WMDs for acquisition of land along streams and water courses.

5. There is little coordinated water research at the state level. However, research is conducted at the university and by the WMDs. One notable example is the contract between the South Florida WMD and the University of California to develop a model for the Kissimmee River restoration project. Considerable research related to water management in agriculture is supported in the Agricultural Experiment Station of the University of Florida.

6. The protection of the state's environmental resources will have to be reconciled with other needs, such as economic development, industrial growth, urbanization, tourism, and agriculture. Our study provides some evidence that Florida has the resolve to create innovative funding mechanisms to support water resource programs. Florida's water policy has already reached a significant level of maturity, providing the state with a firm foundation to deal with its future water resource needs.

Material for this chapter was provided by Mario Melgar Adalid and Fernando Albornoz.

NOTES

1. Department of Environmental Regulation (DER), *Agency Functional Plan* (Tallahassee, Fla: DER, October 1986), p. 84 (hereafter cited as *Agency Functional Plan*).
2. James Brindell and Bram D. E. Canter, "1984 Wetlands Act: A Course Change or Correction," *Florida Environmental and Urban Issues* XII, no. 1 (October 1984), p. 1.
3. South Florida Water Management District, "The Challenge of Water Management," *In Depth Report* 5, no. 1 (March 1980).
4. South Florida WMD, "The Challenge of Water Management."
5. South Florida WMD, "The Challenge of Water Management."
6. Victoria Tschinkel and Gilbert Berguist, "The State Water Use Plan: Where Do We Go From Here?," *Florida Environmental and Urban Issues* XIII, no. 3 (April 1986), pp. 5-9 (hereafter cited as "State Water Use Plan").

7. Edward A. Fernald and Donald J. Patton, eds. *Water Resources Atlas of Florida* (Tallahassee: Florida State University, 1984), p. 252 (hereafter cited as *Water Resources Atlas*).

8. Fernald and Patton, *Water Resources Atlas,* p. 252.

9. Fernald and Patton, *Water Resources Atlas,* p. 9.

10. DER, *Agency Functional Plan,* p. 183.

11. DER, *Agency Functional Plan,* p. 183.

12. DER, *Agency Functional Plan,* p. 28.

13. DER, *Agency Functional Plan,* p. 28.

14. Fernald and Patton, *Water Resources Atlas of Florida,* p. 69.

15. Fernald and Patton, *Water Resources Atlas of Florida,* p. 81.

16. Fernald and Patton, *Water Resources Atlas of Florida,* p. 36.

17. Fernald and Patton, *Water Resources Atlas of Florida,* p. 11.

18. Jeffrey Kahn, "Restoring the Everglades," *Sierra* (October 1986), pp. 38-43.

19. Thomas G. Pelham, *State Land-Use Planning and Regulation* (Lexington, Mass.: D. C. Heath and Co., 1979), pp. 5 and 100 (hereafter cited as *State Land-Use Planning*).

20. Pelham, *State Land-Use Planning,* p. 105.

21. Pelham, *State Land-Use Planning,* p. 107.

22. Jack Osterholt, "Implementing Florida's Planning Process: The State Land Development Plan and the State Water Plan," *Florida Environmental and Urban Issues* XIII, no. 3 (April 1986), p. 3.

23. The Council of State Governments (CSG), *State Water Quality Planning Issues* (Lexington, Ky: CSG, 1982), p. 21 (hereafter cited as *State Water Quality Planning*).

24. Robert C. Apgar, "Florida's State Land Development Plan," *Florida Environmental and Urban Issues* XIII, no. 3 (April 1986), p. 4.

25. Tschinkel and Berguist, "State Water Use Plan," p. 3.

26. Department of Environmental Regulation (DER), *State Water Use Plan* (Tallahassee, Fla: DER, March 1986), p. 1 (hereafter cited as *State Water Use Plan*).

27. DER, *State Water Use Plan,* p. 29.

28. Tschinkel and Berguist, "State Water Use Plan."

29. Tschinkel and Berguist, "State Water Use Plan."

30. Edward Jones, director, Save Our Rivers Program, Department of Land Management, memo (February 10, 1987).

31. DER, *State Water Use Plan,* p. 69.

32. DER, *Agency Functional Plan,* p. 103.

33. DER, *Agency Functional Plan,* p. 103.

34. Tschinkel and Berguist, "State Water Use Plan."

35. DER, *Agency Functional Plan,* p. 103.

36. Pelham, *State Land-Use Planning,* p. 111.

37. Pelham, *State Land-Use Planning,* p. 113.

38. Pelham, *State Land-Use Planning,* pp. 123-125.

39. Pelham, *State Land-Use Planning,* p. 193.

40. CSG, *State Water Quality Planning,* p. 21.

41. CSG, *State Water Quality Planning*, p. 19.
42. CSG, *State Water Quality Planning*, p. 19.
43. Office of the Governor, *Save Our Rivers: Celebrating Five Years of Progress* (October 1986), p. 17.
44. Warren Viessman and Claire Welty, "Water Management and Institutions," *Water Management Technology and Institutions* (New York: Harper and Row, Inc., 1985), pp. 72-73 (hereafter cited as "Water Management").
45. Viessman and Welty, "Water Management."
46. St. Johns River Water Management District, *Quarterly* 6, no. 3 (December 1986).
47. Fernald and Patton, *Water Resources Atlas*, p. 218.
48. James Hearney, *1982-1986 Research and Development Plan, Water Resources Research Center* (Gainesville: University of Florida, October 1980), p. 54 (hereafter cited as *1982-1986 Research and Development Plan*).
49. Northwest Florida Water Management District (NFWMD), *1985 Annual Report* (Havana: NFWMD, n.d.), p. 8.
50. NFWMD, *1985 Annual Report*, p. 8.
51. Fernald and Patton, *Water Resources Atlas*, p. 256.
52. Pelham, *State Land-Use Planning*, p. 153.
53. Pelham, *State Land-Use Planning*, pp. 166-167.
54. CSG, *State Water Quality Planning*, p. 19.
55. Northwest Florida Water Management District (NFWMD), *Tenth Annual Conference on Water Management in Florida, Abstracts*, Public Information Bulletin 86-1 (Havana, Fla.: NFWMD, October 1986), pp. 12-13 (hereafter cited as *Tenth Annual Conference*).
56. Interview with DER officials, Tallahassee, Fla., January 5, 1987.
57. U.S., Congress, Joint Economic Committee, *Hard Choices, Appendix 4, Florida* (February 25, 1984), p. 8.
58. NFWMD, *Tenth Annual Conference*, p. 4.
59. Interview with Warren Viessman, University of Florida, Gainesville, January 7, 1987.
60. Interview with Jim Hearney, director, Water Resources Research Center, November 7, 1986.
61. Interview with Jim Hearney, November 7, 1986.
62. Interview with DER officials, January 5, 1987.
63. Hearney, *1982-1986 Research and Development Plan*, p. 71.
64. Hearney, *1982-1986 Research and Development Plan*, p. 71.
65. Fernald and Patton, *Water Resources Atlas*, p. 154.
66. Fernald and Patton, *Water Resources Atlas*, p. 154.
67. J. Walter Dineen et al., "The Kissimmee River Revisited," *In Depth Report*, Central and Southern Florida Flood Control District, vol. 2, no. 2 (May-June 1974), p. 4.
68. Luther J. Carter, *The Florida Experience: Land and Water Policy in a Growth State* (Baltimore: Johns Hopkins University Press, 1976), p. 83 (hereafter cited as *The Florida Experience*).

69. Frank E. Maloney, Sheldon J. Plager, and Fletcher N. Baldwin, Jr., *Water Law and Administration: The Florida Experience* (Gainesville: University of Florida Press, 1968), p. 306.

70. Dineen et al., "The Kissimmee River Revisited," p. 2.

71. Office of the Governor, *Save Our Everglades: Third Anniversary Report Card* (August 1986), p. 3 (hereafter cited as *Save Our Everglades*).

72. Dineen et al., "The Kissimmee River Revisited," p. 2.

73. Office of the Governor, *Save Our Everglades*, p. 3.

74. Dineen et al., "The Kissimmee River Revisited," p. 2.

75. Carter, *The Florida Experience,* p. 104.

76. Carter, *The Florida Experience,* p. 106.

77. Carter, *The Florida Experience,* p. 154.

78. South Florida Water Management District (SFWMD), "The Challenge of Water Management," *In Depth Report* 5, no. 1 (March 1980), p. 8.

79. SFWMD, "The Challenge of Water Management," p. 4.

80. South Florida Water Management District (SFWMD), *A Closer Look: Lake Okeechobee Backpumping* (West Palm Beach, Fla.: SFWMD, n.d.).

81. Fernald and Patton, *Water Resources Atlas*, p. 154.

82. U.S. Army Corps of Engineers, Jacksonville District, *Central and Southern Florida Kissimmee River, Florida: Final Feasibility Report and Environmental Impact Statement* (October 1985).

83. Office of the Governor, *Save Our Everglades*, p. 4.

84. Office of the Governor, *Save Our Everglades*, p. 6.

85. Office of the Governor, *Save Our Everglades*, p. 6.

86. SFWMD, *Bulletin* 10, no. 2 (Summer 1984), p. 3.

87. SFWMD, *Bulletin* 10, no. 2 (Summer 1984), p. 3.

88. SFWMD, *Bulletin* 10, no. 2 (Summer 1984), p. 3.

89. Fernald and Patton, *Water Resources Atlas*, p. 155.

90. Office of the Governor, *Save Our Everglades*, p. 4.

91. Office of the Governor, *Save Our Everglades*, p. 4.

NORTH CAROLINA

BACKGROUND
Historical Factors

Surface Water

With a statewide precipitation average of approximately 50 inches per year, water supply is not a major problem. However, rainfall varies throughout the state, both regionally and seasonally, and droughts have occurred throughout North Carolina's history. Stream-gauging stations during the recent major drought, in July 1986, registered flows near or less than those during previous major droughts. Many cities issued both voluntary and mandatory restrictions on water use. Stream flows across the state remained below average into November, and major cities, such as Raleigh and Charlotte, were still classified as having severe drought conditions.[1]

Major floods occurred in the state in 1916, 1928, 1940, 1945, and 1954. Flood damage annually amounts to approximately $91 million,[2] and a 1977 flood in the northwestern part of the state killed 13 people and caused more than $45 million in damage.[3] Approximately 11 percent of the land in North Carolina is flood prone and is used for agriculture or forestry.

The federal government, through the U.S. Army Corps of Engineers and the Tennessee Valley Authority, took the lead in building dams for the purpose of flood control. The John H. Kerr Lake and the W. Kerr Scott Reservoir in the Piedmont are two examples of flood control projects that were completed by the Corps in the 1950s.[4] These dams were part of a larger, federal effort at flood control, where the requisite projects were too large or complex to be built and financed by state or local governments. When local governments wanted to increase water supplies and flood control management, they turned to the federal government for assistance.

North Carolina flood control policy was therefore controlled at the federal level, rather than at the state level.[5]

Ground Water

In its early history, North Carolina maintained a laissezfaire approach to water management. Water policy, especially as it concerned ground water--an easily obtainable source of water for industry, agriculture, and local governments--was often forged by the courts. In 1924, the North Carolina Supreme Court adopted the American rule of reasonable use in *Rouse* v. *City of Kinston*. The rule "recognizes the landowner's right to capture and use the water that exists under his land, but limits the quantity of water to that necessary for some useful purpose in connection with the land from which the water is extracted." Thus, reasonable use applies to the land instead of the water. The American rule was challenged in the 1964 case, *Bayer* v. *Nello Teer Co*. In this case, the pumping of vast amounts of water by the defendant's quarry operation resulted in the degradation of the plaintiff's wells through salt water intrusion. The Supreme Court overturned a lower court's ruling, again emphasizing, as in the Rouse case, that the standard requires reasonable use of the land and not necessarily reasonable use of the water. The reaffirmation of the American rule held profound implications for ground water management in North Carolina and eventually led to the first involvement by the state in a similar case three years later.[6]

In 1964, the same year the Bayer-Nello case was decided, the Texas Gulf Chemicals Corp. began phosphate-mining operations along the Pamlico River. A necessary part of its mining operation involved ground water withdrawals, up to 71 million gallons per day, from the Castle Hayne Aquifer. This caused a drawdown in well-water levels in neighboring wells and also increased the possibility of salt water intrusion into the aquifer. Under existing common law, the citizens of Pamlico, Washington, and Beaufort Counties, who relied on the Castle Hayne Aquifer as a principal source of water, could not seek relief under the doctrine of reasonable use, as interpreted by the Supreme Court.[7]

Public concern over the availability of adequate water supplies in the region led to the creation of a legislative study commission to explore the problem. The study commission's report provided the impetus for the general assembly to pass the North Carolina Capacity Use Areas Act in 1967, in response to this dilemma. This represents the first effort by the state to gain control of ground water management through a permitting process. The act limits ground water withdrawals in areas, such as the Pamlico, where demand for water exceeds supply. Once a region has been designated a capacity use area, permits are issued that specifically restrict users of more than 100,000 gallons daily. While the Capacity Use Areas Act is narrow in scope (the capacity use area on the Pamlico River remains the only one of its kind), it represents a critical juncture in North Carolina's water resource management, because it departs from the state's tradition of noninvolvement in ground water matters.

Critical Issues

Water Quality

Many municipalities in North Carolina do not yet comply with state water quality requirements in their treatment of effluent. A survey of utilities for the period 1980-86 revealed that a large number were having difficulty meeting demand for both water supply and waste water treatment. Despite the expansion of waste water facilities by 56 percent of the utilities surveyed, moratoria on new hookups had been imposed on one-quarter of them, and 44 percent failed to meet discharge limits as specified in their permits.[8]

Soil erosion, aggravated by poor soil conservation practices in agriculture, road construction, surface mining, and urban development, is a widespread problem in North Carolina. North Carolina's farms are the chief source of sedimentation. In 1977, for example, 49 million of the 77 million tons of eroded soil in the state originated on cropland. U.S. Soil Conservation Service data indicated that only 16 percent of land subject to erosion in the state in 1982 was being farmed using conservation measures.[9] Federal officials believe that a lack of money on the part of farmers is an obstacle to better soil conservation methods. Sediment reduces reservoir capacities, widens flood-prone areas, increases drinking water treatment costs, and serves as a carrier for pollutants and other toxic substances.

Eutrophication, the overenrichment of water with nitrogen and phosphorus, has also been a major concern in North Carolina. The Chowan River, in the northeastern part of the state, has experienced severe water quality problems caused by eutrophication since the early 1970s. Extensive summer algal blooms on the river are thought to cause the decline in fish catches in the river. In 1982, the North Carolina Division of Environmental Management estimated that nearly two-thirds of the phosphorus and four-fifths of the nitrogen found in the river came from nonpoint sources, such as agricultural runoff.[10] Nutrient problems also have been found in the lower Neuse River in the eastern part of the state. In addition, isolated algal blooms have appeared in the Falls of the Neuse and the B. Everett Jordan Reservoirs in the central Piedmont.

In 1982, the North Carolina Office of Water Resources estimated that 120 million gallons of toxic substances were generated in North Carolina each year, ranking the state fourth overall in the production of hazardous waste. Although there were 16 major chemical spills in North Carolina in 1981, state officials believed that most toxic substances got into the water from publicly owned treatment plants.[11] Textile companies, which make socks impregnated with a chemical that eliminates foot odors, have introduced organic tin compounds into all the major river basins of North Carolina.[12] These compounds have been shown to have an adverse effect on life in marinas and other aquatic environments. Toxic substances that leach from landfills into aquifers are another threat to the state's water. Other nonpoint sources of pollution are also a significant problem. In 1981, for example, high mercury levels in one arm of High Rock Lake resulted in a ban on commercial fishing. The source of the mercury had not been identified scientifically a year later, although high concentrations of the element were found downstream from a battery plant. Another incident of mercury poisoning occurred in 1971 on the lower Cape Fear River. An investigation into the incident concluded that the mercury had accumulated after many years of discharges from industry.[13]

A significant number of the more than 100,000 underground storage tanks in the state, which contain petroleum products, chemicals, and other substances, may be contaminating the ground water. The cleanup costs for each incident can range from several thousand to several million dollars, according to information from the American Petroleum Institute, as quoted in a legislative research commission report. The state, as of December 15, 1986, was investigating 140 separate incidents of underground storage tank leakages that have contaminated 150 water supply wells.[14]

Water Shortages

Although supplies are generally adequate, water shortages are starting to occur at the upper end of the Neuse River Basin. The state is considering whether to control, via the permitting process, surface water withdrawals from tributaries of the Neuse River that serve as public water supplies for small communities such as Hillsborough and Zebulon. Larger cities are opting for other solutions. The city of Durham and the Orange Water and Sewer Authority, which serves Chapel Hill, are about to complete new reservoirs. The proposed Randleman Dam Project, also located in the upper Neuse basin, would provide water for the cities of Greensboro and High Point. The project has been approved by the federal government but has not yet been funded.[15]

In another surface water quantity issue, the state of North Carolina has filed suit against the U.S. Army Corps of Engineers to stop a proposed interbasin transfer of water from Lake Gaston to Virginia Beach, Virginia, a rapidly growing urban area. Lake Gaston is part of the Roanoke River Basin and lies on the Virginia-North Carolina state line. The immediate issue before a federal district court judge in Raleigh is whether there needs to be an additional environmental impact statement before the transfers occur. North Carolina is in favor of an additional study, while the Corps is not. Both sides presented their final arguments on November 7, 1986.[16] A final judgment on this matter is not expected before 1988.

Ground water withdrawals by industry also led to water shortages along the Pamlico River in eastern North Carolina in the 1960s. The state has not suffered serious ground water shortages since then. However, eastern cities, such as Kinston, that rely on ground water, are concerned as withdrawals have produced water-level declines of 150 feet or more in large areas of the eastern coastal plain. The ability of North Carolina's ground water system to meet future demands is largely unknown.[17] Currently ground water accounts for approximately 10 percent of total withdrawals (Table 6.1).

TABLE 6.1 Estimated Water Use in North Carolina, 1965-80

	1965	1970	1975	1980
Population (millions)	4.90	5.08	5.37	5.87
Consumption by use (offstream)				
Total (mgd)	365	473	494	760
Public supply	22	91	97	110
Rural use	280	150	190	170
Irrigation	29	82	87	130
Industrial	34	150	120	350
Per capita (gpd)				
All uses	74	93	92	129
Excl. irrigation	69	77	76	107
Withdrawals by source				
Total (mgd)	3,920	5,730	5,040	8,070
Ground water	420	430	540	770
Surface water	3,500	5,300	4,500	7,300

Source: U.S. Geological Survey, *Estimated Use of Water in the United States, 1965; Estimated Use of Water in the United States, 1970; Estimated Use of Water in the United States, 1975; Estimated Use of Water in the United States, 1980*, Geological Survey Circulars 556, 676, 765, and 1001 (Reston, Va.: U.S. Department of the Interior, 1968, 1972, 1977, and 1983).

STATE INITIATIVES IN WATER RESOURCE MANAGEMENT

Three levels of government--local, state, and federal--each have a role in developing water resource policy in North Carolina. The federal government, with its initiatives in water development, has played the major role in water resource management, while local governments have played the major role in providing water and sewer services. State government in North Carolina has played a less active role, supplementing federal and local initiatives. The historic dominance of federal and local governments in managing North Carolina's water resources has provided little incentive to the state to develop its own planning capabilities. The recent withdrawal of the federal government from regional water policy issues has left a void that could provide the state with an opportunity to contribute to water policy and planning.

Policy Development

In 1937, the North Carolina Planning Board recognized that water pollution affects human activities. It pointed out "the need for a comprehensive and effective policy for use and control of water." In 1945, the State Stream Sanitation and Conservation Committee reported on the first comprehensive assessment of waste water discharges in the state.[18] As a result, the state passed its first comprehensive pollution control legislation, the 1951 State Stream Sanitation Law. It represented a major junction in North Carolina water resources policy for two reasons. First, the state showed leadership by asserting control over water resources management. Second, the law enabled the state to begin building the water institutions necessary for effective water resource management.

Point Source Pollution

Under the legislative mandate provided by the 1951 act, the State Stream Sanitation Committee undertook the development of a pollution abatement program. The main features of the program were the development of water quality standards and the assignment of stream classifications that reflect the "best use" of each segment. It took 12 years to complete and involved the initiation of 335 waste treatment projects at a cost of $118 million. Much of this was accomplished through voluntary compliance, in the case of municipalities with the assistance of construction grants provided under the Federal Water Pollution Control Act of 1956.[19] Federal legislation, notably the Federal Water Pollution Control Amendments of 1972, resulted in more stringent standards and a regulatory role for administrators of the program (currently the Department of Natural Resources and Community Development). The general assembly passed legislation in 1973 giving the state authority to issue permits to point source polluters under guidelines set by the Environmental Protection Agency (EPA). This legislation, called "Control of Sources of Water Pollution; Permits Required," and other antipollution legislation passed by the state are essentially of a regulatory nature. The legislation controls the major point sources of pollution that discharge into surface or ground water and establishes stream and effluent standards. It also regulates septic tanks and other sewage disposal systems that do not discharge directly into surface waters.[20]

The 1974 U.S. Safe Drinking Water Act regulates drinking water by requiring the EPA to establish maximum allowable levels for contaminants. Since enactment of the federal law, North Carolina's regulatory authority has expanded significantly, both in coverage of public systems and degree of control, in order to meet the federal requirements.[21] The North Carolina General Assembly passed the North Carolina Drinking Water Act in 1979, in order to regulate public water systems in accordance with federal requirements. The law required local governments to submit plans for their water systems to the state for approval. It also prohibited any person from discharging sewage above the intake of public water supply system without the approval of the state.[22]

Sedimentation Control

The nation's first soil and water conservation district was organized in Anson County, North Carolina, by Dr. Hugh H. Bennett, who later became the first chief of the U.S. Soil Conservation Service. Agricultural land use was the primary concern of soil conservationists in North Carolina until the post-World War II construction boom brought increased road building and urban development. In the late 1960s and early 1970s, local governments took the first initiatives to protect surface water supplies, petitioning the North Carolina General Assembly for enabling legislation to authorize the adoption of local sedimentation control ordinances. The general assembly, after several years of study and research, passed the Sedimentation Pollution Control Act of 1973. The act finds that sediment is a major pollution problem in North Carolina and that a great deal of it is caused by construction sites and road maintenance. It requires the state to work with local governments on the development of erosion control plans. The act applies to residential, commercial, and industrial development, as well as to highway construction and maintenance.[23] The greatest drawback, however, was that agricultural land--a major, if not the most important, source of sediment--was exempt from the provisions of the act.

In an effort to address pollution from agriculture, the general assembly in 1984 passed a $2 million biennial state cost-share program that provided up to 75 percent funding for agricultural best management practices for farmers. The intent was to encourage the use of good soil conservation practices, in order to reduce the amount of phosphorus contamination from agricultural fertilizers and pesticides. The adoption of a nonpoint source pollution program directed at the state's agricultural interests occurred 11 years after passage of the Sedimentation Control Act and helped to fill the gap created this act. A nonpoint source pollution program, passed in 1986, is an agricultural cost-share arrangement, which will operate in 33 of the state's 100 counties.[24] This demonstrates the supplemental approach that the state has historically pursued when federal and local levels of government failed to act.

North Carolina's antipollution legislation also has been tempered by the inclusion of the "Hardison amendments." These are a series of amendments, named after the sponsor of the first one, that prevent North Carolina from passing any regulations that are stricter than those set by the EPA. The Hardison amendments are significant, illustrating North Carolina's reluctance to assume a leadership role in certain areas of water pollution policy.[25]

Implementation

The 1965 Federal Water Resources Planning Act provided for federal and regional coordination of water development plans, as well as for grants so that states could prepare comprehensive water resources plans. Prompted by federal action, North Carolina established a program of state water resource planning, which coincided with the start of a decade of sustained growth in North Carolina's water administration agencies. The planning program became the responsibility of several different offices within the Department of Natural and Economic Resources. As a result of this fragmentation, North Carolina never completed a comprehensive water plan. However, in March 1977, the Department of Natural and Economic Resources issued the *North Carolina Water Resources Framework Study*. Conducted on a statewide level, the study is aimed at educating policymakers about the water resource planning efforts of the preceding decade, rather than acting as a decision-making document. The study brought together specific water issues such as quality, use, and flood control within a common framework to guide state actions until the year 2000.[26,27]

Water Quality Control
In the absence of a comprehensive state water plan, the general assembly continues to rely on several state agencies and committees to implement and develop the state's response to water management initiatives, such as the Sedimentation Control Act, Federal Safe Drinking Water Act of 1974, and the Federal Water Pollution Control Act Amendments of 1972. The Division of Environmental Management (DEM), within the Department of Natural Resources and Community Development (DNRCD), is the chief governmental unit in North Carolina responsible for implementation and regulation of the standards imposed on the state by the Safe Drinking Water Act and Clean Water Act. As such, the DEM administers the National Pollution Discharge Elimination System permits, as established by EPA guidelines. In addition, the DEM is responsible for the integrated, comprehensive water-planning program established in section 208 of the Clean Water Act.[28]

The Department of Human Resources shares with the DNRCD the important regulatory responsibilities pertaining to safety of public water supplies; transport and disposal of solid wastes, especially toxic and hazardous waste; and ground water absorption sewerage disposal systems of less than 3,000 gallons capacity. It plays a significant role in implementing and enforcing the standards of the 1974 Federal Safe Drinking Water Act and of the Resources Conservation and Recovery Act of 1976.[29] With the sanitary engineering section of the Division of Health Services, it is charged with conducting regional water supply planning, reviewing local water and waste water plans, and administering water supply plans. It also collects data, monitors systems, provides technical assistance, and trains waterworks operators.

Chief among the commissions is the Environmental Management Commission, a 17-member body appointed by the governor and general assembly. The commission hears appeals of fines levied by state regulatory agencies. It is responsible for declaring what areas in the state should be capacity use areas and what areas of the state should be classified as nutrient-sensitive watersheds. This latter designation gives the North Carolina Division of Environmental Management regulatory authority to control point source pollution, particularly phosphorus discharges, from waste water treatment plants. The Environmental Management Commission also plays an important role in North Carolina's new water classification system, which designates the numbers and types of permitted waste water discharges into a watershed. The commission must approve a nonpoint source pollution-control program before the relevant water body can be reclassified. In addition, the commission is involved in a nonpoint source pollution program, which was enacted in 1986 and will be administered by the Soil and Water Conservation Commission. The Environmental Management Commission will help decide which 33 of the state's 100 counties will be included in the program.[30,31]

The North Carolina Sedimentation Control Commission, created by the Sedimentation Control Act, is another commission that implements and regulates water policy in the state. Its other major functions are to work with local governments in developing sediment control programs, review and approve local erosion plans, and work with other state agencies on erosion control. It also implements a public education program focusing on sedimentation and successful techniques for controlling it.[32]

Pollution Prevention Pays Program
The DEM also operates the Pollution Prevention Pays Program, a separate unit within the division that has been funded and staffed by the general assembly since 1982. The program's stated goal is to identify and encourage the adoption of methods and techniques to reduce, prevent, and minimize the production of wastes before they become pollutants. The program attempts to initiate, at the source, the reduction of multimedia waste, including municipal, toxic, solid, and hazardous wastes. The program's primary purpose is to bypass the traditional regulatory path that attempts to reduce pollution by the threat of fines or legal action. By suggesting alternative production methods and new waste reduction techniques for specific manufacturing processes, the state has established a more cooperative and less antagonistic approach to water pollution control.

The Pollution Prevention Pays Program assists industries through the funding of research and technology development and provides research and education grants to the University of North Carolina. The program also provides matching grants to industry and trade associations for workshops and short courses to assist in the implementation of waste reduction projects. Each year, research proposals are solicited from state university faculty members. The proposals go before a review board made up of officials from agriculture, industry, government, and trade associations.

No proposal receives more than $30,000. The general assembly supports the Pollution Prevention Pays Program with a $650,000 annual appropriation, of which education and research receive $350,000. The program represents a case where the state is taking an active, instead of a reactive, stance on water pollution control.[33]

Recognizing the success of the program, the EPA has enlisted North Carolina's help in developing a nationwide program for helping businesses voluntarily reduce their production of pollutants. Under the Intergovernmental Personnel Act, Roger Schecter, head of the Pollution Prevention Pays Program, will spend three to 12 months with the EPA.[34]

Planning

The Division of Water Resources provides planning and technical aid in river basin management. Its plans and studies are developed in cooperation with local governments and other state and federal agencies.[35] For instance, prompted by a request from Kinston city officials, the division began working with the U.S. Geological Survey and 13 cities and local governments on a computer mapping study of the Cretaceous Aquifer. The water table in this aquifer has declined by approximately 120 feet in the Kinston area since 1900. The study, started in 1983 and scheduled for completion in 1988, will be used to advise cities on locations and aquifers for new well fields.[36] Federal, state, and local government units have each contributed financing to the project.[37]

Although water resources planning also takes place in a somewhat fragmented manner, involving federal, state, and local government entities, some regional coordination is provided by the Council of Governments (COGs). Established by Governor Scott in 1970, the COGs are the "lead regional organizations" designated "to plan for the coordinated growth and development of the state...to enhance the supply of services available to the people in each region; to streamline state government by providing one set of regions to be used for administrative and data collection purposes." However, the COGs are structurally weak: "They are composed of local governments, which can renounce their membership at any time. They have no taxing power, no power of property condemnation, and no independent power to implement the plans they draw up." The regional organizations were designed so they would not become another level of government, but rather a vehicle to strengthen local governmental units in carrying out and coordinating state policy under a state effort toward regionalism.[238]

The Triangle J COG is located in the eastern portion of the Piedmont in North Carolina, between the capital city of Raleigh and the university towns of Chapel Hill and Durham. The COG serves Chatham, Durham, Johnston, Lee, Orange, and Wake Counties. Since its inception, it has actively participated in the management of water resources, originally a part of the overall planning function of the agency. Water planning subsumed under its general duties included land-use ordinances, water and sewer master planning for the participating municipalities, and reservoir planning and siting. However, it was not until the mid-1970s that a separate staff position was allocated for the sole purpose of water resources management.[39] In 1975, the Triangle J COG was designated as lead planning agency for one of two areawide section 208 programs in North Carolina created in accordance with provisions of the 1972 Clean Water Act.[40] As a result of its growing responsibilities, the Triangle J COG created a regional water resources program as an adjunct to its general planning operations.

The water resources program has enabled local governments in the Triangle J area to address practical and policy-level issues of water quality and supply protection in the open, coordinated manner essential for interlocal government cooperation.[41] The Water Resources Planning Committee, which establishes the goals and objectives for the program, is comprised of a representative with voting privileges from each member county (usually an elected official) and an unspecified number of other officials, who serve in an advisory role only. The advisory positions are usually held by nonelected professionals in the field of water resources, including university faculty, local government officials, and state water administrators. Within the context of this arrangement, the Water Resource Planning Committee is able to overcome some traditional institutional and bureaucratic barriers, which have consistently inhibited efficient and equitable solutions to water-related problems. Opportunities for new directions in water issues are enhanced considerably by broadening the channels of communication between relevant players in the arena of water resource management.

Current Triangle J COG planning activities that are linked to mitigating water supply problems generally fall under the category of nonpoint source pollution control. Specifically, the COG has been pursuing activities in four areas:

1. Demonstration and evaluation of alternative on-site waste water systems (septic systems);
2. Formal negotiation and designation of local management agencies responsible for nonpoint source pollution control;
3. Inventory of residual waste generation and disposal, including toxic and hazardous wastes to Research Triangle Park, low-level radioactivity waste from hospitals and research facilities, sewage and sludge from water and waste water treatment plants; and
4. Identification and resolution of critical water quality problems in the Falls of the Neuse and Jordan Lake drainage areas.[42]

The fourth activity centers upon the protection of a 2,500-square-mile watershed surrounding the B. Everett Jordan Lake and the Falls of the Neuse Reservoir, discussed in the case study.

Financing

Recognizing that growth of the major urban areas in the United States and the continued degradation of rivers, streams, and oceans demanded adequate treatment of municipal pollution, the U.S. Congress in 1972 authorized $18 billion, through contract authority, to meet this need.[43] Through the 1972 Clean Water Act, the federal government matched local expenditures at a ratio of 75 percent federal to 25 percent local dollars, in order to meet the new, higher quality standards. Federal funding for waste water treatment in North Carolina reached as high as $110 million in 1976. In 1985, federal funding was reduced to $40 million, and the 1987 Clean Water Act authorized only $11 million for water pollution control in North Carolina.[44]

The state helps with one-half of the local share through the North Carolina Clean Water Bond Acts of 1971 and 1977, which authorized the issuance of bonds totaling $150 million and $230 million, respectively. These funds were disbursed to local governments for construction of, and improvements to, waste water treatment facilities, waste water collection systems, and water supply. As a result, local governments have only been responsible for 12.5 percent of the total investment for municipal waste water treatment.[45,46] In addition, in 1985, the North Carolina General Assembly approved $60 million in direct aid to local governments both to replace lost federal funds and to supplement remaining clean water act monies.[47]

In 1985, the North Carolina General Assembly passed into law the North Carolina Cost Share Program for Nutrient-Sensitive Watersheds. The purpose of this program is to reduce the amount of sediments, nutrients, animal wastes, and pesticides entering watersheds that have been declared "nutrient sensitive" by the Environmental Management Commission. The general assembly authorized a $2 million biennial state cost-share program, which includes up to 75 percent funding for implementation of best management practices.[48] The general assembly, in 1983, approved an optional half-cent local sales tax to help local governments to finance their waste water treatment facilities. The tax is expected to raise $164.5 million in the ten-year period ending in 1993.[49]

THE ROLE OF WATER RESEARCH

Early water resources research in North Carolina was conducted primarily by the universities, research foundations, and some federal agencies. Support for water resources research was initially obtained through the state and federal governments. The research projects focused on the traditional issue of water resource management, including structural management of water through reservoirs and dams. The University of North Carolina at Chapel Hill (UNC-CH), Duke University, and North Carolina State University (NCSU) were the prominent institutions of higher education that conducted early water resources research. Engineering research programs included civil, sanitary, and agricultural engineering. North Carolina State University and UNC-CH both conducted research in hydrology, while the Institute of Government at UNC-CH conducted research on the legal and institutional aspects of water policy.[50] The teaching programs in water resources and environmental engineering began to achieve national prominence in the 1920s.

North Carolina has benefited from a tradition of strong university support for water research. Many of the early research dollars from the general research appropriations were channeled into water resources research through the schools of sanitary and civil engineering. The universities also profited from federal grants channeled through all or most of the federal cabinet departments, as well as agencies such as the Tennessee Valley Authority and the National Science Foundation. The substantial expansion of university-based water resources research throughout the 1950s and early 1960s provided the framework for the eventual development of several water research activities based within institutions of higher education in North Carolina.[51]

State agencies did not possess any water-related research capabilities until recently. In 1959, the Department of Water Resources considered the establishment of a division of research and planning. However, this was during the early stages of institutional development in North Carolina and the creation of the Division of Research and Planning was deferred for budgetary considerations. It was not until the mid-1970s, with the creation of the DNRCD, that substantial research capabilities were achieved within state agencies. Until then, the only government agencies conducting research for the state were federal and included the U.S. Geological Survey (USGS) and the U.S. Agricultural Research Service within the U.S. Department of Agriculture.[52]

The North Carolina Water Resources Research Institute

The first and only water research center in North Carolina was created in 1964 as part of the federal Water Resources Research Act.[53] The law contained three grant programs. The first set up state water resource centers at land grant colleges and universities around the country and provided a small, largely unrestricted allotment to the centers. This resulted in the creation of the North Carolina Water Resources Research Institute (WRRI), which is located on the NCSU campus. The second program allowed the federal government to provide 50-50 matching grants to the states to conduct specific research projects. The third program allowed the federal government to provide grants to other universities and federal, state, and local agencies for purposes related to the responsibilities of the Department of the Interior.[54] The legislative intent was to create a binary system that would formulate a research program responsive to state water problems and needs, while providing the federal government with a mechanism to influence state water research, policy, and planning. The mission of the institute is threefold: to identify the state's research needs, to motivate and support research by qualified scientists, and to provide a mechanism for technology transfer.[55]

Research Agenda

Today, major water resources research conducted by the institute covers a wide spectrum of issues, from water quality concerns, such as eutrophication and aquatic weed management, to policy concerns, such as interstate water conflict management and the financing of water and waste water services. Since 1964, the research conducted at the institute has changed considerably in both emphasis and scope. Developments in current research have been influenced by shifts in the national agenda and by the shift in emphasis from water development to water management.

Water quality issues have always been prominent on the WRRI's research agenda. Eutrophication has been a major focus since 1969, and a nonpoint pollution study by Ed Bryan in 1969 helped influence the formulation of the 1972 Federal Water Pollution Control Amendments. In cooperation with the DNRCD, the WRRI continues to aid the state in achieving water quality standards.[56] It is currently trying to identify the factors that contribute most to algal bloom and eutrophication. Such studies complement the efforts of the DNRCD, whose research efforts are more directly concerned with specific problems. The state's water quality legislation provides authority to the DNRCD to collect data, engage in research, and review all relevant public and private projects for water quality consequences.[57] The Water Resources Research Institute also works in cooperation with the DNRCD in advancing state projects.[58]

While the problems of flood, drought, and water pollution have remained unchanged in North Carolina, the methods for solving these problems have not. One of the major changes in water research has been the shift from an emphasis on water development to one of water management. In referring to this water management issue and the complexities of the needed research, Warren Viessman, a professor at the University of Florida, writes:

"The problem is that good water management is a function of more than technology. It involves complex social, legal, political, economic, technological, and organizational systems. In many respects, research related to water management is the application of known technological and imaginative ideas to broad problems involving extensive institutional and technological dimensions. It requires teamwork--an understanding of how the many factions of socio-technological systems interact."[59]

Water research conducted at the WRRI has achieved the level of innovation described by Viessman. For example, over the past 20 years, in addition to its more traditional long-term research, the institute has supported a large body of research that examines issues related to water resources policy, planning, and management. The WRRI has cooperated with different institutions and departments within the North Carolina University system, some of which include: the Institute of Government and the Department of City and Regional Planning, both located at UNC; and the Department of Political Science and Public Administration and the Department of Sociology, both at NCSU. Some of the policy-related studies undertaken were: "Public Participation in Water Pollution," "State Water Resources Planning in North Carolina," "Financing Water Projects in North Carolina," and "Public Policy and Shoreline Landowner Behavior."

By increasing the scope of research to include more nontraditional areas of scientific knowledge, such as those in the social sciences, the range of general knowledge fostered by the institute has been increased. In addition, by opening its doors to new methodologies, difficult technical and institutional water resource problems associated with water management can be resolved at a low economic and environmental cost.[60] The institute's early support of nontraditional research has thus given it an advantage in facilitating the shift from water development to water management research.

Funding

Initially, the WRRI relied solely on the funds provided by the federal allotment, supplementing its budget with federal grant money, which was also part of the Water Resources Research Act. Referring to this federal program started in 1964, David Moreau, director of the Water Resources Research Institute, stated: "At one time, in an extremely competitive era, North Carolina was receiving 10 percent of all federal water research funds available through the matching grant program under the Federal Water Resources Research Act."[61] Recently, federal funds have not increased to keep up with the rate of inflation. However, over the past 20 years, the institute has been successful in broadening its funding base for research.

TABLE 6.2 Funding Levels for WRRI

Fiscal Year	USGS Program Support	Other Federal Support	State Approp.	Other Non-fed. Support	Contributed (Ind. Costs & Cost Sharing)	Total Support
1980	110,000	404,820	255,479	174,811	353,166	1,298,276
1981	15,000	404,781	269,879	252,043	350,520	1,397,223
1982	110,389	162,917	281,347	311,030	337,614	1,203,297
1983	115,000	41,346	303,560	195,367	265,737	921,010
1984	115,000	--	409,626	138,019	263,526	926,171
1985	109,000	--	425,951	261,535	330,490	1,126,976
1986	119,000	23,940	490,664	404,118	404,633	1,442,355

Source: WRRI, Internal document.

In the late 1960s, the state began funding the institute through the university budget. These funds have been continued with annual increases for inflation. Other funding is derived from contracts with the DNRCD and through various cabinet offices, including the governor's office. The institute also currently receives approximately $450,000 annually in nonearmarked funds from the state legislature. In addition, by offering more practical and applied research, the WRRI has been able to increase its support through a cooperative effort with local governments, known as the North Carolina Urban Water Consortium. As of 1985, local government and university contributions totalled $560,000.[62]

The shift in federal and state roles is clearly exemplified by comparing funding levels for the WRRI in fiscal years 1980 to 1986 (see Table 6.2). In 1980, the federal government contributed a total of $514,820 to the WRRI. This included $110,000 in program support from USGS and $404,820 in other federal monies--some 40 percent of the $1,298,276 WRRI budget for that year. In 1984, the USGS program support increased to $115,000, but all other federal monies had been eliminated. Federal funding amounted to only 12 percent.[63] These funding levels have remained steady throughout 1986 and are expected to remain that way in 1987, when Congress is to take up reauthorization of the 1964 Water Resources Research Act. However, if Congress were to discontinue federal funding for the WRRI, it would not devastate the program, since nonfederal funds make up the majority of its water research support.[64]

Intergovernmental Relations

The WRRI has had a long tradition of involvement in the water resources planning and policy process in North Carolina. It has done so by participating in the activities of local, state, and federal governments; publishing informative papers that are understood by the public; interacting with citizens' groups; serving on advisory panels; and designing research specifically to impact on policy issues.[65] David Howells, the first director of the North Carolina WRRI, said that the key ingredient necessary for the institute to have an effect on water policy and planning is cooperation: "It is essential for members of the institute and faculty members to be viewed as colleagues and not as threats to programs and budget prestige by officials in state and local governments and organizations. Cooperative relations are important. By working together with people, over time, a trust is earned and cooperation facilitated."[66]

One very good example of the institute's commitment to multilevel cooperation is manifested in the WRRI advisory and technical committees. The advisory committee, representing state and federal agencies, industry, agriculture, the public at large, and local government, provides program guidance and review of research needs. Similarly, a technical committee, composed of university faculty representing many disciplines, lends professional expertise to institute programs and activities, particularly those related to research.[67]

In addition, these same cooperative efforts have provided the institute with an important mechanism for transferring information and technology, assisting in the North Carolina water policy and planning process. According to David Howells: "Cooperative relationships and people play an important role as a conduit for input that is passed back and forth. As a result, the community of water resource people in the field begin to think of the institute as a separate entity independent of the university. They accept the institute as a normal part of the policy and planning process and actively seek the institute's assistance."[68]

Through its direct participation in legislative hearings, membership on advisory boards and commissions, and teaching at various levels, the institute has been able to tap the knowledge of research clients and to use this knowledge to provide them with the type of information and analysis most suited to their situation.[69] Tangible results of the researcher-user interface include: advice to the DEM on changes in environmental management; assistance in changing the North Carolina Water Code for use of more water-efficient commodes; and provision of research and data to help win passage of the Erosion and Sedimentation Control Act.[70] The institute has also made use of user training sessions, short courses, and workshops. Recent technology transfer events have included dam safety workshops, aquatic weed workshops, a ground water seminar series, and a conference on protecting North Carolina's surface drinking water for use by water managers and/or research faculty.[71] This approach has facilitated a smoother application of research findings.

Since 1964, the WRRI has evolved into the state's prominent water research agency. Through aggressive management, the institute has established a strong community presence, by participating in activities of local, state, and federal governments. After 20 years, the institute has completely incorporated itself into North Carolina's water planning and management process. By fostering intergovernmental relations, the institute has achieved two things: (1) it has broadened both its political and financial base for research, and (2) it has created channels for transferring research into the policy arena. Because of this, the WRRI has established itself as a vital part of state water resources management.

The North Carolina Urban Water Consortium

The North Carolina Urban Water Consortium was established in 1985. The consortium consists of six North Carolina cities or related organizations that have agreed to fund water research organized by the North Carolina Water Resources Research Institute of the University of North Carolina. The cities include Raleigh, Durham, Winston-Salem, High Point, Burlington, and the Orange Water and Sewer Authority, which serves the Chapel Hill area. The purpose of the consortium is to maintain a program of research and technology transfer that will result in higher quality and more cost-effective water supplies and services to urban residents.[72]

With an increasing need for research to support these changes in water resources policy and a decline in federal research dollars, other funding sources were needed. An opportunity to address these needs existed by taking advantage of the climate of cooperation and professionalism that had been fostered by the Water Resources Research Institute over the last 20 years.

The idea of forming the consortium began with David Moreau, the current director of the WRRI. Moreau began exploring alternative means of raising research monies when he arrived at the WRRI in 1983. An engineer with extensive experience in water research, he had been on the faculty of the University of North Carolina since 1968. Moreau also spent seven years on the board of directors at Orange Water and Sewer Authority, serving as chairman for three years.[73] Additional help came from a senior administrator at North Carolina State University. Dr. Franklin Hart, vice chancellor for research, agreed to Moreau's request that the university absorb the consortium's overhead costs indefinitely.[74]

Funding for the consortium comes from several sources. Each participating city contributes a base fee of $10,000 a year to the basic program. These monies will allow several research projects to be funded each year. As described later, cities pay additional costs for research projects that directly apply to them. In addition, the consortium has received a $140,000 grant from the U.S. Environmental Protection Agency to help fund an analysis of toxic substances in the effluent at High Point.[75]

Moreau serves as executive director of the consortium and acts as executive secretary to the consortium's advisory committee. He is responsible for the execution of the research program, communicating with the advisory committee and the researchers. Each member of the consortium is represented on the committee, usually by its utility or public works director. The advisory committee recommends the annual research program to the director; establishes and makes appropriate changes in the consortium's by-laws that are consistent with university rules and regulations; and provides general guidance to the director and oversight of the consortium's operations.[76]

Current Research Projects

The consortium's first two research projects were still under way in the spring of 1987, although they were scheduled to be completed later that year. One was a study of biological ways to remove phosphorus from effluent. The second project was the development of computer software to schedule preventive maintenance for water and sewer facilities.

Existing chemical methods of removing phosphorus are expensive and leave a sludge that is difficult to dispose of. A biological approach offers the prospect of a less expensive way. Burlington, Durham, and Orange Water and Sewer Authority each contributed $66,000 to the project; the state contributed $200,000; and the university agreed to pay $100,000 in overhead costs.[77] The study involves testing effluent samples to determine the most effective biological method of removing phosphorus. Moreau believes that the phosphorus study, while still incomplete, is the consortium's most effective accomplishment to date. "It has already had a significant impact on state policy," he said. "We had enough success with the program to convince the state that they ought to change their standards."[78]

The computer software project would allow the cities to more effectively schedule maintenance for their water and sewer systems. Moreau said that it is difficult to schedule maintenance on water and sewer systems because of their size and complexity. All of the cities in the consortium have participated in this project. By late April 1987, the consortium researchers had begun to train city personnel on how to operate the computer software and were receiving feedback from the cities on how the software worked in practice.[79]

The Institute of Government

The Institute of Government was established in 1932 at UNC in Chapel Hill. Its original founder envisioned the institution as "consisting of a group of men putting their full time and effort into studying, writing and teaching about state and local government in North Carolina for the primary, immediate benefit of public officials and employees who staffed those governments."[80] Throughout its 55-year history, the institute has made extensive contributions to the formulation and implementation of sound government practices. A large portion of senior management personnel in local government throughout the state have received specialized training or continuing education from the institute.[81]

The institute is staffed mainly with attorneys. Other disciplines represented include public administration, political science, accounting, and economics. The institute provides a variety of training programs for local officials by writing, printing, and distributing publications and by working closely with officials in the state legislature and government.[82] While the institute's main concern is not with water resources research, it has, in its role as an extension service, made significant contributions to water resources policy and planning.

In the past, the institute's faculty has served on various resource committees in the general assembly, aiding legislators in the formulation of water legislation and law. Institute faculty also teach courses on water-related subjects in graduate schools. Like the WRRI, the Institute of Government makes extensive use of user training sessions, short courses, and workshops, some of which are presented periodically throughout the year. One such program is the institute's cooperative effort with the School of Public Health. This three-day short school for the state's county sanitarians teaches them what they need to know about permitting for absorption sewerage systems and spray irrigation systems.[83]

Funding for the Institute of Government comes from a variety of sources--the majority through the state's university budget. The remaining

STATE WATER POLICIES / 133

30 percent is divided between state and federal grants, consulting fees, publications, and a state fee system. Under the fee system, which provides over $500,000 annually, each city in North Carolina is charged a voluntary fee, on a per capita basis, for the service provided by the institute. The fee system has been a success in the past and, with increasing revenues from this source, future funding prospects appear good.[84]

CASE STUDY: THE FALLS-JORDAN WATERSHED PROTECTION INITIATIVE

This case study addresses water quality problems in the Falls-Jordan Watershed. Despite development of the water supply, its quality makes its value as a source of potable water questionable. The study illustrates the value of intergovernmental cooperation, facilitated by the Triangle J COG, in coming to a consensus on how to reduce the level of water pollution in the watershed.

The Nature of the Problem

While recent activity centers around the protection of the 2,500-square-mile watershed surrounding the Falls and Jordan Reservoirs, initial quality concerns were focused on problems with B. Everett Jordan Lake. The projected water quality of Jordan Lake has been of considerable concern since the project was first envisioned by the Corps of Engineers around 1945. Water quality also was a concern in the early 1970s when the project was delayed by several legal actions, including a request for an adequate environmental impact statement, as required by the National Environmental Policy Act of 1969. These early water quality concerns were primarily over eutrophication and suitability of water for recreation. In 1979, however, a federal court decision allowed completion of the project, despite continuing concerns about water quality.[85]

The comprehensive protection for the two multipurpose reservoirs (including Neuse Lake) became an issue again in proceedings to reclassify portions of the lake and watershed as a suitable source of drinking water. These proceedings took place during the summer of 1983, as a result of considerable public concern over the unprecedented growth in the Triangle J research area and the adverse impact of new development, which led to eutrophication of the lakes.[86] In October 1983, the North Carolina Environmental Management Commission classified both reservoirs as public water supply sources. However, the commission denied, and continues to deny, authorization of Jordan Lake as a source of potable water until more data are gathered about trace metals and synthetic organic chemicals present in the watershed. In that same year, as a result of excessive algal growth and degraded water quality, the Environmental Management Commission classified the Falls and Jordan watersheds as nutrient sensitive, providing the state with an explicit regulatory mechanism for point source phosphorus control.[87] While local officials in the Triangle J region supported the commission's designation as a preventive measure, they also feared such controls would bring with them added costs in waste water treatment. Although Jordan Lake's immediate suitability as a source of water supply was uncertain, local government officials in the Triangle J region, who were concerned about future water demands, initiated an intensive effort to prevent further degradation of B. Everett Jordan Lake and the Falls of the Neuse Reservoir.

In 1983, the Triangle J COG Water Resources Program Committee passed a resolution requesting state cooperation to help the local governments of the region to work together on water management and land-use ordinances within the Falls and Jordan watersheds. Despite the creation of an ad hoc steering committee of mayors and county board chairmen from 16 jurisdictions in the watersheds, the steering committee has only existed on paper and has never met in the four and one-half years of its existence. This was due largely to the perception that the water resources program of the Triangle J COG would be the primary designer of the watershed protection plan. Its long history of ongoing involvement in the section 208 planning process was recognized throughout the state as the most effective intergovernmental effort of its type.[88]

The Role of the Triangle J COG

The Triangle J Water Resources Planning Committee has played several roles in facilitating the Falls-Jordan watershed initiative. First, the planning committee has acted as a mechanism for identifying policy and related research needs. For example, a major question concerning removal of phosphorus from the lakes centered upon the method of removal. The traditional removal method using chemicals was expensive and produced a sludge of no value.[89] Participants in the Triangle J program recognized a need for an inexpensive alternative to chemical use. Officials of the WRRI, who are regular advisory members on the Triangle J Water Resources Committee, recommended a study on the possibility of biological removal of phosphorus. This study is currently under way.

Another research objective that has been requested by the committee is the development of an aquatic bioassay to measure the toxicity of point source discharges into natural waters. The Triangle J Water Resources Committee requested the Division of Environmental Management (DEM) to apply the bioassay to Jordan Lake and its tributaries to help establish existing levels of toxicity. Data gained would be used to determine the suitability of Jordan Lake as a water supply.

Second, the committee functions as a coordinating mechanism between state and local officials and facilitates the procedures for setting priorities and developing policies. In 1983, officials at the North Carolina Department of Natural Resources and Community Development designed, with local officials in the Triangle J region, a state and local action plan. The three basic targets of the action plan were agricultural runoff, point source phosphorus, and hazardous materials in leaks and spills. As part of the plan, state and local officials agreed to a semiformal action agenda setting basic goals and responsibilities.[90] Policy responsibilities were divided within traditional regulatory and jurisdictional roles.

Finally, the Triangle J Water Resource Committee facilitates the often circuitous process of transferring information on viable alternatives to decision-making bodies. Because the committee consists of both officials from the DNRCD and a representative of the general assembly, local officials and other committee members are given the opportunity to apprise them of viable alternatives in the attainment of social and environmental goals. This interaction was a significant factor in getting a phosphate detergent ban on the state agenda as a possible policy alternative to removal of phosphorus from point sources, such as waste water treatment plants.

Methods to Protect the Watershed

Land Development Controls
A major component of the state and local action agenda for protecting the Falls and Jordan Lakes was the use of stringent zoning and land-use ordinances. While the DNRCD suggested a need for top-down, state-mandated development standards for watershed protection, the historic role of local control and regulation in zoning and land-use ordinances, combined with the perceived expertise of the Triangle J water resources program in the section 208 nonpoint source program, supported the contention that development standards for watershed protection should remain in the hands of local governments and should be implemented on an voluntary basis.[91]

Specifically, the Triangle J COG developed a three-tiered set of recommendations for the type and location of new development in the Falls-Jordan watersheds, based on the principle of providing greater protection to areas closest to the lakes. These guidelines included the designation of water quality critical areas for one mile around each lake, limiting new development to a low-density, rural, residential character with no industrial development. Beyond the critical areas, but within public water supply portions of the watershed, industrial development would be limited. Basinwide guidelines attempted to control new development throughout the 2,500-square-mile watershed, with recommendations as to impervious cover limitations and vegetated buffer zones along streams.[92] According to Ed Holland, director of the Triangle J Water Resources Program, the cities and counties closest to the Falls and Jordan Lakes have made substantial progress, modifying local ordinances to comply with the recommended guidelines.[93]

Agricultural Cost-Share Program

Another major policy component of the state and local action plan is the agriculture cost-share program. It was recognized early on in the section 208 planning process carried on by the Triangle J COG, that utilization of good soil conservation practices was the key to reducing the phosphorus that results from the use of fertilizers and pesticides. The need to aid farmers in soil conservation practices was an urgent, vital part of a comprehensive nonpoint agenda. The DNRCD's involvement with the Triangle J Planning Committee further reinforced their support for the state-funded cost-share program for agriculture.[94] Although federal funds to aid farmers in soil-conservation practices were available under the 1977 Clean Water Act Amendments, few farmers found them attractive, as they were required to enter into five- to ten-year contracts with the Department of Agriculture. Moreover, federal support for the national 208 program was phased out by 1981. Consequently, in 1984, the DNRCD requested that the general assembly appropriate $2.45 million for cost-share grants to farmers.[95] The general assembly authorized a $2 million biennial state cost-share program, which provided up to 75 percent funding for agriculture best management practices.

Point Source Phosphorus

As mentioned earlier, heavy nutrient loading led to the Environmental Management Commission's classification of the Falls Jordan watershed as nutrient sensitive and provided the state with an explicit regulatory mechanism for point source phosphorus control. Concerned about additional waste treatment costs, citizens and local officials in the Triangle J area immediately supported an effort to ban the use of laundry detergents containing phosphates. It is important to note that the idea for a phosphate ban originated from a study in the DNRCD. However, it drew little attention until officials from the DNRCD presented the alternative to the Triangle J Planning Committee.[96] Local officials on the Triangle J Water Resource Committee were able to promote the phosphate ban as an alternative to legislation. Congressman Joe Hackney, a member of the Natural and Economic Resources Committee, initiated the legislation for a clean detergent bill in the State Assembly, while serving as a state senator. In 1984, the North Carolina House of Representatives passed legislation banning the sale of household detergents containing more than 0.5 percent phosphorus in the Falls and Jordan watersheds. However, vigorous opposition, led by the Soap and Detergent Association, stalled the bill in the Senate.[97] Subsequent attempts to implement such a ban resulted in passage of the bill by the Senate in 1987, followed by approval in the House, making it law immediately.[98]

In addition, the state has offered an alternative to those localities that have been required by the nutrient-sensitive designation to remove phosphorus from effluent. The secretary of the DNRCD proposed a basic tradeoff: "if you [local governments] take certain actions to reduce nonpoint runoff then we [state government] might not have to require phosphorus removal at your treatment plants...."99 This alternative has sparked local interest in the Falls-Jordan watershed protection plan and the aggressive implementation of the local land-use guidelines.

Funding

The increasing involvement of state and local government in the policy process has contributed significantly to its success. However, little progress could have been achieved without a firm financial commitment. As mentioned earlier, the Triangle J COG was one of the first areawide agencies in the country to qualify for section 208 funding. In fact, early federal funding was expressly in anticipation of the completion of the Falls and Jordan Reservoirs. As Ed Holland, director of the Triangle J Water Resources Program stated: "This was the beginning of the initiative to protect these two bodies of water. Much of the earlier effort of the 208 process was an attempt to get arms around the scope of the problems administratively."100

In 1981, the Triangle J COG experienced a 70 percent loss of external funding for its water resources activities. From 1981 to 1985, it relied on an annually decreasing share of 208 support passed through the North Carolina DNRCD, as part of the Clean Water Act Amendments. The local governments comprising the Triangle J COG expressed their support for the water resources program by increasing the percentage of their general COG dues from $6,000 in 1978 to over $50,000 in 1985. When federal pass-through money for "areawide" programs was cut off in 1985, the state assembly appropriated $70,500 to the Falls-Jordan watershed protection program.101

CONCLUSIONS

1. Floods and droughts have been intermittent problems in North Carolina, and the federal government took the lead in building large water development projects. With a growing population, it is likely that additional water supplies for public consumption, industrial use, and agriculture will be necessary. As the federal role declines, the state will have to play a more active role.

2. North Carolina traditionally has been more active in water quality issues. Both point and nonpoint source pollution is a problem, and in 1951 the state passed its first antipollution legislation. However, a great deal of the initiative has come from the local level, as in the case of the 1973 Sedimentation Control Act.

3. The Council of Governments, and in particular the Triangle J COG, has provided a valuable forum for the resolution of water quality problems. Under its auspices, local governments were able to agree on land-use controls and the need to reduce phosphorus contamination. To this end, the general assembly passed legislation restricting the sale of laundry detergents

containing phosphorus and provided funding for a cost-share program, enabling the implementation of agricultural best management practices.

4. The North Carolina WRRI's aggressive and interdisciplinary approach to water resource issues has shown that it can affect the state's policies and planning. In particular, the Urban Water Consortium has helped in the development of a program of research and technology transfer that will result in higher quality and more cost-effective water supplies and services to urban residents. In addition, its member cities provide financial support to the WRRI for research of problems of mutual interest. This will help to insulate the research efforts of the consortium from fluctuations in government funding.

5. Traditionally, North Carolina has not taken the initiative in developing water policy for the state. Most of the activity occurred at the federal level or was initiated locally. There is some evidence that this is changing. If North Carolina can continue to foster its research efforts and integrate them into the policymaking process, it will be in a good position to solve its future water problems.

Material for this chapter was provided by Bryan Murdock and Henry Welles.

NOTES

1. Department of Natural Resources and Community Development (DNRCD), "Drought Advisory Bulletin" (Raleigh, N.C.: DNRCD, November 17, 1986), p. 4.

2. Lawrence S. Earley, "Water: The Looming Crisis," *Wildlife in North Carolina* (August 1982), p. 22.

3. Water Resources Research Institute of the University of North Carolina (WRRI), *Floods and Droughts* (Raleigh, N.C.: WRRI, 1978), p. 4.

4. Interview with David Moreau, director, Water Resources Research Institute, Raleigh, North Carolina, January 12, 1987.

5. Department of Natural Resources and Community Development (DNRCD), *Water Quality and Urban Stormwater: A Management Plan* (Raleigh, N.C.: DNRCD, Division of Environmental Management, 1979), p. 2.

6. Milton S. Heath, "Ground Water Quality Law in North Carolina," draft of article for *Popular Government* (Chapel Hill, N.C., n.d.) (hereafter cited as "Ground Water Quality Law").

7. Heath, "Ground Water Quality Law," p. 3.

8. Raymond Burby, David Moreau, and Edward J. Kaiser, *Financing Water and Sewer Extensions in Urban Growth Areas: Current Practices and Policy Alternatives*, WRRI Report no. 232 (Raleigh, N.C.: WRRI, September 1987), pp. 14-18.

9. Earley, "Water: The Looming Crisis," p. 16.

10. Earley, "Water: The Looming Crisis," p. 14.

11. Earley, "Water: The Looming Crisis," p. 21.

12. Interview with David Howells, former director of WRRI, Raleigh, N.C., January 14, 1987.

13. Earley, "Water: The Looming Crisis," p. 21.

14. Legislative Research Commission, "State Infrastructure Needs," Report to the General Assembly of North Carolina (Raleigh, N.C., 1986), p. K2.

15. Interview with John Morris, director, North Carolina Division of Water Resources, Raleigh, N.C., January 12, 1987.

16. Interview with John Morris, January 12, 1987.

17. U.S. Geological Survey, *Activities of the U.S. Geological Survey Water-Resources Division in North Carolina, 1985-86* (Raleigh, N.C.: 1986), p. 3.

18. Maynard Hufschmidt, *State Water Resources Planning and Policy in North Carolina* (Raleigh, N.C.: WRRI, February 1979), p. 9 (hereafter cited as *State Water Resources Planning*).

19. David H. Moreau, "Water Quality Planning in North Carolina," July 1977, unpublished manuscript.

20. *The General Statutes of North Carolina* (Charlottesville, Va.: The Michie Co., 1986), Section 143-215.1.

21. *Congressional Quarterly Almanac*, 93d Congress, 2d session, 1974, vol. XXX (Washington, D.C.: Congressional Quarterly, Inc.), p. 423.

22. *The General Statutes of North Carolina*, Section 130A-311.

23. Hufschmidt, *State Water Resources Planning*, p. 10.

24. U.S. Environmental Protection Agency, Office of Water Regulations and Standards, *Proceedings of a National Conference, Perspectives on Nonpoint Source Pollution*, Kansas City, Missouri, May 19-22, 1986, p. 96 (hereafter cited as *Proceedings of National Conference*).

25. North Carolina Public Interest Research Group, *Citizens Guide to Water Quality in North Carolina* (Durham, N.C.: pamphlet, n.d.).

26. Hufschmidt, *State Water Resources Planning*, p. 5.

27. North Carolina Department of Natural and Economic Resources (NCDNER), *North Carolina Water Resources Framework Study* (Raleigh: NCDNER, 1977), pp. 1-2.

28. Hufschmidt, *State Water Resources Planning*, p. 50.

29. Hufschmidt, *State Water Resources Planning*, p. 5.

30. Interview with David Howells, January 14, 1987.

31. Department of Natural Resources and Community Development, "Is Your Water Supply Protected?" (Raleigh, N.C., n.d., pamphlet).

32. *The General Statutes of North Carolina*, Section 130A-54.

33. Interview with Roger Schecter, director, Pollution Prevention Pays Program, North Carolina Department of Natural Resources and Community Development, March 27, 1987.

34. WRRI "EPA Borrows Director of NC's Pollution Prevention Pays Program," *WRRI News* 247 (November/December 1987), p. 4.

35. North Carolina Department of Natural Resources and Community Development, "NC Department of Natural Resources and Community Development" (Raleigh, N.C.: brochure, n.d.).

36. Interview with Allen Brochman, hydrologist, North Carolina Division of Water Resources, Raleigh, N.C., January 14, 1987.

37. Interview with William Lyle, hydrologist, U.S. Geological Survey, Raleigh, N.C., January 15, 1987.

38. Brad Stuart, "Making North Carolina Prosper: A Critique of Balanced Growth and Regional Planning," A report (Raleigh, N.C.: North Carolina Center for Public Policy Research, 1979), p. 63.

39. Interview with Ed Holland, director, Triangle J Water Resources Program, Research Park, N.C., March 14, 1987.

40. Public law 92-500.

41. Legislative Research Commission, "Haw River and Jordan Reservoir Water Quality," Report to the 1985 General Assembly of North Carolina (Raleigh, N.C.: December 1986), p. G-1.

42. Terry D. Edgmon, "Municipal Intergovernmental Relations and Water Resource Decision Making in the Triangle J Region," WRRI Report no. 166, (Raleigh, N.C.: WRRI, June 1981), p. 29.

43. *United States Code Congressional and Administrative News*, 95th Congress, 1st session, 1977, vol. 3 (St. Paul, Minn.: West Publishers, 1977-78), p. 4328.

44. Sheron K. Morgan, "Seven Policy Options for Financing Water and Waste Water Facilities in North Carolina," *Popular Government* (Spring 1986), p. 44 (hereafter cited as "Seven Policy Options").

45. Legislative Study Commission on Alternatives for Water Management, "Alternatives for Water Management," Report to the 1980 General Assembly of North Carolina (Raleigh, N.C.: March 1980), p. E-1.

46. Morgan, "Seven Policy Options," p. 45.

47. Interview with Joe Hackney, representative, North Carolina General Assembly, Chapel Hill, N. C., January 14, 1987.

48. Legislative Research Commission, "Haw River and Jordan Reservoir Water Quality," p. H-4.

49. Morgan, "Seven Policy Options," p. 45.

50. David Godschalk and Milton Heath, *Water Resource Planning in North Carolina* (Chapel Hill: Institute of Government, 1964), pp. 76-77.

51. Interview with David Moreau, January 12, 1987.

52. Godschalk and Heath, *Water Resource Planning in North Carolina*, pp. 76-77.

53. Public law 88-379.

54. *Congressional Quarterly Almanac*, 87th Congress, 1st sess., 1964, vol. XXI, p. 508.

55. Water Resources Research Institute, *1986-87 Program* (Raleigh, N.C.: University of North Carolina, n.d.), p. 1.

56. WRRI, *1986-87 Program,* p.1.

57. Hufschmidt, *State Water Resources Planning*, p. 39.

58. Interview with David Moreau, January 12, 1987.

59. Warren L. Viessman, Jr., "Research as an Aid to Decision Makers: Policy Implications and Processes for Implementation," National Water Resources Research Conference (draft working paper, n.d.), p. 6 (hereafter cited as "Research as an Aid to Decision Makers").

60. Viessman, "Research as an Aid to Decision Makers," p. 10.

61. Interview with David Moreau, January 12, 1987.

62. Interview with David Moreau, January 12, 1987.

63. Water Resources Research Institute, "Institutional Commitment," mimeographed (Raleigh, N.C.: University of North Carolina, 1986), p. 1.

64. Interview with David Moreau, January 12, 1987.

65. Viessman, "Research as an Aid to Decision Makers," p. 4.

66. Interview with Howells, January 14, 1987.

67. WRRI, 1986-87 Program, p. 1.

68. Interview with David Moreau, January 12, 1987.

69. Viessman, "Research as an Aid to Decision Makers," p. 12.

70. Interview with David Moreau, January 12, 1987.

71. WRRI, 1986-87 Program, p. 21.

72. David Moreau, "The North Carolina Urban Water Consortium: A New Approach to Research on Urban Water Resource Problems" (Paper delivered at the annual meeting of the University Council on Water Resources, Amherst, Mass., July 1985) (hereafter cited as "North Carolina Urban Water Consortium").

73. Interview with David Moreau, Austin, Tex., March 13, 1987.

74. Interview with David Moreau, April 27, 1987.

75. Interview with David Moreau, January 12, 1987.

76. Moreau, "North Carolina Urban Water Consortium."

77. Moreau, "North Carolina Urban Water Consortium."

78. Interview with David Moreau, April 27, 1987.

79. Interview with David Moreau, April 27, 1987.

80. John Sanders, "The Institute of Government at Fifty," Popular Government (Winter 1981), p. 1.

81. Interview with Milton Heath, assistant director and professor of public law and government, Institute of Government, Chapel Hill, N.C., January 14, 1987.

82. Institute of Government, "Institute of Government" (Chapel Hill: University of North Carolina, pamphlet, n.d.).

83. Interview with Milton Heath, January 14, 1987.

84. Interview with Milton Heath, January 14, 1987.

85. Department of Natural Resources and Community Development (DNRCD), Division of Environmental Management, Water Quality Section, "Toxic Substances in Surface Waters of the B. Everett Jordan Lake Watershed and September 1985 Update" (March 1985), p. 6 (hereafter cited as "Toxic Substances").

86. DNRCD, "Toxic Substances," p. 7.

87. EPA, Proceedings of National Conference, pp. 97-99.

88. Interview with Ed Holland, January 15, 1987.

89. Interview with Ed Holland, January 15, 1987.

90. EPA, *Proceedings of National Conference,* p. 97.

91. Legislative Research Commission, "Haw River and Jordan Reservoir Water Quality," p. D-8.

92. EPA, *Proceedings of a National Conference,* p. 97.

93. Interview with Ed Holland, January 15, 1987.

94. Interview with Ed Holland, January 15, 1987.

95. Legislative Research Commission, "Haw River and Jordan Reservoir Water Quality," p. E-4.

96. Interview with Ed Holland, March 14, 1987.

97. EPA, *Proceedings of National Conference,* p. 98.

98. Interview with Congressman Joe Hackney, September 15, 1987.

99. Interview with Congressman Joe Hackney, September 15, 1987.

100. Interview with Ed Holland, January 15, 1987.

101. Legislative Research Commission, "Haw River and Jordan Reservoir Water Quality," p. G-2.

TEXAS

BACKGROUND
Historical Factors

Flooding

Flooding is a significant problem in Texas, causing millions of dollars worth of damage annually to urban and rural areas. Flooding along coastal areas can also be serious, resulting from periodic heavy inland rains, hurricanes, high tides, and insufficient natural drainage. Because of the diversity of topography in the state, different methods have been used in different regions to protect against the effects of flooding. Structural methods used to control both inland and coastal flooding include levees, flood storage in reservoirs and channelization. Nonstructural methods, such as regulating the development of flood-prone areas, advance warning systems, and evacuation plans, have also been used.

Between 1913 and 1915 the state experienced cataclysmic floods and droughts. As a result, a conservation amendment that formed the basis of Texas water resources financing from 1917 to 1957 was adopted. This amendment gave local and regional agencies, such as cities, water districts, and river authorities, primary responsibility for the financing of water projects. Until 1957 there was no state role in water resources planning.[1] While these regional entities provided some relief from flooding during this period through the construction of reservoirs, local interests also petitioned the federal government for assistance. The first Corps of Engineers project in the state was Denison Dam, which formed Lake Texoma on the Red River and was completed in 1943. Since that time, the Corps has constructed many of the major reservoirs, providing approximately half of the total storage capacity in reservoirs with a capacity of 5,000 acre-feet or more.[2]

Today, water demand is increasing such that reservoirs, which were once built primarily for flood control, are increasingly facing pressure to be used as water supply "storage tanks". As more water is stored, there is less reservoir capacity left in reserve to contain runoff, increasing the possibly of flooding. Floods caused by dams unable to hold the excess water have already occurred in several states.

Development below dams, or even near the normal conservation pool level of impounded lakes, has encroached into zones that have the potential to flood during severe storms. One example of this is the extensive residential development along the Colorado River on Lake Austin and Lake Travis above Austin. The most severe storm of record above Lake Travis occurred on September 10, 1952. This led to the water level in Lake Travis rising 56 feet in about eight hours, from a level of 619 to 675 feet mean sea level.[3] Fortunately, this storm occurred at a time when Lake Travis was at its lowest level since its initial filling, enabling it to capture a storm volume of 720,400 acre-feet. Had the storm occurred when the lake power storage was full, the flood pool would have filled, and homes below the spillway crest would have been flooded. Also, releases through the floodgates would have been made, and these would have caused millions of dollars worth of damage downstream.

Research is under way to develop computerized methods, using real-time data collection systems, to assist decision makers in the management of the reservoir systems on the Colorado River during these extreme storm events. Yet these procedures can only minimize the severity of flood damage risk. Flood damage is likely at some future date because of development in flood-prone zones. Water planners in Texas will face continual pressure regarding the tradeoff in reservoir capacity usage between water supply storage and flood control.

State Water Planning

After an extended drought in the 1950s, broken by extensive heavy rains and flooding in the spring of 1957, the legislature, in special session, adopted the Water Planning Act of 1957. The first report under this act, entitled "Texas Water Resources Planning at the End of the Year 1958," was submitted to the 56th Texas Legislature.[4] However, the first major effort in water planning began in Texas in August 1964. It was initiated when Governor John Connally included the following words in an official document: "Therefore, by authority granted me under Article V, Section 22, House Bill 86, 58th Texas Legislature (the General Appropriations Act), I hereby request the Texas Water Commission to use any available moneys appropriated under that Act to begin at once to develop a comprehensive State Water Plan."[5]

This planning function was shifted to the Texas Water Development Board (TWDB) and became effective on September 1, 1965. The preliminary report on the first Texas Water Plan was published in May 1966. It included numerous proposed reservoirs and a scheme to transfer surplus surface water from northeast Texas to Dallas, and ultimately to the

Lower Rio Grande Valley via sections of the Trinity and Brazos Rivers and canal systems. The plan proposed that water from the Colorado River would be transported via a canal from the Austin area to San Antonio. The initial scheme included no provision for transfer of water to water-short west Texas, either from within or outside the state.

Public discussion on the preliminary plan resulted in numerous changes, which were incorporated in the final plan, published in the fall of 1968.[6] It proposed a canal parallel to the Gulf Coast in order to transfer water from the Sabine River north of Port Arthur to the Lower Rio Grande Valley, providing water to Corpus Christi and other locations along the way. In the final plan, San Antonio would not get water from the Colorado River near Austin, but from Canyon Reservoir on the Guadalupe River and other proposed reservoirs. Another change was the inclusion of a proposed Trans-Texas Division, transferring water from northeast Texas due west to a proposed distribution point, Bull Lake, to be located in the High Plains, northwest of Lubbock. Proposed spur canal systems would provide water to San Angelo, Abilene, and other cities in that western part of the state.

The 1968 plan emphasized the need for out-of-state water in Texas. It said, "Importation of water from out-of-State sources is essential to the future development of Texas, and must begin no later than 1988. Planning indicates that by 2020 as much as 12 to 13 million acre-feet per year may need to be imported."[7] The plan suggested that this imported water should come from the lower Mississippi River. The capital cost estimate, exclusive of the out-of-state structures for importation and the appurtenant irrigation distribution facilities, was approximately $6.3 billion. Irrigation distribution facilities were to be a local responsibility and were estimated to be $250 to $300 per irrigated acre.

The referendum to broaden the powers of the TWDB and to finance the implementation of the water plan was placed on the ballot in 1969.[8] The referendum narrowly failed, with 49.5 percent voting for and 50.5 percent against it. As a result, schemes for water importation were given a significant setback.

However, water transfer schemes continued to be debated at both the state and federal levels. In 1976, the Six-State High Plains-Ogallala Aquifer Regional Resources Study was authorized by Congress under PL 94-587, section 193, at a cost of $6 million. One purpose of the study was to develop plans to increase water supplies in the six-state High Plains area of the Ogallala Aquifer. The study area covered all of Texas from the Pecos-Odessa-Midland area northward to Amarillo and extended on to include much of Nebraska.[9] Several important policy issues were considered in the study. Some mentioned by Harvey Banks, who was the study director for the project's consortium of consulting firms, were as follows: Should promotion of, or a requirement for, conservation of water and energy in irrigation enterprises be a major federal objective and program? Would it be in the public interest to legally restrict current usage of the ground water with near-term economic detriment in order to prolong the availability of water for future economic benefit?[10]

The economic studies of the five alternate routes considered for importing water to the High Plains, two of which would bring water to Texas, were reported by William R. Pearson of the Southwestern Division of the U.S. Army Corps of Engineers. He estimated the annual cost of systems to transfer 8.7 million acre-feet to a point near Lubbock to be as high as $3.8 billion.[11] The unit cost of water at a central distribution point on the Texas High Plains in 1977 dollars ranged from $308 to $569 per acre-foot, depending on the amount of water and the route selected.[12] Landford estimated that an additional $200 to $400 per acre-foot would be needed to construct the local distribution systems to deliver water from a terminal storage facility to the farmer's headgates. Further, Landford states, "Farmers can only afford to pay about $150 per acre-foot."[13] It is apparent that the cost of importing water to replace depleted ground water for irrigation cannot be justified unless there are major changes in economics of the farming enterprise. The voters have not been willing to support the needed subsidy for such projects.

Because the High Plains-Ogallala Aquifer study involved Texas officials, this added to the perception that state leadership was linked to water transfer plans. There was fear that large funding authorizations would ultimately be used to initiate large-scale water transfer activities. In 1976, a proposal for water development bonds was rejected by 57 percent of the voters. The same result occurred in 1981 on a proposal to allocate a portion of the excess revenues of the state for water development, again by 57 percent opposition, at a time when the state financial condition was rather good. Voting pattern analysis clearly showed that those residents in the more populous humid east Texas counties strongly opposed the proposition, while the opposite was true in the High Plains counties where more than 75 percent supported it.[14]

Critical Issues

Projected Future Water Demands
Precipitation is highly variable from month to month and year to year. On the average, from east to west, precipitation decreases about one inch per 15 miles.[15] For the period from 1950 to 1979, rainfall averages ranged from eight to ten inches per year in the far west Texas desert region near El Paso, to over 56 inches per year in southeast Texas, near the Gulf of Mexico.[16] Thus, although overall the state expects to have only minor shortfalls in water supply, several areas are expected to have regional water shortages in the near term (Figure 7.1).

The upper Rio Grande and far west Texas region, where rainfall is scarce, just barely met water demands in 1980 and cannot meet low demand projections by 1990. The west central region cannot meet high projections in 1990 nor low projections in 2020.[17] It should be noted that the economic base in these areas is dominated by irrigated agriculture, which accounts for 72 percent of the total water consumption in the state (Table

7.1). The total value of Texas agricultural production in 1984 was $3.6 billion. Although only 30 percent of all cropland was irrigated, those acres contributed 50 to 60 percent of the total crop value.[18]

The recent population boom in Texas has directly increased municipal water needs. Texas cities rely either on surface water, ground water, or a combination of the two. Municipal use accounted for 16 percent of all water used in Texas in 1980. Many Texas cities could be facing water shortages in the near term if water-use projections are correct. High population projections suggest water consumption in some cities, such as Austin, will more than double by 2020. Even under a low projection scenario, Austin's water use will double by 2030.[19]

TABLE 7.1 Estimated Water Use in Texas, 1965-80

	1965	1970	1975	1980
Population (millions)	10.60	11.20	12.24	14.23
Consumption by use (offstream)				
Total (mgd)	12,180	9,650	12,800	10,940
Public supply	470	510	730	640
Rural use	170	240	300	400
Irrigation	11,000	8,100	11,000	8,000
Industrial	540	800	770	1,900
Per capita (gpd)				
All uses	1,149	862	1,046	768
Excl. irrigation	111	138	147	207
Withdrawals by source (fresh water only)				
Total (mgd)	19,600	19,200	24,000	14,300
Ground water	13,000	9,200	11,000	8,000
Surface water	6,600	10,000	13,000	6,300

Source: U.S. Geological Survey, *Estimated Use of Water in the United States, 1965; Estimated Use of Water in the United States, 1970; Estimated Use of Water in the United States, 1975; Estimated Use of Water in the United States, 1980,* Geological Survey Circulars 556, 676, 765, and 1001 (Reston, Va.: U.S. Department of the Interior, 1968, 1972, 1977, and 1983).

**FIGURE 7.1 Projected Water Demand as a Percent
of Supply for Texas by Region for 2020**

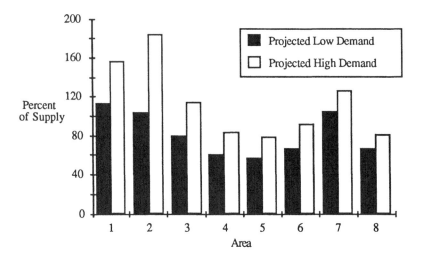

Area: 1. Upper Rio Grande and Far West Texas
       2. High Plains and Trans-Pecos
       3. West Central Texas
       4. North Texas
       5. Northeast Texas
       6. South Central Texas
       7. South Texas and Lower Gulf Coast
       8. Southeast Texas and Upper Gulf Coast

Source: Texas Department of Water Resources (TDWR), *Water for Texas:
A Comprehensive Plan for the Future*, Volume 1 (Austin Tex.: TDWR,
November 1984).

Texas has an extensive coastline, which makes an important
contribution to the Texas economy. The value of commercial seafood
harvested in 1983 was $192 million.[20] Many of the ocean-based plants and
animals that provide an integral part of the coastal food chain are dependent
on fresh water inflows to bays and estuaries at critical times during their life
cycle. This same water might otherwise have been used inland. In the eyes
of some inland users, this water is all but "wasted." Water released for this
purpose is not included in the water consumption figures given earlier, but it
is nevertheless a significant part of Texas' overall water needs. Compared
with Texas' 17.85 maf of water used inland in 1980, estuary fresh water
requirements are reported to range from 4.7 maf for minimum survival of
the coastal ecosystem, to 13.6 maf per year to provide maximum
enhancement of the coastal food chain.[21] There is a continuing battle

between upstream users and coastal interests, including environmentalists, over how much water should be reserved for this purpose.

Surface Water

Approximately 64 percent of the state's surface water is being used to meet current water needs.[22] These water supplies are not distributed evenly across the state, and some areas are projected to be unable to meet their future needs. The state water plan delegates most planning authority to river authorities and water districts, but cities are also required to plan for their own water needs. Thus, conflicts between the various water planning entities, sometimes operating in the same river basin, arise. Although the TWC has some power to settle these disputes, TWC commissioners, who "perform the legislative and judicial functions of the Texas Water Commission,"[23] are not well equipped to do this.

A major dispute between two authorities operating on different stretches of the Colorado River may foretell future water supply problems. A permit to the Colorado Municipal Water District for the construction of Stacy Reservoir, issued by the Department of Water Resources, was contested by the Lower Colorado River Authority on the basis that there was insufficient unappropriated water in the Colorado River to meet all of the outstanding appropriations. The issue was whether water that had been authorized to be appropriated under a certified filing or a permit, but had never been beneficially used, became unappropriated water that could be reassigned without cancellation of all or part of the original permit.[24] Heavy political pressure was applied to both parties to resolve the situation, which threatened to destroy the emerging political consensus necessary for the development of comprehensive water legislation. Thus, despite a Texas Supreme Court ruling in favor of the Lower Colorado River Authority, Stacy Reservoir is currently under construction.

In Texas, allocation of surface water rights is based on two criteria: prior appropriation and beneficial use. Prior appropriation is a "first in time, first in right" approach. However, the criteria of beneficial use is superimposed onto the prior appropriation criteria, stating that water rights can be listed according to priority of use, as well as seniority of right or length of ownership. For example, municipal use has a higher priority than recreational use. The first seven priority uses were enumerated in the 1931 Wagstaff Act,[25] while number eight was added by the 69th legislature in 1985. Table 7.2 lists the beneficial use categories for surface water in Texas by priority.

The addition of category eight is important, not only for the fishing industry, but also because it represents progress in the state's attitude toward a more comprehensive outlook and management system. It is the one important result of the TWDB Bays and Estuaries Program begun in 1971.[26] For the first time in Texas, fresh water needs for bays and estuaries must be considered in relation to the states' other water needs. Nevertheless, a great deal remains to be done and a well-organized, cohesive, statewide water management system is far from reality today.

TABLE 7.2   Beneficial Use Priorities for Texas Surface Water

Priority	Use
1	Domestic and Municipal
2	Industrial Processing
3	Irrigation
4	Mining and Mineral Recovery
5	Hydroelectric Uses
6	Navigation
7	Recreation and Pleasure
8	Bays and Estuaries (1985)

Source: Water District and River Authority Study Committee, *Report to the 70th Texas Legislature*, vol. 1 (Austin, Tex.: December 1986), p. 31.

Ground Water

More than 50 percent of Texas is underlain by seven major and 16 minor aquifers. In the mid-1930s, this ground water supplied approximately 670,000 acre-feet annually, or about 22 percent of annual consumption.[27] With the development of large-scale irrigation in west Texas in the 1950s, the growth in ground water usage was extremely rapid. By 1980, ground water supplied 10.85 maf annually, which was 61 percent of all water used in Texas. Annual natural recharge of these aquifers averages only 5.3 maf per year. This ground water overdraft has been a long-standing and increasingly severe problem in Texas. In 1980, irrigated agriculture alone withdrew 8.96 maf. It is predicted that if the statewide consumption of such underground water continues at the present rate, the supply available for irrigation use will decrease by 50 percent by 2030.[28] For instance, the Ogallala in the Panhandle region, the Alluvium and Bolson deposits clustered in west and north Texas, and the Trinity Group and Carrizo-Wilcox aquifers, which run parallel from northeast to southwest Texas, are all experiencing a decreasing underground water supply. Pumping costs are increasing as the water table declines and water becomes more difficult to withdraw.

Texas ground water law is based on the "absolute ownership rule," which states that "percolating waters are the private property of the landowner." That is, stationary ground water deposits underneath a property owner's land are completely at the disposal of the landowner, who may pump water at any rate he wishes, so long as the withdrawal is not done maliciously to harm a neighbor. Even though underground streams or aquifers are legally state property, just as surface streams and rivers are, Texas courts have held that the question of a defined underground stream must be conclusively proven.[29] The practical result is that landowners pump ground water as though it were truly owned by them. However, many think that ground water regulation is inevitable if Texas is to meet the challenges of growth and a falling water table.

In some areas, another consequence of overdrafting is subsidence, which is a gradual sinking of vast areas of land as the water underneath is pumped out. Ground water pumpage in the Houston-Galveston area has caused both subsidence and salt water intrusion.[30] The Harris-Galveston Coastal Subsidence District was established by the state legislature in order to regulate the pumping of ground water as a means of controlling subsidence in the Houston area. This district was given unusual powers by Texas standards in an effort to bring the costly subsidence of already low-lying and flood-prone lands under control. It has been successful in arresting the subsidence process in its area of jurisdiction, although the land remains lower than it was before overdrafting began. Areas outside the district boundaries still are experiencing significant subsidence.

Interstate and international conflicts over ground water use pose a challenging problem. For example, the city of El Paso won the first round of a suit against New Mexico regarding importation of water from another state. El Paso was permitted to draw water from a nearby underground water source, located primarily in New Mexico and used as a local supply in southern New Mexico. This decision regarding the interstate commerce of water paralleled an earlier decision in the Sporhase case.[31]

Water Quality
Besides diminishing the water supply, overdrafting of ground water may cause other problems such as salt water intrusion. Like surface rivers, most aquifers "flow" to a sea outlet; when these aquifers are severely overdrafted, the normal fresh water gradients to the sea may be reversed. Sea water may flow toward producing wells, causing salt water pollution of the aquifer and making the water unfit to drink. Other sources of ground water pollution are runoff from city streets and agricultural drainage. The use of nitrogen-rich fertilizers is thought to be a major cause of increasing nitrate concentrations found in ground water.

Another major concern is industrial pollution. Texas has made some progress in controlling traditional industrial pollution relating to oxygen-demanding wastes. For example, the biochemical oxygen demand loading on the Houston Ship Channel, once among the nation's most polluted bodies of water, is now less than a third of the 1970 level.[32] Although Texas has avoided the serious pollution problems associated with heavy industry in the northeast and north central United States, increasing industrialization is making pollution control more difficult, particularly in regard to the highly toxic wastes. In and around Houston, the heart of Texas industry, lie several of the high-priority toxic waste sites on the U.S. Environmental Protection Agency's (EPA) superfund cleanup waiting list. There have also been isolated cases of chemical dumping within the state. A future concern will be safe disposal of radioactive waste, such as from the nearly completed South Texas Nuclear Project.

Deep-well injection is the currently preferred means of disposing of toxic wastes in Texas. Such wastes are injected into a well that extends deep below the earth's surface, below currently tapped ground water supplies. One problem is that the deep-well injection process is relatively new, and as a result, many are concerned about how stable these formations are and whether they will hold these deadly pollutants for the indefinitely long period of time that is needed. Improperly designed deep-well injection deposits could be a potential "pointsource" pollution problem.

To the surprise of some, industry has made greater strides in recent years in the control of traditional pollutants (oxygen-demanding substances) than cities. To some extent this has been the result of EPA regulations and assistance programs during the 1970s. However, Texas was, until recently, experiencing a booming growth rate. Many cities found it impossible to finance and construct waste water treatment facilities rapidly enough to keep up with demand. Inadequate planning, defeat of bonding programs, and other factors contributed to the problem, but the end result was periodic spills and releases of insufficiently treated waste water in the receiving streams. The resulting general perception in the early 1980s was that the Texas Department of Water Resources (TDWR), the state pollution control agency, was not being sufficiently rigorous in pursuing and correcting pollution problems.

STATE INITIATIVES IN WATER RESOURCE MANAGEMENT
Policy Development

In 1981, following a series of unsuccessful referenda to finance water development projects, a new approach to water planning began to emerge in Texas. It was apparent that a base for statewide support must evolve if support for water development activities was to emerge. Greater attention to the fresh water needs of bays and estuaries was necessary to gain support of coastal county voters. Complex environmental issues must be better expressed. Also, conservation of water and reuse emerged as a key to meeting future needs instead of depending so heavily on new supplies.

Lieutenant Governor Hobby exhibited strong interest in a balanced approach to water planning. Recognizing the need for a more comprehensive approach to water resource management, he worked with a task force on water use and conservation, appointed by the governor to develop recommendations on water policy. Despite attempts to craft a balanced package of water legislation that would accommodate all interest groups (at least to some extent) the package did not make it through the 68th (1983) legislative session. The House of Representatives modified the package in favor of traditional development interest, and the conference committee was unable to come to an agreement.

Meanwhile, the TDWR sensed its problems, and for the first time, a major organized effort was undertaken to get public input regarding the

Texas water planning activity, utilizing a formal survey by Beldon Associates and TDWR questionnaires on key issues.[33] A draft of a new water plan was released by the TDWR in 1983, followed by a final report in two volumes. The plan, entitled *Water For Texas: A Comprehensive Plan For the Future*, was formally published in 1984, following a period of public comment. It is based on the 1969 Texas Water Plan, and utilized public input and the recommendations of three committees that had been formed to review and update the plan. These committees were organized into three areas: finance, water resources use and conservation, and water importation.[34] The plan emphasizes water conservation and a broad range of statewide water issues, scarcely mentioning water importation. Also, the flexibility of the plan is stressed. This plan has been adopted by the Texas Water Development Board (TWDB) and is now the official plan for the state.

In order to pave the way for better success in the 1985 legislative session, the legislature appointed a Joint Committee on Water Resources, and it held statewide meetings in late 1983 and 1984. With much preparatory work behind it, the draft legislation introduced into the 69th legislative session was generally received with favor. Again, there were areas of disagreement between the two houses, with the Senate being much more supportive of strong environmental provisions than the House. The lieutenant governor, working with the Senate, took the lead in keeping the effort on track and not letting the elements of disagreement balloon into a major regional conflict that could kill the chances of meaningful water legislation. The bill that emerged from the conference committee was a compromise, winning approval from divergent groups, despite a high level of controversy. The general consensus was that, given the diversity of interest groups concerned with water issues, this was probably the best that could be expected from the Texas legislature in the current political climate. Most agree that it could not have happened without astute political leadership, which included the crafting of a resolution to the Stacy Reservoir conflict.

The package of water legislation approved by the Texas legislature in 1985 included a state-backed loan program for local water projects, emphasizing conservation as a first order of business. Flood control, water quality, and the development of regional water and sewer systems were also highlighted. In the required referendum, more than 70 percent of the voters supported a constitutional amendment authorizing $980 million in state general obligation bonds, plus an additional $450 million in bond insurance. Other legislation passed by the legislature in 1985 related to the institutional aspects of water management. The state water agencies were reorganized, and the regional water districts and river authorities, which had been created on an ad hoc basis to address specific problems, were placed under review.

The concern about the conflict between the Colorado Municipal Water District and the Lower Colorado River Authority over Stacy Reservoir, and the fact that the river authorities tended to take a strictly regional view, as opposed to a statewide perspective, appeared to be the catalyst for legislative review of the operations of river authorities and water districts. The Water District and River Authority Study Committee was authorized and directed to determine if the powers of water districts and river authorities were too great and if changes in their operations were needed. Members of the committee were appointed by the governor, lieutenant governor, and speaker of the house. One issue was whether organizations in Texas were working together or operating independently. Also of concern was whether conservation was being adequately encouraged and sufficient attention was being given to environmental issues. The committee was directed to report its recommendations, including needed changes in state law, to the legislature before the 70th session started in January 1987.

The study committee held statewide meetings throughout the year and drafted six pieces of legislation, none of which were enacted. They encompassed three general areas pertaining to the operations of river authorities and water districts. The Texas Water Commission (TWC) would have been strengthened significantly, by giving it greater powers to enhance the overall management of the state's water resources. In addition, a Texas water resources management oversight committee would have been created to provide continuing supervision over the operations of each entity and to examine the relationships between them. While two of the bills related specifically to management of ground water, S.B. 673 authorized the TWC to adopt rules to promote conservation of water, regionalization, and protection of the environment.[35] Again, opposition came from the water districts, who wanted to keep rule making at the local level. They argued that each locality can better tailor such rules to the individual needs of the district. However, the evidence clearly suggests that in some cases districts have been formed with the major intention of preventing direct intervention by the legislature.

Implementation

Reorganization of State Water Agencies
The history of the state water agencies is long and varied. In 1913 the state's first water agency, the Board of Water Engineers, was created by the 33rd legislature. It was responsible for regulation of water rights, based upon the prior appropriation doctrine. The Texas Water Pollution Advisory Council, established by the legislature in 1953, was responsible for coordinating the state's water pollution control activities. In 1957, at the end of the worst drought in Texas history, the Texas Water Development Board was formed. The board was to coordinate development of water supplies statewide and to administer the Water Development Fund, which is the state's primary means of financing water projects. The Texas Water Planning Act of 1957 created the Texas Water Resources Planning Division in the Board of Water Engineers.

In 1977, following several organizational changes, all of the water agencies were combined to form the TDWR. The Water Quality Board (originally the Water Pollution Control Board) was disbanded, and the Water Rights Commission (originally the Board of Water Engineers) was replaced by the Texas Water Commission. However, a statutory sunset review of the TDWR in 1984 brought legislative attention to water quality issues, among other things. It became apparent that the agency should be more aggressive in pursuing polluters. Only eight years after its creation, the 69th legislature in 1985 abolished the TDWR as an agency and created the TWC and the TWDB.

The Texas Water Commission (TWC) is the state agency with primary responsibility for implementing state water law, including regulation and enforcement policy. The TWC is also responsible for water rights, water pollution control, including water quality planning, and for administering Texas's portion of the National Pollution Discharge Elimination System. The commission is the state supervisory agency for river authorities, ground water districts, water control and improvement districts, municipal utility districts, and other water districts.[36] However, the commission does not provide direct supervision of these organizations. Its new duties under reorganization also include responsibility for regional solid waste planning, solid and hazardous waste regulation, and in a catch-all phrase in Senate Bill (SB) 249, all functions formally delegated by law to the TDWR except for those specifically assigned to the TWDB.

As a result of its increased powers granted by the legislature at the time of reorganization, it has the authority to impose administrative fines of up to $10,000 per violation for noncompliance with waste water discharge permits.[37] In addition, the TWC is required to bring enforcement action any time an entity is substantially in noncompliance for four consecutive months.[38] In 1986, the TWC assessed a total of $1,131,819 in administrative fines against municipalities in Texas, not including a fine of $500,000 against the City of Houston for previous violations.[39]

The Texas Water Development Board (TWDB) also received new responsibilities in 1985 as a result of SB 249. Authority over application and designation of local sponsors for federal projects was transferred from the TWC to the board. The TWDB retained control over the state water plan, all state-funded research and planning, and financial assistance programs, including the new Agricultural Trust Fund and the Pilot Loan Program created by the passage of House Bill 2 in 1985 and subsequent voter approval (see section on funding). This program relates to a new state initiative and loan program to promote better water conservation in irrigated agriculture. The TWDB remained the state's liaison with the U.S. Army Corps of Engineers and the U.S. Bureau of Reclamation.

The state's expanded role in conservation is illustrated by provisions in the 1985 legislation that require cities to delineate a conservation program in order to qualify for financial assistance from the TWDB for water development projects. In addition, the TWDB has a conservation education program utilizing pamphlets on topics such as: "A Homeowners Guide to Water Use and Water Conservation" and "Water Savings Ideas for Business and Industry." The TWDB is coordinating its public education program with the Texas Education Agency and the Texas Agricultural Extension Service.

Water Planning

Although the legislature relies on the TWC and TWDB to implement state and federal laws, it has also created other governmental entities that deal with local and regional water issues more directly. Historically, Texans have preferred to keep power and authority at home--preferably in the hands of individual citizens or, for necessary governmental functions, at the local level.[40] The management of Texas' water resources has followed this pattern, the operational aspects of water resources management being mostly at the local or regional level. By giving localities the freedom to implement their own water regulations, the state has attempted to avoid the political battles associated with state-imposed regulation of water resources. These governmental units can be classified into three types: municipalities, river authorities, and water districts.

Water institutions have been created under general law authorization or by a specific act of the legislature to address problems as they have emerged. The districts operate as semiautonomous political entities, under the supervision of a governing board. Texas now has over 1,200 water districts, 20 river authorities, and several larger municipal water supply districts. In several cases, there is more than one river authority or district operating in different segments of the same river basin, providing the seeds for conflict and misunderstanding. It is generally agreed that these local entities have, in the past, done a good job in carrying out their assigned functions. Nonetheless, there have been recent cases of serious conflict leading to litigation.

Two examples of the conflicts that could occur illustrate the problem. One concerns surface water rights when two river authorities operate in the same basin and both aspire to develop and market additional supplies. Such a case occurred in the dispute between the Lower Colorado River Authority (with jurisdiction on the lower portion of the Colorado River) and the Colorado River Municipal Water District (operating on the upper reaches) over the proposed Stacy Reservoir. Another example is the potential conflict between a ground water management district and a river authority with overlapping service areas. The district's function may include augmenting ground water recharge, and it may want to build detention structures to facilitate recharge with surface water. The river authority has interest in capturing that surface water in its reservoirs for sale and hydropower generation. The potential for conflict is evident, and too often costly and time-consuming litigation is the result.

Municipalities. Cities have responded to water challenges in several ways. Several cities operate extensive water supply systems and own reservoirs. In some cases, such as Dallas, the city developed a long-range supply plan in response to the severe drought of the early 1950s, and have an ensured supply for many years to come.[41] Other cities buy water from regional river authorities or water supply districts, usually under long-term contracts. Some cities have developed their own programs for water conservation. Since 1968, El Paso has had a water conservation program, which includes a building code requiring newly constructed bathroom fixtures to meet water-saving specifications, an inverted rate structure, and a yearly contest to encourage desert landscaping in residential areas. The city has saved over 5 million gallons of water per day with a pipe replacement program to reduce leakage.[42]

Lubbock has been using municipal waste water for irrigation purposes since 1925. Amarillo sells waste water, instead of treated potable water, to a power plant and refinery, saving the city money and reducing demand for treated water. Dallas has a summer surcharge rate structure, which discourages high summer water use.[43] Austin has adopted both voluntary and mandatory water rationing over the past several years, primarily as a response to inadequate water treatment capacity, rather than supply shortages. Austin also provides water-saving devices, such as toilet dams and low-flow shower heads, to water customers who want them.

River Authorities. River authorities in Texas date back to 1929 and were created out of the perceived need to coordinate federal, state, and local flood control and water storage projects within a single river basin. Created by the state, river authorities are autonomously governed bodies and a principal means for surface water policy implementation in Texas. River authority directors are generally appointed by the governor, approved by the senate, and serve six year terms. In a few cases, directors are elected. Despite the fact that most of them have taxing authority, they rely almost exclusively on user fees and bond revenues for their operating budgets.

The river authorities vary greatly in size and scope of activity. The largest employs over 1,700 people and the smallest only two. Annual operating budgets vary from $200,000 to over $300 million. Their functions include water supply, electric power generation, flood control, recreation, and water quality. In general, river authorities were created on an ad hoc basis in response to specific problems and not as part of a master plan for water management in the state. Details of the operations of river authorities and water districts in Texas are provided in a recent study at The University of Texas at Austin.[44]

Water Districts. Water districts can be broken down into eight types, covering various areas, such as ground water, water improvement, navigation, irrigation, and municipal utility districts. Only ground water districts and municipal utility districts will be discussed here.

Ground water districts are increasingly important, as the state attempts to improve management of its numerous aquifers, several of which are subject to severe overdraft. Texas has attempted to use these districts, first created in 1949, to implement state ground water policy without direct state involvement.

These districts can only be created if:

1. The TWC designates that an underground reservoir existed;
2. The TWC or local county commissioner's court decides that such a district is desirable and feasible; and
3. The local voters approve it in a majority of the counties involved, or the legislature passes a special act bypassing these procedures.[45]

However, several bills were introduced into the 70th Texas Legislature to assist in the formation of these districts and strengthen the protection they afford to ground water supplies. Similar bills were introduced by Senator Montford, a member of the Water District and River Authority Study Committee, by Representative Guerrero, a member of the National Groundwater Policy Forum chaired by Governor Babbitt; and several other legislators. In general, these bills, which were defeated in the House, had two major provisions:

1. In order to expedite the formation of additional ground water districts, the TWC would be given the power to create interim districts if the voters failed to approve such districts in critical ground water areas, as designated by the TWC. The TWC then acts as the district directors until the voters in the district area vote to form their own ground water district.
2. The TWC would be given the authority to set minimum district pumping standards and to order noncomplying districts to enforce their regulations, including the minimum standards set by the TWC. This is an important step toward ground water regulation, as many districts often do little either in the realm of creating regulations or enforcing them. In some cases, they may have been created to keep the Texas legislature from passing stronger legislation that could mean direct state control.

Municipal utility districts have all of the functional responsibilities attributed to water districts, except for irrigation and drainage. Typically, they are created to raise low-cost funds to pay for the water and waste water infrastructure for houses being built by private developers. The initial investment is paid for by bonds, which may be repaid over a 20-year period. In theory, the recipients of the services repay this debt. However, as the municipal utility district's area grows and merges with an adjacent city, the debt will be transferred to the public sector as a part of the annexation process.[46]

Financing

Water Development Fund

The state's primary means of funding water projects is through the Water Development Fund, administered by the TWDB. According to Sue Clabaugh, supervisor of the Financial Section of the Water Development Fund, TWDB, "this Fund was created in 1957 by a constitutional amendment, and was originally funded at $200 million in state bonds. This figure was raised to $400 million in 1966, and to $600 million in 1984."[47] This money, in the form of general obligation bonds, is to assist local communities and "political subdivisions" in developing water supplies.

On November 5, 1985, the voters approved $980 million worth of state general obligation bonds as provided by the 69th legislature in House Joint Resolution 6 and House Bill (HB) 2. The Water Development Fund consists of four separate accounts, as shown in Table 7.3:

    1. The Water Development Account, which provides loan funds for water supply projects and for projects enabling a switch from ground water to surface water use;

    2. The Water Quality Enhancement Account provides loan funds for waste water treatment systems;

    3. The Flood Control Account provides loan funds for flood control projects, both structural and nonstructural; and

    4. The Acquisition Account allows the state to buy a share of the storage capacity in regional reservoirs for resale to political subdivisions at a later date, and to acquire parts of regional water and waste water treatment systems. One purpose of this provision is to ensure that projects are developed to their optimum size, even if the local sponsor does not require the entire supply. This latter option came about as a result of HB 2 and is the first time that the TWDB could use a state-participation account for this type of acquisition.[48]

TABLE 7.3 69th Texas Legislature HB 2 Funding for Water Development Fund

Account	Amount Authorized
Water Development	$190 million
Water Quality Enhancement	$190 million
Flood Control	$200 million
Acquisition	$400 million
Total	$980 million

Source: Texas Water Development Board.

While the authorization of the $980 million in state bonds appeared to be good for Texas water agencies, the economic downturn in the state in the two years since the 1985 approval has been detrimental to bond sales. According to Sue Clabaugh, "the first sale of bonds under the 1985 appropriations took place on March 19, 1987. A total of $150 million was approved: $110 million for the Water Development account and $40 million for the Flood Control account. However, the funds have not been delivered yet."[49]

House Bill 2 also directed the TWDB to establish a bond insurance program. Under this program, the state would pledge $250 million in credit to insure certain local water-related bonds against default. The bond insurance program would use an initial leverage ratio of two to one and limit the total amount of bonds insured in any fiscal year to $100 million.

Another new feature, introduced by HB 2, was the directive that all loan applications above $500,000 for state aid must also submit a water conservation plan that shows "reasonable diligence" in conserving water. The conservation plan may restrict discretionary uses, such as lawn watering and car washing, and may include educational programs, drought contingency plans, and water rates that encourage conservation. Subject to availability of funds, the TWDB must provide technical assistance to help local governments draw up conservation plans. This money would come from the Water Assistance Fund's Research and Planning Fund.

Water Assistance Fund

This second major fund administered by the TWDB was created in 1981 by the 67th legislature and financed with $40 million in appropriations. This is a holding fund from which the board may distribute money to three separate subfunds:

1. Water Loan Assistance Fund, which provides loans for water, sewer, and flood control projects;
2. Storage Acquisition Fund for state acquisition of portions of reservoirs; and
3. Research and Planning Fund, which supports a regional water supply and sewage collection and treatment planning grant program. Funds are available for up to 50 percent of the cost of developing plans for regional water supply and flood control systems.[50]

As part of the legislative program to implement agricultural elements of the Texas Water Plan, HB 2 created an Agricultural Trust Fund and a Pilot Loan Program within the Water Assistance Fund, financing them with $15 million.[51] This money provides grant and loan funds, respectively, for the improvement of irrigation techniques. The 69th legislature also gave authority to either the 70th (1987) or 71st (1989) legislatures to approve future sales of state bonds worth $200 million, for further water conservation loans, if the Pilot Loan Program yields positive results.

THE ROLE OF WATER RESEARCH
Research in State Institutions

In general, state agencies do not have their own research programs. The TWDB is the primary state agency financing water research and planning, by distributing funds from the Water Research and Planning Fund. For the two-year period ending March 31, 1987, $9 million was spent. The TWDB has an additional budget, amounting to $4.1 million in 1986, for data collection and analysis.[52] The TWDB's role in water research is mainly one of keeping abreast of the status of research throughout the state and distributing its research funds to universities, municipalities, river authorities, and other entities that conduct the actual research.

The state university network is composed of 33 Texas colleges and universities, all of which have researchers who indicate some degree of involvement in water research.[53] The state legislature appropriates funds specifically for water research to only three universities: Texas A&M University, Southwest Texas State University, and Texas Tech University. A summary of state support for water research at each of these three institutions is shown in Table 7.4. In addition, The University of Texas at Austin earmarks some of its own money for water research.

TABLE 7.4 Specific State Support of Water Research at Texas Universities, Fiscal Year Ending August 31, 1987

Institution	Research center/project	Appropriation (dollars)
Agriculture Experiment Station (Texas A & M University)	Water Resources Research	2,113,428
	Texas Water Research Institute (includes $109,000 of federal funds)	309,126
Texas Tech University	Research in water, water conservation and reuse	168,790
	Research in alternate energy sources, including agricultural irrigation	358,795
	Research on problems of arid and semiarid lands	74,173
Southwest Texas State University	Edwards Aquifer Research and Data Center	206,562

Source: *Vernon's Texas Session Law Service 1986*, vol. 16 (St. Paul, Minn.: West Publishing Co., 1986), p. 457.

Texas A&M University is a key actor in the state's water research effort. This is mainly due to the university's focus on agriculture and the fact that it contains the only state-supported agriculture research center in Texas: the Texas Agriculture Experiment Station. As its name implies, its water research efforts revolve around agricultural applications. Given the importance of agriculture to the overall state economy, it is not surprising that the Agriculture Experiment Station receives substantial state funds. For the fiscal year ending August 31, 1987, the state appropriated $42,291,069, of which $2 million is designated for water-related agricultural research. There are 14 research centers in Texas that receive money through the Agricultural Experiment Station, which serves as a conduit for research funds and keeps abreast of their individual research activities. Each center tends to specialize on research topics that cater to regional needs.[54]

The state also contributes funds to the Texas Water Resources Institute (TWRI) at Texas A&M. Its 1986-87 budget was $309,126, which included federal formula funds of about $109,000. The TWRI is administratively a part of the Agriculture Experiment Station, but sets its own research agenda, distributing funds to other institutions. For the fiscal year ending September 1, 1988, 23 preproposals were received by the TWRI. Following review by the TWRI advisory committee, eight full proposals were requested by the director. Of the eight full proposals requested, four received funding from the TWRI. These grants are generally too small to complete most water research projects. Rather they are used as "seed" funds so that researchers can collect preliminary data in order to better compete for federal or other funds.[55]

In the past, the TWRI's close association with the Agriculture Experiment Station resulted in an emphasis at the institute on agriculture-related water research. However, recently there has been a shift in focus to water quality research, due to a continuing emphasis at the federal level on water quality and an awareness that the state faces significant water quality problems.[56]

In addition to the three universities that received state funds, many other Texas colleges and universities participate in some level of water research activity. The largest is The University of Texas at Austin, which has the Center for Research in Water Resources. The 1986-87 state appropriation for the university included $185,869 allocated to the center.[57] The focus of the center is on improving water management and water-related environmental problems of Texas. In recent years, topics of particular concern have been hazardous waste management, ground water pollution, and better management of existing water resources through conservation and optimization of reservoir operations. The total water research budget was nearly $1.4 million in fiscal year 1987.[58]

Texas was part of the five-state Southern Plains Region of the Water Research Institute Program, administered by the U.S. Geological Survey. In November 1985, the five-year plan for the region was published. Included in this plan were the water research priorities seen by representatives from this region. These were broken down into water quality, water supply, and socioeconomic and legal interactions. The inclusion of socioeconomic and legal interaction indicates that multidisciplinary water research is recognized as essential to maintaining sufficient supplies and adequate water quality to meet future needs.

Initiatives at the Local Level

There is evidence of water research being done by local and regional governmental entities, such as cities and river authorities. This research is primarily geared to specific problems encountered by these groups. For example, the City of Austin is involved in a waste water research center at its Hornsby Bend sludge treatment plant.[59] As part of a $40 million municipal bond package for improvements at the plant, Austin has established the Center for Environmental Research adjacent to the plant. This center will be devoted to applied research, primarily focusing on environmental water issues faced by municipalities, such as providing cheaper and higher quality waste water treatment. The center will solicit funds for various research projects, with faculty and students being provided by The University of Texas at Austin and Texas A&M University. The city will pay for the center director, as well as all construction costs. According to Andrew Covar, the center's director: "While most major universities have research centers, this is the first time, as far as we know, that two major universities have combined with a municipality to conduct long-term environmental research."[60]

The Lower Colorado River Authority (LCRA) has budgeted $500,000 to determine the value of investing in new waste water treatments methods. Some of the possible methods to be evaluated include: water hyacinths, artificial wetlands, rock reed filters, and intermittent sand filtration. The objective is to find ways to treat waste water more cheaply and better than traditional, chemical-based methods.[61] The LCRA is also involved in research on private disposal systems, such as septic tanks and drain fields. It is responsible for maintaining water quality levels in the Highland Lakes, which are subject to the pressures of increasing urban development. Homeowners must provide their own waste water disposal systems, subject to approval by the LCRA, if located within 2,200 feet of the lakes. In particular, the LCRA is evaluating new, less expensive systems developed by private waste water disposal companies.[62]

Both the LCRA and Austin cases illustrate the various levels at which water research is conducted and needed in the state. Austin's Center for Environmental Research is being built by the city, with limited, indirect state support, through The University of Texas and Texas A&M University systems. The LCRA's pilot treatment project follows a similar pattern. The LCRA budgeted $500,000 for the project, with the possibility of an additional 10 percent funding from the EPA and state funds. It would seem appropriate for the state to finance such centers, as the research results could be used statewide. The fact that cities, such as Austin, and river authorities, such as the LCRA, are attempting to fill these gaps indicates a need for such research and highlights the somewhat limited state role in funding water research.

CASE STUDY: A WATER EDUCATION PROGRAM INITIATED BY THE TEXAS SOCIETY OF PROFESSIONAL ENGINEERS

This case study describes an innovative program, initiated and partially funded by a nongovernmental entity, to address water resource management through an education program. The Texas Society of Professional Engineer's (TSPE) Water Education Program for Texas is aimed at educating the people of Texas about water issues. It hopes to create the public awareness necessary to find and implement solutions to Texas' water problems, with conservation being an important element. The TSPE felt that water issues in the state have not received the public support commensurate with their importance. The program is directed toward education of the Texas youth to help the next generation better understand the future problems. Also, the children will in turn educate their parents.

Background

The Governor's Task Force on Water Resources report of 1981 contained the following recommendations, which form the basis for the Water Education Program for Texas:

Successful resolution of complex water resource problems is often dependent upon the degree of public understanding of the problem and the degree of public support for the solution. Given the importance of elective public participation in finding and implementing solutions to water resource problems, the State should actively support education and technical assistance efforts that will enhance the public's understanding of water resource problems and issues. The State, working with local and regional government, should assist in the development of and provide funding for curricula and educational materials and technical assistance in water conservation, water reuse and recycling, water quality management, water supply development, environmental management, and flood protection.[63]

Accordingly, special emphasis was placed on education as a means to increase conservation and water quality improvement efforts. Based on a statewide public opinion survey regarding the Texas Water Plan, it was discovered that the people of Texas felt that education was an appropriate response to the state's water challenge. In this questionnaire, one out of three Texans with an opinion on the issue felt that education was the best approach to encouraging water conservation, while 81 percent felt that education would be an effective method of controlling consumption.[64]

It was realized that it was cheaper and easier to educate schoolchildren through existing schools, than to try to educate the Texas populace at large. It was hoped that educating schoolchildren would result in an increasing awareness among their parents, thereby educating both present and future voters about statewide water concerns.[65]

Implementation

Phase I
The Texas Society of Professional Engineers (TSPE) was the instigator of the present Texas water education effort. The TSPE represents all 19 engineering disciplines and has about 9,500 members statewide. It is the largest state engineering society in the nation. The society was founded in 1936 to promote "engineering professionalism," and began its water education efforts in 1954, when the first TSPE Water Education Committee was formed. Then in 1983, a new Water Education Committee was created in order to study and evaluate ways to educate Texans about water issues within the state.[66] It had the "ultimate goal" of getting a "water curriculum integrated into the standard school curriculum on a self-sustaining basis,"[67] eventually reaching "every child in every grade (kindergarten through grade 12) in every school in the state for the rest of the century."[68]

In early 1983, the Water Education Committee of the TSPE initiated a pilot water education program in selected Texas schools, funded entirely by a $9,000 grant from the TSPE. The pilot program was the first phase of the TSPE's effort to evaluate the prospects for a statewide water education program. Its curriculum was developed for the TSPE by Water and Man, Inc., of Salt Lake City, Utah.[75] Three school districts--Midland, Richardson, and Kilgore--representing three distinct areas of the state, were chosen to field test the water education program.[70] The program was soon endorsed by the Texas Education Agency and teachers from grades 4, 6, 9, and 11 were instructed on the Water and Man curriculum, beginning in May 1983. Further teacher training and classroom instruction began in the fall of 1983.[71]

The results of questionnaires sent to participating teachers showed that the pilot project was a resounding success. Teachers and school superintendents alike were enthusiastic about the project,[72] which also earned the endorsement of the Texas Department of Water Resources, Texas Water Conservation Association, Texas Water Utility Association, American Water Works Association, and Texas Education Agency.[73] Following this wave of support, the TSPE Water Education Committee moved on to phase II of its education program.

Phase II

Phase II of the water education program was designed to determine if data obtained in phase I were truly indicative of success if implemented in a large-scale, statewide effort. It was budgeted at $249,500 and was to utilize 10 percent of the state's school districts (100-110 districts) and 1,500 of its teachers.[74] This dramatic budget increase was made possible by a $125,000 "challenge" grant from the TWDB in April 1984, which required matching private sector contributions. Over $70,000 of this matching amount has been raised, and the TSPE continues to obtain private support for the ongoing phase II process.[75]

The response to phase II was equally positive. Water education was being delivered to an increasing number of Texas schoolchildren, who had previously received little, if any, water-related instruction. As a result of efforts by the TSPE and the success of phase II of the project, the Texas State Board of Education implemented the TSPE Water Education Council's recommendation to have water education incorporated into the standard public school curriculum in Texas. The vehicle for this process was Proclamation 63, a February 6, 1986 directive issued to textbook publishers by the Texas State Board of Education. It specified that textbooks must include subject matter that empowers schoolchildren to do the following:

-- identify rivers and bodies of water (grade 2);
-- understand that water is managed for public and private benefit (grade 3);
-- locate and identify major rivers and bodies of water within and adjoining Texas (grade 4);
-- understand that the availability of resources such as water influence economic growth (grade 5); and
-- understand the effects of rivers and bodies of water on the development of culture and regions (grade 6).[76]

In addition, high school introductory physical science textbooks are directed to include information on water conservation, waste disposal, chemical disposal, and water management within the context of acquiring scientific skills and knowledge of scientific applications.[77]

The TSPE's dedication to water education was further demonstrated by a separate initiative started in the early 1980s. The TSPE committee worked with the National Forensic League in an effort to get the subject of water placed on the ballot to be considered as the national high school debate topic. They were not successful initially, but the committee persisted and water was selected as the 1985-86 high school debate topic. It was formally expressed as: "What is the most effective water policy for the United States?" The relatively rapid acceptance of the water issue as a debate topic indicates the importance and relevance of water issues to the nation, as well as Texas.[78]

Status of the Program

In 1986, the TSPE Water Education Council sought and received accreditation by the Texas Education Agency for its water education training sessions so that teachers receiving such training could get credit for their "career ladder," which is a Texas teacher promotional advancement program. Obviously, this strengthens the water education program, by providing an incentive for teachers to become qualified to teach water education courses. There are 20 Regional Education Centers in Texas providing consultants who plan and conduct teacher in-service training for nearly 90 percent of all Texas teachers.[79] These same centers are used for water education training for teachers.

Phase II of the Water Education Program for Texas is still in progress. The TSPE continues to provide educational materials and travel expense reimbursement for Texas schoolteachers desiring water education training and continues to conduct water education workshops for these teachers.[80] The TSPE also has a statewide network of educators who provide help and information to schoolteachers interested in water education. The society enjoys state cooperation from the TWDB, the Texas Education Agency, and the Texas State Board of Education and continues to work with textbook publishers to ensure that they are complying with the requirements of Proclamation 63.[81]

In addition, the water education concept seems to be spreading to other Texas water-related agencies. The Texas Water Development Board prints coloring booklets depicting Texas schoolchildren's thoughts on water conservation. These drawings were taken from the 4100 entries submitted by Texas schoolchildren for the State Water Conservation Logo Contest. Each of the nine finalists received letters of recognition from the governor and their drawings were displayed in the capitol building in Austin during October 1986.[82]

Further evidence of the expanding water education effort is apparent in education topics related to coastal water resource questions. In January 1987, two marine science workshops were conducted at The University of Texas Marine Science Institute in Port Aransas: one for elementary and one for secondary Texas schoolteachers. Two more workshops were scheduled in April and May 1987. Among other things, the teachers learned about constructing and maintaining salt water aquariums. The marine education program at Texas A&M had two seminars scheduled for junior high instructors in March and for senior high teachers in April 1987. These seminars were designed to show teachers how to focus on the skills needed to build and maintain salt water aquariums, as well as to understand the technological equipment that makes viewing of marine life in the classroom possible. The Texas A&M Sea Grant Program also publishes *Marine Education*, a quarterly pamphlet designed to inform elementary and secondary teachers about research and activities in the marine environment.[83]

Summary
There appears to be a genuine student interest in learning about water. This should go a long way toward educating the people of Texas about the importance of water and its limited available supply. The purpose of water education, as stated in *Water and Man Conceptual Framework for Water Education*, is to "help citizens understand the nature and importance of water, and the necessity for wise water management." Clearly, this education process will help Texas address its water issues in the future as Texas schoolchildren grow up. However, the extent of any near-term impact that this education will have on the political climate surrounding Texas' water problems depends not only on how well Texas schoolchildren learn, but also on how well they teach their parents. Nevertheless, the TSPE's Water Education Program for Texas is an important element in the state's attempt to solve its water problems.

CONCLUSIONS

1. A state with considerable geographic diversity, Texas is susceptible to both droughts and floods. As in other states, the federal government played a significant role in the early development of water supply and flood control projects. As this source of financial assistance began to wane, the state attempted to develop other sources for the financing of water development projects, including the importation of water from other states. Attempts to authorize bonds to finance water projects that could support such schemes were rejected by Texas voters in 1969, 1976, and 1981.

2. More recently, there has been a growing realization that better management of existing supplies must be a part of any proposed water development project. This was reflected by the passage in 1985 of a package of legislation, including bonding authority, which was approved by the voters and provided financing for water projects of several types. This legislation, which supported the Texas Water Plan, acknowledged the fact that water should be treated as a finite resource and that environmental concerns, such as the needs of bays and estuaries, should be addressed. Although the steps taken to deal with these problems were much less than many desired, most agree that they were moves in the right direction.

3. Despite the fact that ground water overdrafting is a serious problem in many areas, the formation of local ground water management districts is at the discretion of local inhabitants. Even when formed, the power of such districts to control overdrafting is often very limited. Likewise, attempts to manage the state's surface water supplies, by coordinating the efforts of the semiautonomous river authorities, so far have been unsuccessful.

4. The need to conserve existing water supplies has been addressed at several levels. The Texas Water Plan requires that requests for state assistance in the development of water supplies be accompanied by plans for conservation programs. In addition, some municipalities and river authorities have instituted their own, often voluntary, conservation

programs. A unique education program, initiated and partially funded by the TSPE, is designed to instill a conservation ethic in the state's schoolchildren and, hopefully, convey some of the information to their parents.

5. Although Texas has set up a fund in the Texas Water Development Board, relatively little money is spent on water research in Texas. Most of the existing projects are funded through the university system. With the current economic slump, it is unlikely that much-needed research into issues such as drought contingency planning and fresh water needs of bays and estuaries will receive needed attention.

6. Texas is slow to respond to social and environmental concerns, and this is reflected in its inability to develop progressive water policies and the necessary institutional framework for their implementation. The progress that has been made in the last few years has been the result of efforts on the part of particular interest groups. If this pattern holds for the future, changes in water policy in Texas likely will continue to be slow and incremental in nature.

Material for this chapter was provided by Pat F. Dalton and Stattler A. Mood.

NOTES

1. Donald L. Howell, "Financing Water Resources Projects in Texas," in *Water Resources, The Need for a Water Research Agenda,* ed. Ernest T. Smerdon, Water Resources Symposium No. 11 (Austin: Center for Research in Water Resources, The University of Texas at Austin, 1984), p. 55.

2. John McNeely and Ronald Lacewell, *Surface Water Development in Texas* (College Station, Tex.: Texas Agricultural Experiment Station, 1977), pp. 511-577.

3. Interview with David Maidmont, Department of Civil Engineering, The University of Texas at Austin, Austin, Tex., July 8, 1987.

4. Texas Water Development Board (TWDB), *Texas Water Development Board* (Austin, Tex.: TWDB, November 1968).

5. Texas Water Development Board (TWDB), *Water for Texas, A Plan for the Future,* preliminary draft (Austin, Tex.: TWDB, May 1966).

6. TWDB, *Texas Water Development Board,* p. vii.

7. Texas Water Development Board (TWDB), *The Texas Plan - Summary* (Austin, Tex.: TWDB, 1968), pp. 35-36.

8. Howell, "Financing Water Resources Projects in Texas," p. 54.

9. Harvey O. Banks, "Six-State High Plains-Ogallala Aquifer Regional Resources Study--An Overview," *WRRI Report no. 145* (Las Cruces, N.M.: New Mexico State University, May 1982), pp. 8-25.

10. Given Texas ground water laws, whether such an approach would be legal in the state poses an interesting question.

11. William R. Pearson, "High Plains-Ogallala Aquifer Study--Water Transfer Element," *WRRI Report no. 145* (Las Cruces, N.M.: New Mexico State University, May 1982), p. 147.

12. Robert M. Sweazy, "West Texas Water Resources: Beyond 2000," *Proceedings of Conference on West Texas Natural Resources: Economic Perspectives for the Future* (Lubbock, Tex.: ICASALS, Texas Tech University, 1983), p. 32.

13. Robert R. Lansford, "High Plains-Ogallala Aquifer Study, New Mexico--Economic Impacts," *WRRI Report no. 145* (Las Cruces, N.M.: New Mexico State University, May 1982), p. 63.

14. Robert A. Peterson, "1981 Constitutional Amendment Election--Voter Turnout and Voting Patterns" (Austin, Tex.: Office of the Secretary of State, January 1982).

15. Texas Department of Water Resources (TDWR), *Water Planning in Texas* (Austin, Tex.: TDWR, April 1984), pp. 1-2.

16. Thomas J. Larkin and George W. Bomar, "Climatic Atlas of Texas," *Texas Department of Water Resources (TDWR)* (Austin, Tex.: TDWR, December 1983), p. 18.

17. Texas Department of Water Resources (TDWR), *Water for Texas, A Comprehensive Plan for the Future, Volume I* (Austin, Tex.: TDWR, November 1984), pp. 45-47 (hereafter cited as *Water for Texas*).

18. Ernest Smerdon, "Irrigation Demands Need Conservation Technology for Next Century," *Texas Professional Engineers* (March/April 1987), pp. 6-8.

19. TDWR, *Water for Texas, Vol. I*, p. 26.

20. Herbert W. Grubb, "Water Resource Needs of the Texas Economy" (Paper delivered at the Water Law Conference, The University of Texas School of Law, October 3-4, 1985).

21. TDWR, *Water for Texas, Vol. I*, p. 36.

22. TDWR, *Water for Texas, Vol. I*, p. 12.

23. Texas Water Commission (TWC), *The Texas Water Commission* (Austin, Tex.: TWC, February 1986), p. 1.

24. Frank R. Booth, "Implications of the Stacy Dam Case," (Paper delivered at the Water Law Conference, The University of Texas School of Law, October 3-4, 1985).

25. Water District and River Authority Study Committee, *Report to the 70th Texas Legislature*, vol. 1 (Austin, Tex.: December 1986), p. 31.

26. Interview with Herman W. Hoffman, P.E., supervisor, Municipal and Commercial Conservation Unit, TWDB, Austin, Tex., March 10, 1987.

27. TDWR, *Water Planning in Texas*, p. 15.

28. "Shaky Economy Endangers Texas' Water Future," *Austin American Statesman*, October 19, 1986.

29. Ronald A. Kaiser, *Handbook of Texas Water Law: Problems and Needs* (College Station, Tex.: Texas Water Resources Institute, Texas A&M University, 1986), p. 32.

30. TDWR, *Water for Texas, Vol. I*, p. 7.

31. Sporhase v. Nebraska, 458 U.S. 941 (1982).
32. Bernhard Johnson, Inc., *Regional Asessment Study: Houston Ship Channel--Galveston Bay* (Houston, 1975).
33. Texas Department of Water Resources (TDWR), "An Overview of Texas Water Resources Problems and Water Resource Issues: As Related to Securing Public Input to Revise and Amend the Texas Water Plan," (Austin, Tex.: TDWR, February 1982). The results are provided in "Report of Findings: Public Input to Amend the Texas Water Plan," by Intergovernmental Work Group, June 1982. The Beldon Associates' results are in "A Statewide Public Opinion Study Regarding the Texas Water Plan--Summary Report," conducted for the Governor's Task Force on Water Resource Use and Conservation and TDWR, 1982.
34. TDWR, *Water for Texas, Vol. I*, p. 7.
35. Water District and River Authority Study Committee, *Report to the 70th Texas Legislature*, pp. 95-125.
36. Texas House of Representatives, *House Study Group Special Legislative Report*, no. 121, Austin, Texas, September 18, 1985, p. 24 (hereafter cited as *Special Legislative Report*).
37. Tex. Water Code, Chapter 26, section 26.136.
38. Tex. Water Code, Chapter 5, section 5.117.
39. Trinity Improvement Association, *Update*, March 1987.
40. E. T. Smerdon, J. A. Gronouski, and M. S. Hunt, "Institutional Arrangements to Facilitate Better Water Resources Management," *Public Affairs Comment* 33, no. 2 (1987).
41. Texas Department of Water Resources (TDWR), *Water for Texas, Technical Appendix, Vol. II* (Austin, Tex.: TDWR, November 1984), p. III-8-15.
42. TDWR, *Water Planning in Texas*, p. 20.
43. TDWR, *Water Planning in Texas*, p. 19.
44. John Gronouski and Ernest Smerdon, eds., *Texas Water Management Issues,* Policy Research Project No. 77 (Austin: The University of Texas at Austin, 1987).
45. Becky Marie Bruner, *Groundwater Law and Management in Texas*, Professional Report (Austin, Tex.: The University of Texas of Austin, August 1985), pp. 25-27.
46. David Eaton and Russell Hedge, "Institutions for Water Aquisition and Management in Texas," *Public Affairs Comment* 30, no. 3 (1984).
47. Interview with Sue M. Clabaugh, director, Financial Section, Water Development Fund, TWDB, Austin, Tex., March 20, 1987.
48. Texas House of Representatives, *Special Legislative Report*, p. 2.
49. Interview with Sue M. Clabaugh, March 20, 1987.
50. Interview with Jim Fries, director, Water Data Collection, Studies, and Planning Division, TWDB, Austin, Tex., March 20, 1987.
51. Texas Water Development Board (TWDB), *Statement to Water District and River Authority Study Committee* (Austin, Tex.: TWDB, September 19, 1986), pp. 5-6 (hereafter cited as *Statement to Water District*).

52. TWDB, *Statement to Water District.*
53. Texas Water Resources Institute, *Water-Related Researchers at Texas Universities* (College Station, Tex.: Texas A&M University, 1986), p. 1.
54. *Vernon's Texas Session Law Service 1986*, vol. 16 (St. Paul, Minn.: West Publishing Co., 1986), p. 457.
55. Interview with Wayne Jordan, director, Texas Water Resources Institute, Texas Agricultural Experiment Station, College Station, Texas, March 18, 1987.
56. Interview with Wayne Jordan, March 18, 1987.
57. The University of Texas at Austin, *1986-87 Operating Budget, Volume I* (Austin: The University of Texas at Austin, June 6, 1986), p. 961.
58. Office of Executive Vice President and Provost, "Center for Research in Water Resources," Report on Organized Research, vol. 3, Special Items (Austin: The University of Texas at Austin, 1987).
59. Interview with James King, engineer II, City of Austin, Water and Wastewater Department, May 11, 1987.
60. "Dedication of Center Scheduled," *Austin-American Statesman*, April 5, 1987.
61. Interview with Quintan Martin, water policy and programs manager, LCRA, Austin, Tex., May 11, 1987.
62. Interview with Dennis Haverlow, air/water quality manager, LCRA, Austin, Tex., May 14, 1987.
63. Texas Society of Professional Engineers (TSPE), *Water Education Program for Texas* (Austin, Tex.: TSPE, 1984), p. 9 (hereafter cited as *Water Education Program*).
64. TSPE, *Water Education Program*, p. 9.
65. Interview with E. D. Dorchester, P.E., division engineering manager, Texas Electric Service Company, former chairman, Texas Society for Professional Engineers, Water Education Council, May 18, 1987.
66. TSPE, *Texas Professional Engineers* (September-October 1985), p. 9.
67. TSPE, *Water Education Program*, p. 2.
68. TSPE, *Engineering Times* (September 1984), p. 8.
69. TSPE, *Engineering Times* (September 1984), p. 8.
70. Texas Water Development Board, *TWDB News*, May 22, 1986, p. 30.
71. TSPE, *Water Education Program*, pp. 2-3.
72. TSPE, *Water Education Program*, pp. 2-3.
73. TSPE, *Engineering Times* (September 1984), p. 8.
74. Interview with Leroy Goodson, general manager, Texas Water Conservation Association, and chairman, TSPE Water Education Council, Austin, Tex., May 20, 1987.
75. Interview with E. D. Dorchester, May 18, 1987.
76. Texas State Board of Education (TSBE), *Proclamation 63* (March 8, 1986), pp. 22-80.

77. TSBE, *Proclamation 63*, pp. 81-82.
78. Interview with E. D. Dorchester, May 18, 1987.
79. Texas Society of Professional Engineers (TSPE), *TSPE Insider* (May 1986), p. 1.
80. Interview with Jennifer Carr, special projects coordinator, TSPE, Austin, Tex., May 18, 1987.
81. Interview with Leroy Goodson, May 20, 1987.
82. TSPE, *TSPE Insider* (May 1986), p. 1.
83. Texas A&M Sea Grant Program, Texas A&M University, *Marine Education* 7, no. 3 (March 1987), pp. 1-7.

WISCONSIN

BACKGROUND
Historical Factors

Wisconsin is a water-rich state. It contains 15,000 lakes, more than 43,000 miles of rivers and streams, including the Wisconsin, Fox, and Mississippi Rivers, and portions of Lakes Michigan and Superior. Beneath the surface lies a series of four overlapping aquifers, which together encompass the entire state. Except in the southeastern part of the state, the aquifers are gaining more water through recharge than is removed for municipal, industrial, commercial, and agricultural use.[1] In contrast to other states in this study, Wisconsin does not face water supply problems in the near future.

The major uses of water in Wisconsin are: pulp and paper processing, animal and plant agriculture, municipal, fruit and vegetable processing, beer brewing, cheese making, electroplating, meat processing, and recreation and tourism.[2] Table 8.1 displays a breakdown of water users in Wisconsin. The importance of self-supplied water, that is, water not obtained through a government authority, is particularly evident. These uses interact and conflict through their effects and demands on water quality. Some demand high-quality water to meet their water needs, some pollute the water, and some fall into both categories. For instance, vegetable processing and beer-brewing industries require high-quality water because water is used directly in the processing of foods. Dairy cattle also require high quality water as fat-soluble pollutants will enter dairy products produced for human consumption. Both agriculture and industry can be a significant source of pollution if wastes are inadequately treated.

TABLE 8.1   Estimated Water Use in Wisconsin, 1965-80

	1965	1970	1975	1980
Population (millions)	4.14	4.42	4.59	4.71
Consumption by use (offstream)				
Total (mgd)	163	176	240	307
Public supply	44	48	46	57
Rural use	80	78	77	82
Irrigation	29	40	56	77
Industrial	10	10	61	91
Per capita (gpd)				
All uses	39	40	52	65
Excl. irrigation	32	31	40	49
Withdrawals by source				
Total (mgd)	4,760	6,290	3,160	5,810
Ground water	460	490	460	610
Surface water	4,300	5,800	2,700	5,200

Source: U.S. Geological Survey, *Estimated Use of Water in the United States, 1965; Estimated Use of Water in the United States, 1970; Estimated Use of Water in the United States, 1975; Estimated Use of Water in the United States, 1980*, Geological Survey Circulars 556, 676, 765, and 1001 (Reston, Va.: U.S. Department of the Interior, 1968, 1972, 1977, and 1983).

    Recreation and tourism account for one-quarter of all retail trade in the state.[3] Sports fishing alone generates $49 million a year.[4] Most of the tourism in the state is dependent upon clean water, and water pollution control programs provide major benefits to this industry. When a "fish consumption advisory" is issued or a beach is closed to swimmers because of pollution, the entire recreational industry is negatively affected.
    Wisconsin has a long history of water pollution control, starting in the 1860s. The earliest efforts were aimed at limiting the spread of disease, preventing massive fish kills related to municipal and industrial discharges, and controlling discharges that might interfere with navigation. The Slaughterhouse Offal Act of 1862 made it illegal to construct or maintain a slaughterhouse on the banks of a river, and during the 1880s, several laws were enacted to limit the discharge of lumbering and commercial fishery wastes. The powers of the State Board of Health, created in 1876 to administer pollution control laws, were strengthened in the early 1900s, in

order to investigate deaths from typhoid fever in Lakes Superior and Michigan communities.[5]

Surface water pollution continued to attract attention in the 1920s. Starting in 1926, the pulp and paper industry and state agencies sought to develop a cooperative solution to the stream pollution resulting from mill wastes. Initial efforts focused on ascertaining the extent of fiber loss at each mill and reducing the amount of waste produced to a minimum. In 1929, field laboratories were established at several mills, and a number of parameters, including five-day biochemical oxygen demand and pH, were assayed at each mill in the immediate vicinity.[6]

Chapter 264, from the Laws of 1927, created the Committee on Water Pollution as a policymaking body and to coordinate all state activities on water pollution control. The committee consisted of the state sanitary engineer, the state chief engineer, and representatives from the Board of Health, the Conservation Department, and the Railroad Commission. In 1950, a full-time director for the committee and staff were hired. This marked the beginning of a systematic approach to pollution control in the state's 28 major drainage basins. Further consolidation of pollution control functions occurred in the 1960s with the enactment of the Water Resources Act, Chapter 614, Laws of 1965; and Chapter 75, Laws of 1967, which created the Department of Natural Resources.[7]

Critical Issues

Surface Water Pollution
Point source pollution from factories and municipalities was the principal water issue in Wisconsin in the 1960s and 1970s. Polluted surface water in rivers and streams, along with accelerated eutrophication of the Great Lakes, brought point source pollution to the attention of politicians, administrators, and the general public. Although sewage has been treated in the state since the 1920s,[8] major efforts to control point source pollution began in the 1970s in response to the Federal Clean Water Act. The building of municipal plants was financed through a combination of local revenues, matching funds provided from state general revenue funds, and federal funds. Today, 90 percent of the state's municipalities are in compliance with federal sewage treatment standards.[9] However, the largest city in the state, Milwaukee, is not in compliance at the present time.

Milwaukee has been under a court order since 1977 to renovate its sewage treatment facilities and comply with permits established by the Department of Natural Resources (DNR). The city has a combined sewage system that, when inundated with storm water, is discharged into Lake Michigan. A $1.6 billion program to renovate the system involves constructing a large underground reservoir that will store excess storm water until treatment plants have the capacity to process it.[10]

Industrial polluters, including the pulp and paper industry, also contribute to point source pollution. The discharge of organic wastes results in a high level of biochemical oxygen demand (BOD). For instance, the Fox and Wisconsin Rivers, which have the highest concentration of paper-processing mills in the world, were unable to support fish and other aquatic life. However, pollution controls installed by paper mills and municipal dischargers have reduced BOD loads from more than 218,000 pounds per day in 1973 to less than 40,000 pounds per day in 1981. This has led to the reestablishment of fisheries on both the Lower Fox and Upper Wisconsin Rivers.[11]

When the goals of the point source pollution control program were close to being met, nonpoint source pollution became the major focus of the state's water resources programs. The reasons for this were threefold. Government officials felt that it did not make sense to spend additional millions of dollars on further controlling point source pollution if the waters of the state continued to fall below water quality standards because of nonpoint source pollution. In addition, the state did not receive any assurances that the federal government would address the problem in the foreseeable future. From a political standpoint, urban legislators had an incentive to support a nonpoint source program; they could trade their support of the nonpoint source program for rural legislators' support of point source programs.

In 1986, the DNR reported that approximately 30 percent of the state's streams and 40 percent of the state's lake surface area are degraded by nonpoint sources. In addition, about 70 percent of Wisconsin's Great Lakes coast is degraded.[12] Major sources of nonpoint source pollution are sediment from cropland, construction sites, streambanks, and grazed woodlots; nutrient loads associated with barnyard runoff, cropland erosion, runoff from city streets and lawns; and heavy metals and other toxic substances from a variety of sources.

Ground Water Pollution

Ground water is particularly susceptible to nonpoint source pollution, especially that originating in agricultural areas. For instance, the central part of the state, with its sandy permeable soils, is particularly suitable for irrigated crops. Irrigation allows repeated cropping on the same land, necessitating application of fertilizers and pesticides, which, with repeated watering, drives nutrients, fertilizers, and pesticides into the ground water. As a result of contamination of wells with aldicarb at levels exceeding ten parts per billion, the use of this pesticide has been severely restricted since 1982.[13]

Other sources of ground water contamination are landfills. Older sites, particularly those that have been abandoned, may be a source of leachate contamination of drinking water in municipal areas where they are most concentrated. Ponds and lagoons may be used to store and dispose of municipal and industrial wastewater. Unless adequately lined with plastic or clay-type soils, these areas also provide a source of contamination.[14]

Metallic mining activity may pose a threat to ground water, both from waste materials and from the processes used to extract the ore. In northern

Wisconsin, sulfur-containing pyrite would be present in the tailings of proposed copper mines. Abandoned lead and zinc mines in the southwestern part of the state allowed oxidation of exposed sulfides, which now contaminate the ground water as it flows into previously dewatered areas.15

Two other sources of contamination are leaking underground petroleum storage tanks and industrial and commercial volatile organic compounds. Many of these compounds are no longer in use but continue to be detected through the DNR's community water supply sampling program. Figure 8.1 shows contaminant sources by numbers of wells with contaminant levels exceeding ground water quality enforcement standards. However, while leaking petroleum storage tanks are the smallest in number, the toxicity level of petroleum constituents (i.e., benzene) found in ground water is the greatest.16

FIGURE 8.1 Contaminant Ground Water Sources, 1986

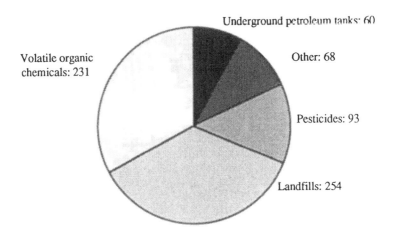

Volatile organic chemicals: 231

Underground petroleum tanks: 60

Other: 68

Pesticides: 93

Landfills: 254

Source: Department of Natural Resources (DNR), "Wisconsin Water Quality: Report to Congress, 1986," PUBL WR-137 (Madison, Wisc.: DNR, June 1986)

The Changing Role of the Federal Government

Wisconsin's existing water resources programs have not been greatly affected by recent federal inactivity in water resources policy. The state has never benefited from large federal investments in water supply projects, such as dams, canals, and reservoirs. Most of the federal monies it received were a result of the Clean Water Act and were devoted to rehabilitating municipal sewage treatment plants. Approximately 90 percent of these plants have already been rehabilitated. The state's most expensive remaining rehabilitation project, involving the City of Milwaukee, is partially financed by the federal government, and these funds show no sign of being cut back.

In general, it was agreed that the federal government, and specifically the EPA, has been taking a less active stance in enforcing environmental regulations since 1980. Wisconsin's water officials are concerned about the federal pullback from setting and enforcing national water quality standards and the effect this may have on its own water quality. Not only do they fear that high quality water within the state will be degraded by pollution entering from other states with lower pollution control standards, but also that a relaxation of federal standards will put pressure on a state to relax its programs. When standards are uniform throughout the country, it is easier to implement and enforce pollution control laws without providing industry with an economic incentive to move to another state with less stringent standards. Another area of concern for which federal action is necessary is acid rain. Wisconsin is in a position to control the 35-50 percent that originates within the state and has acted to reduce sulfur dioxide emissions by 50 percent by 1993. However, much of the remainder originates in the Midwest.[17]

All of the people interviewed in Wisconsin agreed that there was less federal money available to support water resources research in the state than in the past. While Wisconsin's politicians are aware of a lessening of federal commitment to water resources research, they have not responded by providing more support for basic research. They feel that basic water resources research is a federal responsibility for two reasons. First, it is too expensive for an individual state to finance. Second, each state has similar water problems, and research would be duplicated, leading to a waste of effort and money.[18] The state has put pressure on the federal government to increase support of basic water research through the actions of Senators William Proxmire and Robert Kasten, who are strong advocates of environmental protection programs. They have initiated or participated in congressional hearings on dioxin contamination of rivers, the Milwaukee sewage situation, acid rain, and pesticide contamination of ground water supplies.[19]

STATE INITIATIVES IN WATER RESOURCE MANAGEMENT
Policy Development

Nonpoint Source Pollution Abatement Act
Created by the Wisconsin legislature in 1978, it is one of the country's oldest and largest state-run nonpoint source pollution control programs. It

operates by designating priority watersheds to be eligible for the disbursement of state funds to support the implementation of best management practices for curbing nonpoint source pollution. The program, developed primarily by the DNR and then presented to the legislature for approval, was based on the following three premises:

1. Because pollutants can originate from many different nonpoint sources, effective controls must be comprehensive.
2. The goals of soil conservation programs are not necessarily the same as the state's water quality goals. Thus, an effective program to control pollution cannot rely solely on existing water conservation programs.
3. As nonpoint source pollution control is a water quality program, it requires strong technical involvement and leadership by the state water quality agency.[20]

The major objectives of the program are to identify the most effective approaches for achieving specific water quality standards and to provide the necessary financial assistance for the installation of approved nonpoint source control practices. Such efforts are coordinated with other elements of the state's water quality program, and limited technical and financial resources are concentrated in critical geographical areas. The latter are defined in terms of hydrological units rather than political boundaries. The DNR has developed a systematic process for identifying, ranking, and selecting critical watersheds to receive comprehensive attention.[21]

The state government's role is to devise an initial planning document for each watershed, including designating areas of significant nonpoint source pollution as primary management areas. It also provides the majority of cost-sharing funds and consults with localities over technical problems. It exercises a minimum amount of central control; the work of managing the watersheds is handled by local designated management agencies. The work of installing the best management practices is performed by individual landowners, who sign cost-sharing agreements. Acceptable practices are listed in Table 8.2.

The Groundwater Bill

Ground water contamination became a dominant issue in the early 1980s as the DNR's monitoring efforts revealed the extent of contamination of drinking water wells. The legislature, under the guidance of the Assembly Committee on Environmental Quality, proposed comprehensive ground water legislation. The committee spent two years formulating the bill, soliciting input from environmentalists, private industry, and various state agencies.

The 1983 Wisconsin Act 410, the Groundwater Bill, was signed into law in May 1984. A total of $2.3 million per year was appropriated, of which $500,000 was devoted to drilling new wells and providing alternate water supplies to victims of contamination.[22] The rest of the money was

TABLE 8.2 Best Management Practices

Code	Practice	Capital Cost	Private On-site	Maximum State Contribution (%)
C1	Contour Cropping	Low	Moderate	50***
C2	Strip Cropping	Low	Moderate	50***
C3	Diversions	Moderate	Moderate	70
C4	Terraces	Moderate	Moderate	70
C5	Waterways	Moderate	Moderate	70
C6	Minimum Tillage	Low	Moderate	50***
C7	No-till	Low	Moderate	50***
M1	Critical Area Stabilization	High	Low	70*
M2	Grade Stabilization Structure	High	Low	70*
M3	Shoreline Protection	High	Low	70*
M4	Settling Basins	High	Low	70*
L1	Barnyard Runoff Management	Moderate	Moderate	70
L2	Manure Storage Facilities	High	Moderate to High	70**
L3	Livestock Exclusion From Woodlots	Low	Low	50
U1	Leaf Collection	Low	Low	50
U2	Street Sweeping	Low	Low	50
U3	Infiltration System	Moderate	Low	70

Notes: C=generally used in cropland but may be applicable in urban areas, M=applicable to both urban and rural areas, L=livestock, U=urban; *=cost may be increased to 80 percent if 10 percent county cost is provided, **=dollar ceiling of $6,000; ***=a flat rate per acre equal to the cost-share rate applied to an average installation may be used.

Source: Department of Natural Resources (DNR), *The Wisconsin Nonpoint Source Water Pollution Abatement Program,* a report to the governor and legislature (Madison, Wis.: DNR, March 1982), p. 16.

divided between water quality standards monitoring and cleanup activities. An attempt to include funds for research other than monitoring was rejected by the legislature.

The Groundwater Bill set up a two-tiered standards approach for state regulation of ground water contamination. The higher level, called the enforcement standard, is a conventional measure of human harm; if ground water reaches this level of contamination, the DNR is mandated to intervene to control pollution. The lower level is the preventive action limit, which aims to protect the environment at contamination levels below those designated as harmful to humans. All state agencies are required to design pollution control measures to attain these goals for the activities they regulate.

The formulation of the Groundwater Bill is illustrative of the state's method of creating legislation. It was developed over a two-year period by a consensus committee composed of legislators, industry representatives, environmental lobbyists, and the prospective enforcers of the law--the DNR and other state agency personnel. A primary focus of the committee was the difference of opinion between environmentalists and industry representatives, who would fund the program through user fees. These differences of opinion were partially resolved when the DNR proposed specific statutory language to allay business' uncertainties over the original, generic regulatory language. The chairman also included Wisconsin's public intervenor as a member of the committee, which further facilitated a compromise.[23] The legislature was aided by the advice of nonpartisan water issues experts employed by the legislative council. This organization researches issues for individual legislators, staffs study committees when the legislature is not in session, and drafts bills for individual legislators. Scientific staff members were originally hired by the legislative council using funds from a National Science Foundation (NSF) grant and have since been retained with state funds.[24]

Implementation

The DNR bears primary responsibility for implementing water policy in the state. Created by the legislature in 1967, it incorporated all of the agencies with natural resource responsibilities and now has about 2,600 employees. In 1965, the water quality and regulatory activities of the Committee on Water Pollution, State Board of Health, and Public Service Commission were transferred to the Department of Resource Development. In 1967, this department was consolidated with the Conservation Department.[25] The DNR is responsible for the implementation of both conservation and environmental regulation policy. Initially, it devoted a great deal of its effort toward conservation policy,[26] but since 1975 its functions have become more evenly divided between these two responsibilities. The department is divided into four divisions: enforcement, environmental standards, resource management, and management services.

The DNR is administered by a seven-member natural resources board appointed to staggered six-year terms by the governor and approved by the Senate. The board is geographically distributed by statute, and appointments to the board are influenced by political considerations. However, it is dominated by individuals who respect the need for environmental quality. The board appoints the department secretary, who is directly accountable to it. Much of the success of the DNR's programs is attributed to the fact that all of the natural resource management and environmental protection programs are housed in one agency under a common secretary appointed by a citizens' board. This means that resources can be managed more comprehensively and that management is less subject to political pressure.[27]

Nonpoint Source Pollution Abatement
Administered by the DNR, this is a voluntary cooperative program with local authorities and landowners. In selecting priority watershed projects, the DNR uses input from state, federal, local, and regional interests. The process emphasizes projects where water quality problems are critical and land-management practices are the most feasible means of control. By 1984, planning had been initiated on nine new projects, in addition to the 17 already ongoing. Of the first five priority watershed projects, two (the Hay River and Elk Creek) had concluded the period for landowners to sign cost-sharing agreements. One hundred fifty cost-share agreements were signed in the Elk Creek project and 141 in the Hay River project, and represent 67 and 70 percent of the animal units, respectively. Thus, although significant improvements in water quality are expected, the voluntary nature of the program means that water quality problems from uncontrolled sources will remain. So far, pollution load reduction in participating watersheds has been reduced by 50 to 70 percent.[28]

Ground Water Quality
Chapter 160 of the Wisconsin Statutes, was created as part of the state's comprehensive ground water legislation: 1983 Wisconsin Act 410. Based on recommendations from the Wisconsin Department of Health and Social Services, the DNR is required to adopt state ground water standards, both an enforcement standard and a preventive action limit. By June 1987, standards had been established for 39 substances of health concern and ten of welfare concern.[29]

Chapter 160 also established the Groundwater Coordinating Council, consisting of the governor's representative and the head of all state agencies with some responsibility for ground water management. The DNR, through its bureaus of Water Resource Management, Water Supply, Wastewater Management, Solid Waste Management, and Office of Technical Services, is the lead agency. Other agencies with specific responsibilities are the Department of Transportation (for storage of road salt); University of Wisconsin (for eduction, research, and technical assistance); Wisconsin Geological and Natural History Survey (for inventorying and mapping geologic and hydrologic resources); Department of Health and Social Services (epidemiology and toxicology studies); Department of Industry, Labor, and Human Relations (for regulation of septic and underground petroleum storage tanks); and Wisconsin Department of Agriculture, Trade, and Consumer Protection (for pesticides, fertilizers, and animal waste management).[30]

One way of judging the effectiveness of the Wisconsin ground water program is to compare it with the recommendations of the National Ground Water Policy Forum. This commission listed ten recommended components, both required and optional, for a state ground water plan. Wisconsin, primarily through the efforts of the Wisconsin Geological and Natural History Survey (WGNHS), has met all six of the required components and has partially met one of the optional criteria. These components and Wisconsin's position are as follows:

1. The mapping of aquifers and recharge-discharge areas. The WGNHS has mapped all of the state's aquifers on a 1:500,000 scale, with one-quarter at 1:100,000.
2. The classification of aquifers by use. Wisconsin has set uniform standards for each of its four aquifers.
3. The setting of ambient ground water standards. The 1983 Wisconsin Act 410 mandates the DNR to develop a two-tiered approach--enforcement and prevention.
4. The authority to impose controls on all significant sources of potential contamination. Chapters 144 and 147 of the Wisconsin Statutes delegate this responsibility to the DNR.
5. Programs for monitoring, data collection, and analysis must be established. The DNR is assigned this responsibility under Chapter 160.27.
6. Enforcement provisions must be established. The DNR has been granted enforcement powers by the legislature.

In an attempt to implement surface water restrictions to protect ground water, the WGNHS works on a cost-sharing basis with counties, at their request. The WGNHS and county extension agents map the aquifers and educate county leaders about the qualities and vulnerabilities of the recharge-discharge areas located within their jurisdiction. The educational effort is aimed at convincing country officials about the need to adopt zoning laws to protect sensitive ground water areas.[31]

Relations with the Federal Government
Wisconsin is often ahead of the federal government in legislating water policy. The Nonpoint Source Pollution Abatement Program was developed and funded without any significant federal involvement.[32] However, on a daily management basis, priority watershed administrators often cooperate with federal representatives, particularly Soil Conservation Service personnel, in implementing best management practices. On the other hand, the chairman of the legislative consensus committee, which formulated the Groundwater Bill, does not welcome federal ground water legislation. She believes that federal standards would be less stringent than the existing state law and might deter ground water cleanup processes in Wisconsin.[33] Wisconsin has had a difficult time getting the EPA's Region V field office to

approve innovative transferable discharge permits and variable ambient water quality standards on the Fox River.[34]

Wisconsin has a complex relationship with the federal government. Its water agencies are always grateful to receive federal funds, but occasionally resent federal intransigence in accepting innovative water policy initiatives geared expressly for Wisconsin's particular environmental problems.[35]

Financing

General funds finance the majority of the state's water programs. In the past, the state's citizens have been willing to approve bond issues and cigarette tax increases to finance water programs.[36] In general, programs that benefit a limited constituency, or that are devoted to solving problems for which the responsibility can be apportioned, are increasingly financed by user fees. Programs that are more controversial are financed on a cost-sharing basis. These programs, such as the Nonpoint Source Pollution Abatement Program and the WGNHS aquifer mapping program, are usually voluntary.

User Fees

User fees have been utilized in the state for a number of years to support water programs, but had never provided a substantial amount of funds until the passage of the 1983 Groundwater Bill. This water quality program is totally financed by user fees, amounting to $2.3 million per year,[37] and is levied against potential ground water polluters. These funds finance the monitoring of threatened aquifers, replacement of contaminated water supplies, and cleanup of ground water hazards. The bill also established a ground water trust fund to finance compensation of well-contamination victims and reauthorized an environmental repair fund.[38]

When the legislature decided to finance the act with user fees, it made an effort not to create new fees and to make the fees "no fault." Solid waste disposers were targeted because it was felt that solid waste facilities were responsible for more ground water contamination than any other identifiable group. The disposers, lobbying against the fees, presented the following arguments: (1) they were being forced to pay to solve problems that they did not create; (2) wastes produced because of pollution control restrictions, such as fly ash and wood sludge, should not be included; (3) municipal dumps, which were providing a public service, should not be included; and (4) wastes burnt in incinerators, which were polluting the air, should be included. Legislators considered these arguments and limited the fee increase to 35 cents per ton (from 3 cents per ton). A staff analyst at the Wisconsin Legislative Council stated that this fee was too low to alleviate ground water contamination, claiming that at least two dollars per ton is needed.[39]

Federal Programs

Some water programs in the state have been partially financed by federal funds, particularly as a result of the Federal Clean Water Act. These funds, along with state monies from the Wisconsin Fund, financed the rehabilitation of municipal sewage facilities, including the Milwaukee sewage system. Federal funds, originating with the United States Geological Survey (USGS), also help finance WGNHS activities. The WGNHS prefers not to use USGS matching funds because USGS provides its share of the cost in kind, not in real dollars.[40] On the whole, aside from financing the construction of sewage facilities and supporting research at the university, federal money does not play a significant role in Wisconsin's water programs.

Cost Sharing

Many water programs in the state are partially financed through cost-sharing arrangements, in which the state provides a portion of the necessary funds and the participating municipality provides the rest. The Wisconsin Fund, create in 1978, was the first of the cost-sharing programs. Financed from general revenues, it was established to assist in the renovation of municipal sewage treatment plants so that they could meet the standards established for 1983 by the Federal Clean Water Act. State monies, raised through general taxes, matched local investments at a ratio of 1:1. As of 1987, the state had expended $723 million through the Wisconsin Fund.[41] Maintaining the wastewater treatment infrastructure built with federal and state grants will be a major expense. The governor is currently studying how best to finance this need and to determine the respective roles of state and local government.

More recently, the Nonpoint Source Pollution Abatement Program and certain WGNHS programs have been financed through cost-sharing arrangements. In the WGNHS cost-sharing programs, the counties pay 50 percent of the cost for mapping their aquifers (usually $50,000). The WGNHS encourages cost sharing, because it provides the WGNHS with funds to carry out its work and because it acts as proof to the legislature that the counties want the mapping completed. This gives the legislature justification for providing more funds to the WGNHS.[42]

THE ROLE OF WATER RESEARCH

There is a great deal of water-related research conducted in Wisconsin. Most of this research is done in programs connected with the University of Wisconsin (UW) system. Some programs are training programs that, in addition to performing practical research, are designed to provide experience to graduate students. Other programs are purely research programs and range from being broadly interdisciplinary to exclusively technical. Funding is achieved through competitive grants or customer financing.

Institutional Arrangements

The Institute for Environmental Studies
The Institute for Environmental Studies is a large, interdisciplinary environmental instruction and research program located on the University of Wisconsin-Madison campus. It operates separate research centers in environmental remote-sensing technology, biotic systems analysis, climatic research, human systems (presumably in some way related to water use and quality), land information studies, and marine studies.[43] The institute offers an undergraduate certificate in environmental studies, along with four graduate study programs. Its environmental monitoring and land resources programs award both Ph.D. and master's degrees, while its energy analysis-policy and water resources management programs award M.S. degrees.

There are more than 60 faculty members on the teaching staff, representing about 25 different departments. Its master's degree program in water resources management is intensively interdisciplinary. Graduate students in this program must become familiar with biological and physical sciences, engineering, law, and social sciences, along with techniques of quantitative analysis. The final component of a student's curriculum is a summer-long group research workshop, in which an interdisciplinary water resources planning and management project is performed for a paying client. During the early 1980s, the institute's students and staff participated in management studies for lake property owners' organizations and developed cost-effective animal waste-management techniques for Dane County, Wisconsin.[44]

The Water Resources Center (WRC)
In comparison with the Institute for Environmental Studies, the Water Resources Center (WRC) is a much smaller, more specialized research organization. Although it is a part of the University of Wisconsin system, it does not operate a teaching program. The WRC's director works for the research center 65 percent of the time, with his remaining work hours being devoted to more traditional university departmental tasks. There is also a half-time associate director, a full-time research coordinator, and five support staff members.[45] The state pays a portion of the salaries of center employees and maintains the center's facilities, but seldom funds any research projects directly. Created in response to the federal Water Resources Research Act of 1964, the center receives an annual allotment from the federal government of approximately $105,000.

In recent years, the WRC has concentrated on ground water contamination studies, nonpoint source pollution analysis work, and various toxicological projects in water chemistry.

Other University of Wisconsin Research Programs
The university operates a joint state-federal Sea Grant Program, which usually has a budget in the range of $3 million per year. This is primarily a

research effort focused on the Great Lakes. Approximately 20 percent of its budget is devoted to a small extension service. Like the WRC, the Sea Grant Program is not jurisdictionally confined to UW-Madison. It has sponsored research projects with, for example, UW-Green Bay, UW-Milwaukee, and UW-Superior campuses and with Marquette University in Milwaukee.[46]

The Sea Grant Program has close ties to UW-Madison's graduate program in water chemistry.[47] It is chaired by WRC's director and includes the associate director of the Sea Grant Program on its staff. The program involves the Department of Civil and Environmental Engineering and the Department of Chemical Engineering. It is a good example of the interweaving of personnel from a variety of departments in the university system's water resource programs.

The Center for Limnology, which focuses on the study of fresh water lakes and ponds, is also located on UW-Madison's campus. This center is run by the Department of Zoology and has been cooperating with the Department of Geology and Geophysics on several, federally-sponsored, ground water research projects.[48]

Finally, UW-Madison operates an interdisciplinary Center for Environmental Toxicology, which involves faculty from several departments. This center is operated cooperatively by the Medical School, the College of Agricultural and Life Studies, the School of Pharmacy, and the School of Veterinary Medicine.[49]

Although only the Madison and Milwaukee campuses of the UW system offer Ph.D. degrees in water-resources-related fields, faculty from many other UW campuses perform water resources research. The University of Wisconsin at Stevens Point is an important facility for ground water research because of its location in the central sands region of Wisconsin. The faculty at the Eau-Claire, Green Bay, and River Falls campuses are also performing ground water research. The Sea Grant Program has provided research grants to UW-Green Bay to study the economic impact of the Great Lakes. Lake Winnebago is also an important research subject in the state and attracts grant money to UW-Oshkosh and UW-Green Bay.

Conclusions about Research at the UW System

Water resources research activities in the UW system benefit from the presence of a multitude of interdisciplinary programs and centers that unite the efforts of diverse academic fields. When it was founded in 1970, the Institute for Environmental Studies was one of the first higher educational institutions designed to address the growing national consciousness of environmental issues. The institute has been successful because it integrated itself directly and unobtrusively into the existing departmental system. It does not award any undergraduate degrees so it cannot "steal" other departments' undergraduates. It also concentrated on bringing together faculty under a broad environmental mandate, not as a relatively small and strictly water-oriented program. The University of Wisconsin-Madison also has a very strong faculty government, which may be conducive to interdisciplinary research and the success of nondepartmental programs. Departmental chairs at UW-Madison are democratically elected for short tenures. This may contribute to the success of interdisciplinary programs by avoiding the empire building that can occur under long-term departmental heads.[50]

Another reason why the university system has produced so much water resources research has to do with the type of individual attracted to the state university. Wisconsin is an environmentally concerned state with abundant recreational resources that attract people who are interested in the environment. Wisconsin also has a progressive political culture and a pattern of activist environmental regulation. Although the legislators of Wisconsin do not feel that it is the state's duty to fund water research directly, these same legislators have built a strong university system that provides researchers with the tools necessary to attract federal research dollars. Although the university receives only a small part of its research budget from local sources, researchers have been cognizant of the state's needs and have secured federal grant funds to conduct research that will benefit Wisconsin.

Research at State Government Agencies
Department of Natural Resources. Approximately 90 percent of the DNR's research activities concern conservation, not environmental issues. However, within the department's Bureau of Research, a Water Resources Research Section has major applied research projects on acid rain and lake management. Other environmental protection programs include nonpoint source monitoring and modeling, ground water studies, and the development of lake management practices. Another major effort, aimed at improving fish and game productivity and funded by federal Dingell-Johnson or Pittman-Roberts Grants, revealed high levels of mercury in fish from the relatively "pristine" northern Wisconsin lakes. This finding has led to additional monitoring of these lakes and has made determination of the cause a research priority. In 1986, the proposed research project investigating the cause of high levels of mercury in northern pike, walleye, and other fish, was ranked number one by the DNR's Research Review Committee.[51] However, the DNR has not always been able to secure the funding that it deemed necessary from the legislature. Despite the importance placed by DNR personnel on this research proposal, the legislature did not provide the $480,000 requested.[52]

Department of Agriculture, Trade, and Consumer Protection. This department has developed a number of research projects, which are selected on the basis of their potential usefulness to regulatory mandates. It is surveying pesticide use in Wisconsin, examining pesticide persistence in ground water supplies, and estimating the leaching potential of various pesticide practices, largely as a result of the 1983 Wisconsin Act 410. It is also developing a model county animal waste-management plan with the

UW-Stevens Point faculty and Portage County. This project may prove useful to the DNR's nonpoint source pollution project.[53]

Other State Departments. The Department of Industry, Labor, and Human Relations is cooperating with UW-Madison's small-scale waste management project to investigate the use of new private sewage systems. The goal of this program is to delineate the inspection responsibilities assigned to the department under the Wisconsin Administrative Code. This work has received direct state funding. The Department of Health and Human Services is conducting epidemiologic investigations of the effects of toxic compounds in ground water. These compounds were designated by the DNR, under the Wisconsin Act 410, as hazardous to human health.[54]

State-Level Coordination of Research
Water resources research in Wisconsin is a decentralized process; there is no one agency coordinating the activities of other state agencies and the University of Wisconsin system campuses. However, there is extensive contact between state agency and university personnel. One notable example was Professor Gerard Rohlich, who worked closely with the DNR and was a Resource Development and Natural Resources Board member for six years. Joint research projects between the university, WGNHS, and DNR are common. University graduates also secure jobs in the DNR or other state agencies after graduation.

There are no general water research goals for the state government. A coordinated effort is most likely to arise in response to a specific problem, such as the need for research to support the 1983 Wisconsin Act 410. To aid in the act's implementation, the legislature has formed the Ground Water Coordinating Council, an organization that will, among other things, "advise and assist state agencies in...the exchange of information related to ground water including...ground water monitoring,...laboratory analysis and facilities, research activities, and the appropriation and allocation of state funds for research."[55] The council does not make decisions, nor does it oversee programs. Chaired by a representative of the DNR, it is a consensus-forming body with a diverse organizational membership. Other entities represented on the council are the governor; the University of Wisconsin system; the Department of Health and Social Services; the Department of Agriculture, Trade, and Consumer Protection; the Department of Transportation; and the WGNHS. In its first annual report, dated August 1985, the coordinating council instructed its subcommittee to "prepare a research plan that identifies the most important ground water research needs of the state, estimate the fiscal requirements to meet these needs, and assist decisionmaking in the budget process."[56] As of early 1987, the subcommittee had not issued its plan.

Research Funding Sources

Funding for water resources research in Wisconsin originates from state, municipal, county, private, and federal sources. Research funded by the state government is almost always short-term, applied research that can meet political demands of legislative constituents, particularly in conjunction with the ground water law. The most important source of research dollars is the federal government, specifically the USGS, NSF, and EPA. Federal dollars pay for the research behind Milwaukee's sewer reconstruction program and UW-Superior water researchers cooperate with the EPA's Great Lakes laboratory.

The research budget at the WRC is largely dependent on obtaining competitive federal and private research grants. Between 1973 and 1983 the WRC secured funds for three to four large-scale research projects, each in the $1-3 million range. However, fiscal austerity has resulted in a decrease in the center's budget in recent years. Large million-dollar grant programs from the EPA no longer appear to be available, so the WRC has obtained a greater number of smaller grants from diverse sources, including the Wisconsin Power and Light Company, the Upper Mississippi River Basin Commission, The Great Lakes Basin Commission, Union Carbide Corporation, NSF, and the U.S. Department of Agriculture. In securing private research dollars, it must be careful not to appear to be "too close" to private funders, in order to avoid an appearance of conflict of interest. The sensitivity of this issue is illustrated by the fact that the WRC was accused of "being in bed with companies" after accepting Union Carbide funds to conduct research on aldicarb.[57]

Although not strictly research, industry may be required to participate in and fund monitoring efforts. For instance, the DNR initially banned the land disposal of wood-pulp sludge because of the possibility of dioxin contamination. Based on the results of initial studies, the ban has been lifted for one mill on the condition that monitoring and evaluation of risk continue, but remains in effect for those that have not provided adequate information to assess the risk.[58]

CASE STUDY: THE WISCONSIN AND FOX RIVERS WASTE DISCHARGE CONTROL PROGRAM

The Fox and Wisconsin Rivers are the focus of an innovative pollution control program initiated by the state of Wisconsin. This program attempts to control water pollution through application of the principles of equity, efficiency, and effectiveness. The program works through a process assigning allowable BOD loadings for individual river segments, using a cooperatively developed model of the rivers' assimilative capacities. Research leading to the development of such models for the Wisconsin River was begun at the University of Wisconsin in 1967. These results were used by the DNR as the basis for the development of a pollution control program, in which the assimilative capacity of the river was established. Policymakers, with public participation, were then responsible for assigning wasteload allocations.

Background

Characteristics of the Rivers

The Wisconsin River drains the central region of the state, beginning at the northern border with Michigan and flowing south into the Mississippi River. Approximately 320 miles long, it evolves from a slow-moving, swampy river into a swift river with rapids and waterfalls. Its average flow is 8,500 cubic feet per second, and its record low flow is 2,000 cubic feet per second.[59] The Fox River drains east-central Wisconsin from Lake Winnebago into Lake Michigan. It has a length of 40 miles and is a highly developed industrial river interrupted by a series of dams. Its average flow is 4,000 cubic feet per second and its record low flow is 950 cubic feet per second.[60]

The proximity of these rivers to the state's forests has made them prime locations for pulp- and paper-processing mills. This concentration of industry has, in turn, led to the development of population centers along the rivers. The Fox River valley has the second highest population density in the state[61] and the highest concentration of pulp- and paper-processing mills in the world.[62] The municipalities located along both rivers depend on the pulp and paper industry for their economic base.

Environmental Degradation

Municipal and industrial waste discharges have degraded the environmental quality of both rivers. The most severe problems are high biochemical oxygen demand, high concentrations of suspended solids, and increased turbidity. These problems, common in many industrially developed rivers, are accentuated in the Fox and Wisconsin Rivers by the organic quality of pulp and paper waste discharges. River water is used to flush wood sludge from the mills, which leads to increased levels of suspended organic solids in the water. These solids provide an increased food supply for bacteria, which deplete the oxygen supply in the water. Stretches of the Fox River had dissolved oxygen levels of zero in the 1970s. Municipal waste discharges and hydroelectric stations on the rivers accentuate the turbidity problem.

Early Attempts by the DNR to Regulate Discharge

The DNR began the process of monitoring the rivers in 1969. The department contracted for mathematical modeling work on the lower Fox River to determine stream conditions expected under varying flows, temperatures, and waste loadings. In-house mathematical modeling capabilities were subsequently developed, and in 1971, a $125,000 automatic water quality monitoring system of six stations of the Wisconsin

River and five on the lower Fox River was installed. Dissolved oxygen, temperature, conductivity, and pH were recorded hourly and the data were used in river-modeling studies.[63] The DNR, under its mandate from the state's water pollution control legislation, began the process of establishing standards and enforcing them.

However, the pulp and paper industry began to exert pressure on the DNR. The industry did not trust the department to develop cost-effective regulations nor to take its needs into account.[64] Industry representatives, distressed by the lack of opportunity for input into the development of the regulations, hired a consultant in order to challenge any DNR regulations in court. Economic arguments also formed the basis of opposition by municipalities, local businesses, and labor organizations. Together, these groups formed a strong constituency that pressured elected representatives into persuading the DNR to moderate its position. On the other hand, environmentalists and the tourist industry wanted strong regulations, but the political leadership to support such a position was lacking.

Development of Regulations

The Wisconsin River Study
A solution to the stalemate began to emerge in 1967, four years before DNR moved to regulate discharges into the two rivers. An interdisciplinary team of researchers, headed by Irving Fox and Anthony Dorsey at the University of Wisconsin, began working in 1967 to develop a systems approach to alleviate the environmental degradation of the Wisconsin River.

The Wisconsin River Study team had 43 participants, including hydrologists, sanitary engineers, statisticians, economists, lawyers, and political scientists.[65] Its $250,000 budget came from a federal grant through the Water Resources Center. The four-year study resulted in recommendations to the legislature at the same time the DNR had reached a stalemate in its efforts to get its regulatory proposals enacted.

The study had three goals:

    1. to advance the knowledge about policy alternatives and institutional need for water quality management on the Wisconsin River;
    2. to provide results for dealing with water quality management problems on the Wisconsin River; and
    3. to provide useful educational experiences for graduate students.[66]

The team used a systems approach to attain these goals. It attempted to take into account economic forces, the formal institutional framework, cultural factors, and technological capabilities.[67] The study team believed that in order to meet goal number two, representatives of industry and the DNR should be involved in the study at all times. The DNR and industry did attend meetings early in the study, but as time passed they lost interest and stopped attending.

The study concluded that any successful program to restore environmental quality to the river must account for equity, efficiency, and effectiveness. The team defined those terms as follows. Equity meant that each polluter should bear a burden of cleanup equal to the share of pollution it caused. Efficiency meant that no money should be wasted. Effectiveness meant that pollution should be controlled. To fulfill these requirements, the following conclusions and recommendations were made:

1. It would be more efficient (less expensive) to control industrial waste than municipal waste or to provide instream aeration.

2. Effluent charges would be an efficient way to regulate industrial discharges.

3. To ensure equity, each discharger should pay in proportion to the amount that its discharge degrades the water.

4. The regulatory institutional structure should be strengthened by establishing an investigation and planning agency and a quasi-judicial agency to set standards.

The conclusions of the study, presented to the state legislature in 1971, were ignored, possibly because the state expected forthcoming federal Clean Water Act amendments to supersede anything it legislated. In addition, the study did not have DNR and industry support because of lack of involvement.[68] Nonetheless, the study had a much greater long-term impact on the Fox River Program and led to legislation addressing pollution of the Fox and Wisconsin Rivers. This legislation closely followed the Wisconsin River Study's format and recommendations.

The Fox River Negotiations

The Fox River negotiations were initiated by the DNR in 1972 in response to the stalemate over regulation. They were formatted on the recommendations of the Wisconsin River Study. Participants included agency representatives, industry representatives, and two University of Wisconsin-Madison professors, Dr. Erhard Joeres of the Civil Engineering Department and Dr. Martin David of the Economics Department. The negotiations, which included DNR and industry representatives, lasted eight years. A majority included university personnel as well. Industry reacted positively to being involved in the development of regulations and felt that the participation of university personnel would increase the chances of its interests being taken into account. Over time, the three groups developed a working relationship.

The negotiators' first task was to formulate a model for the assimilative capacity of the river and the waste outputs of industry and cities. Industry and the municipalities felt that the model, initially proposed by the DNR in 1971, was flawed, and they threatened to challenge it in court. Their complaint was that "the model was based upon a 'worst case' scenario of simultaneous low flow and high temperature that had never occurred in the forty-four years of Fox River flow and temperature monitoring."[69] In consultation with industry representatives, the DNR modified its model, in order to determine the amount of biochemical oxygen demanding (BOD) material that could be discharged to attain the 5 mg/l dissolved oxygen standard under different conditions of temperature and water flows. (Lower flows and higher temperatures reduce the river's assimilative abilities.) The DNR agreed to set quarterly standards that met EPA requirements. Different standards were set for different portions of the river, based on their assimilative capacities.

It was decided to ration the allowable load of BOD among the industrial and municipal dischargers through a process known as "wasteload allocation." In 1976, the governor designated the Fox Valley Water Quality Planning Agency to provide a local forum for the development of policy recommendations based on technical information defining the allowable BOD loading. The wasteload allocation process was codified[70] and in 1983 was adopted by the DNR. The lower Fox River was divided into two segments (clusters I and II), and the total maximum daily load for each was determined by calculating the total amount of BOD allowable as a function of river flow and temperature. A formula was developed for allocating this load between each of the dischargers, and discharge permits were issued accordingly.[71]

Chapter NR 212.115 allows for the transfer of wasteload allocations between point source dischargers. Permits issued to dischargers could be rented to other waste dischargers for a period not to exceed the term of the seller's permit. However, this provision has never been implemented.

Evaluation of the Program

In general, the river has not been degraded below EPA standards, and waste disposers have been able to save money. Because most dischargers fluctuate their discharge levels daily, water in the river usually exceeds the minimum allowable dissolved oxygen concentration. However, one example illustrates the controversy that still surrounds the issue of wasteload allocation.

In late 1982, Consolidated Paper Company-Appleton Division (CPI) ceased discharging into the cluster II region. Since the DNR approved the concept of allowing the full use of the assimilative capacity of the river, the remaining six dischargers in cluster II requested that the "surplus" assimilative capacity be "reallocated" to them. Charged with recommending a resolution of the issue, the Fox Valley Water Quality Planning Agency solicited input from the public over a two-year period. Available options also included withholding the allocation, either as a permanent reserve for the purpose of improving water quality or for future industries or municipal growth. It was decided to modify the permits of the existing cluster II dischargers.

This response angered environmentalists, who argued that there was no reason to relax permits at a time when incremental steps should be taken toward improving water quality. The whole issue of antidegradation and the zero discharge goal has received renewed attention as a result of this case. Currently, there is no legal mechanism for making effluent limitations more restrictive than those that the water quality standards allow; the DNR would have to upgrade the water quality standards on cluster II to reflect higher ambient dissolved oxygen or establish an antidegradation policy.[72]

CONCLUSIONS

1. Wisconsin is a water-rich state and has not had to face the water allocation decisions typical of arid western regions. Major water concerns in the state focus on water quality problems associated with both surface and ground water sources.

2. Throughout its history, Wisconsin has been characterized by a strong institutional infrastructure, including the University of Wisconsin system, legislature, and state agencies. These institutions have enabled the state to confront, in a comprehensive manner, water issues that the federal government has ignored or withdrawn from. For example, the 1983 Wisconsin Act 410 supplements the federal superfund program, and the Nonpoint Source Abatement Program was a precursor to the recent federal inclusion of nonpoint source monies in the 1987 Clean Water Act.

3. The DNR is a well-funded agency with the power to enforce existing regulations. It takes an integrated approach to problem solving and is often ahead of the EPA in its implementation mechanisms. This has sometimes been a source of conflict between the two agencies. Decentralization of programs within the DNR has also increased its efficiency and facilitated communication with localities.

4. Success in addressing the water quality problems of the Fox and Wisconsin Rivers can be attributed to a cooperative effort between state regulators, industrial polluters, and other interests. The development of wasteload allocations was an attempt to address industry's concerns regarding costs, while meeting EPA clean water standards. It is anticipated that such an agreement, arrived at in cooperation with industry representatives, will be easier to enforce.

5. The University of Wisconsin system is a large, well-respected institution with a significant research effort in water and environmental issues. One-third of the state's budget is devoted to higher education, and this has made the federal withdrawal from research less devastating for Wisconsin. The university programs result in well-qualified personnel for the DNR, enabling the development of monitoring programs. In addition, university researchers have addressed some of the pressing issues in

Wisconsin, most notably providing background information that facilitated the development of wasteload allocations for the Fox River.

6. Because of the strong nature of its legislature, university, and regulatory agencies, the State of Wisconsin has been able to develop strong water management policies and to fill some of the gaps created by federal inactivity in water resource programs. The development of a strong institutional infrastructure could serve as a model for other states. However, inherently unique to Wisconsin is its progressive heritage and its conservationist background. It is difficult to evaluate the importance of this heritage and to predict the applicability of this model to other states.

Material for this chapter was provided by Pamela M. Nachamie and Robert D. Sommerfeld.

NOTES

1. Department of Natural Resources (DNR), *Groundwater, Wisconsin's Buried Treasure, DNR Special Report* (Madison, Wisc.: DNR, 1985), p. 8.

2. Department of Natural Resources (DNR), "Groundwater Quality in Wisconsin: Wisconsin's Buried Treasure," PUBL WR-156-87 (Madison, Wisc.: DNR, June 1987) (hereafter cited as "Groundwater Quality").

3. DNR, "Groundwater Quality."

4. W. C. Richardson, "Learning in the Great Lakes Lab," *EPA Journal* 11, no. 2 (March 1985), p. 14.

5. L. F. Warrick and K. M. Watson, "Pollutional Surveys in Wisconsin Paper Mills," *Paper Trade Journal* (June 12, 1930) (hereafter cited as "Pollutional Surveys").

6. Warrick and Watson, "Pollutional Surveys."

7. Pat Schraufnagel, "Water Quality Management in Wisconsin," unpublished manuscript, n.d.

8. U.S., Congress, Senate Committee on Small Business, Hearing Before the Subcommittee on Entrepreneurship and Special Problems Facing Small Business, 98th Congress, 2d Session, 1984.

9. Jeff Smoller, "An Extra Effort Wins Water Quality Payoff," *EPA Journal* 11, no. 3 (April 1985), p. 14.

10. Interview with David Grundy, water quality planner, Milwaukee Metropolitan Sewage District, Milwaukee, Wisc., January 9, 1987.

11. Department of Natural Resources (DNR), "Wisconsin Water Quality: Report to Congress, 1986," PUBL WR-137 (Madison, Wisc.: DNR, June 1986), p. 85 (hereafter cited as "Wisconsin Water Quality").

12. DNR, "Wisconsin Water Quality," p. 1.

13. Lynn Entine et al., "Groundwater--Wisconsin's Buried Treasure," *Wisconsin Natural Resources Magazine*, supplement, n.d., p. 11 (hereafter cited as "Groundwater").

14. Entine et al., "Groundwater," p. 12.

15. Entine et al., "Groundwater," p. 14.
16. DNR, "Wisconsin Water Quality," p. 29.
17. DNR, "Wisconsin Water Quality," p. 54.
18. Interview with Joseph A. Strohl, majority leader, Wisconsin State Senate, Madison, Wisc., January 7, 1987.
19. U.S., Congress, House Committee on Agriculture, Testimony of Senator William Proxmire, Hearings before the Subcommittee on Department Operations, Research, and Foreign Agriculture, on H.R. 3254 and H.R. 3818, 98th Congress, 1st Session, 1984.
20. Interview with Joseph Strohl, January 7, 1987.
21. John G. Conrad, James S. Baumann, and Susan E. Bergquist, "Nonpoint Pollution Control: The Wisconsin Experience," *Journal of Soil and Water Conservation* 40, no. 1 (January-February 1985) (hereafter cited as "Nonpoint Pollution Control").
22. Correspondence with Bruce J. Baker, director, Bureau of Water Resources Management, DNR, December 1987.
23. Interview with Mary Lou Munts, commissioner, Public Service Commission, and former state legislator, Madison, Wisc., January 7, 1987.
24. Joint interview with Mark Patronsky, senior staff attorney, Wisconsin Legislative Council, and Anne Bogar, staff analyst, Wisconsin Legislative Council, Madison, Wisc., January 6, 1987.
25. Pat Schraufnagel, "Water Quality Management in Wisconsin."
26. Interview with Lyman Wible, administrator, Division of Water Resources, DNR, Madison, Wisc., January 7, 1987.
27. Correspondence with Bruce Baker, December 1987.
28. Conrad, Baumann, and Bergquist, "Nonpoint Pollution Control."
29. DNR, "Groundwater Quality," p. 8.
30. DNR, "Groundwater Quality," pp. 9-12.
31. Interview with Ron Hennings, assistant director, Wisconsin Geological and Natural History Survey, Madison, Wisc., January 8, 1987.
32. Interview with John Conrad, chief, Land Management and Nonpoint Division, DNR, Madison, Wisc., January 8, 1987.
33. Interview with Mary Lou Munts, January 7, 1987.
34. Joint interview with Erhard Joeres, professor of civil engineering, and Martin David, professor of economics, University of Madison, Madison, Wisc., January 6, 1987.
35. Interview with Mary Lou Munts, January 7, 1987.
36. W. C. Richardson, "Learning in the Great Lakes Lab," p. 14.
37. Correspondence with Bruce Baker, December 1987.
38. Harvey E. Wirth, "Wisconsin's Groundwater Law and Regulation, A History: 1948-1985," document presented to the Water Resources Center, University of Wisconsin-Madison, 1986, p. 127 (hereafter cited as "Wisconsin's Groundwater Law").
39. Wirth, "Wisconsin's Groundwater Law."
40. Interview with Ron Hennings, January 8, 1987.
41. Correspondence with Mary Jo Kopecky, Bureau of Community Assistance, December 1987.

42. Correspondence with Mary Jo Kopecky, December 1987.

43. Institute for Environmental Studies, University of Wisconsin-Madison, "Water Resources Management Graduate Program," (Madison, Wisc., pamphlet, n.d.).

44. Joint interview with Erhard Joeres and Martin David, January 6, 1987.

45. Interview with Dr. Gordon Chesters, director, Water Resources Center, and professor of soil science, University of Wisconsin-Madison, Madison, Wisc., January 5, 1987.

46. Interview with Gordon Chesters, January 5, 1987.

47. Interview with Gordon Chesters, January 5, 1987.

48. Wisconsin Ground Water Coordinating Council, *Wisconsin Ground Water Coordinating Council Annual Report to the Legislature* (Madison, Wisc., August 1985), p. 19 (hereafter cited as *Wisconsin Ground Water*).

49. Interview with Gordon Chesters, January 5, 1987.

50. Joint interview with Erhard Joeres and Martin David, January 6, 1987.

51. Correspondence with Bruce Baker, December 1987.

52. Interview with Lyman Wible, January 7, 1987.

53. Wisconsin Ground Water Coordinating Council, *Wisconsin Ground Water*, pp. 23-24.

54. Wisconsin Ground Water Coordinating Council, *Wisconsin Ground Water*, pp. 24-25.

55. Wisconsin Ground Water Coordinating Council, *Wisconsin Ground Water*, p. 3.

56. Wisconsin Ground Water Coordinating Council, *Wisconsin Ground Water*, p. 18.

57. Interview with Gordon Chesters, January 5, 1987.

58. Correspondence with Bruce Baker, December 1987.

59. U.S., Congress, Senate Subcommittee on Air and Water Pollution of the Committee on Public Works, *Restoring the Quality of Wisconsin's Rivers*, 92d Congress, 1st Session, 1971, p. 1516.

60. Joint interview with Erhard Joeres and Martin David, January 6, 1987.

61. Joint interview with Erhard Joeres and Martin David, January 6, 1987.

62. Interview with Gordon Chesters, January 5, 1987.

63. "Bureau of Water Quality Activities, A Decade of Change, 1967-1977," unpublished manuscript, 1977.

64. Joint interview with Erhard Joeres and Martin David, January 6, 1987.

65. Ernest J. Flack, ed., *Proceedings of the Conference on Interdisciplinary Analysis of Water Resource Systems* (Boulder, Colo.: University of Colorado, 1973), p. 332 (hereafter cited as *Proceedings*).

66. Flack, *Proceedings*, p. 328.

67. U.S., Congress, *Restoring the Quality of Wisconsin's Rivers*, p. 1527.

68. Flack, *Proceedings*, p. 338.

69. Joint interview with Erhard Joeres and Martin David, January 6, 1987.

70. Chapter NR 212, Wisconsin Administrative Code.

71. Michael T. Llewellyn, "The Zero Discharge Debate: Wisconsin's Wasteload Allocation Program," *Wisconsin Academy Review* 32, no. 1 (December 1985) (hereafter cited as "Zero Discharge Debate").

72. Llewellyn, "Zero Discharge Debate."

CONCLUSIONS

We have studied the water management policies of six states. Our goal was to determine to what extent states independently take the initiative in water resource management and research, or whether the recent withdrawal of the federal government from such issues has resulted in a policy void. We have focused on the water policy issue that appears to be dominant in each of the chosen states. Based on our limited study, we have come to the following conclusions:

1. There is an increased awareness among the states that water is a valuable resource, which must be prudently managed if long-term economic objectives are to be realized. For more arid states, where supplies are limited, the emphasis in water policy has changed from one of structural measures to enhance supplies to that of better management of existing supplies. In general, there is also a greater emphasis on water quality, with an increasing awareness of the importance of protecting ground water supplies from contamination.

2. In the absence of federal initiatives, all states are realizing that it is incumbent upon them to manage this resource, as they are each individually responsible for establishing a sound base for economic development. There is less evidence of state initiatives in the area of water research.

3. There is a great diversity of approaches in addressing the issues facing each state. This does not necessarily result only from the diversity of problems facing different states, but also stems from different cultural and institutional backgrounds. In general, more money is needed to fund new programs, and a variety of funding mechanisms are being devised, often involving new actors, such as the private sector.

Wisconsin is a state with a long history of addressing natural resource issues and has strong political and educational institutions that provide leadership in public policy issues. The state has often taken the initiative in protecting water quality, most recently that of ground water supplies. Other states, such as California, have received considerable assistance in the past from the federal government. However, they have also taken the initiative in water policy issues, most notably in planning the Central Valley Project in the 1930s. Thus, the recent withdrawal of the federal government has not left an institutional void.

In Arizona, the impetus for better management of existing ground water supplies came from the federal government. Using financial assistance for completion of the Central Arizona Project as leverage, the federal government insisted that Arizona address the problem of ground water overdrafting. The state developed a ground water management plan that included the formation of new institutions and appropriate funding mechanisms. A somewhat adversarial relationship between the state and federal government has also developed in Florida. The state determined that federal drainage and land channelization projects on the Kissimmee River had adverse environmental consequences that had not been anticipated. The state is taking steps to remedy the situation, but the role of the U.S. Army Corps of Engineers, which constructed the project, is not yet settled.

In North Carolina, an innovative funding mechanism, involving local government entities, has been developed to enhance resources available for water research. In another example of new funding mechanisms, Texas has enlisted the help of the private sector in developing a water education program instituted in the public schools.

It is impossible to say, based on a study of six states, how extensive initiatives in water resources management at the state level are across the nation. However, it is evident that the states are uniquely qualified to address the issues specific to their region, and that many states have already developed solutions to some of their water management problems. It is less obvious whether they are also willing to provide the funds necessary to supplement inadequate federal funds for water resources research activities.

INDEX

204 / INDEX

About the Authors

JURGEN SCHMANDT, Ph.D. is Professor of Public Affairs at the LBJ School of Public Affairs, University of Texas at Austin. Since 1985, he has also served as director of the Woodlands Center for Growth Studies, which is the policy research division of the Houston Area Research Center. His previous appointments include senior environmental fellow at the U.S. Environmental Protection Agency, associate director at the Harvard University Program on Technology and Society, and head of the national science policies unit, Organization for Economic Cooperation and Development, Paris.

ERNEST SMERDON, Ph.D. is Dean of the College of Engineering and Mines at the University of Arizona, Tucson and a member of the National Academy of Engineering. Until 1987 he was director of the Center for Research in Water Resources at the University of Texas at Austin. His previous appointments include chairman of the Department of Agricultural Engineering, University of Florida, and director of the Water Resources Institute, Texas A&M University.

JUDITH CLARKSON, Ph.D. is an environmental policy analyst, having recently completed the Masters in Public Affairs program at the LBJ School of Public Affairs, University of Texas at Austin. She was formerly employed as associate biologist at the University of Texas System Cancer Center, where she directed a research program in radiation biology.